Visit our website to:

- Calculate your own Five Elements in seconds
- Get a personalized report
- Book a consultation
- Learn about bringing **The Five Elements** into your organization

my5elements.life

An East Asian Approach to Achieve Organizational Health,
Professional Growth, and Personal Well-Being

The Five Elements

Kevin John Fong

The Five Elements: An East Asian Approach to
Achieve Organizational Health, Professional
Growth, and Personal Well-Being
©2023
By Kevin John Fong

Triple Earth LLC
San Francisco, CA
my5elements.life

The intent of the author is to offer information of a
general nature. Every effort has been made to verify
the accuracy of the historical names, dates and
events stated herein. In some cases, names have
been changed to protect the identity of private parties.
The author assumes no responsibility for errors,
inaccuracies, omissions, or any other inconsistencies.

Cover design and interior layout: Jody Luzier
Interior art: Vanessa Bowen, Jody Luzier, James Kwolyk
Editor: Gina Mazza
ISBN-13: 9 798989 373239
Set in Roboto, Candara, and Sofia Sans

*"Our world is in need of creative
new insights, born of curiosity and
nurtured by the wisdom of different
world views. The time has come to
see a problem with new eyes and to
unfold a deeper ecology of life. We are
all created from the elements, and it
is necessary that we produce designs
that reflect our origins."*

KATHERINE METZ
The Art of Placement

PRAISE FOR **THE FIVE ELEMENTS** AND THE WORK OF KEVIN JOHN FONG

Kevin John Fong is a masterful teacher and heart-opener; his book born of twenty years of teaching and laboring for justice, is a gift. **The Five Elements** revitalizes timeless wisdom, teaching us how to be in greater harmony with ourselves, and in doing so, steward a just and joyful world.
Valarie Kaur | author and activist, *See No Stranger*

As Kevin writes in the Preface, his grandmother who inspired **The Five Elements** lived to the age of 102. This is literally age-old wisdom he's received, worked through, tested and now made available to you and me. If you want old-new views to open your old-new heart, open to this elemental journey.
Dan Mulhern | distinguished lecturer at University of California Berkeley and author of *Everyday Leadership: Getting Results in Business, Politics and Life*

For years, Kevin John Fong has been a guide to me and so many others who care about equity and justice in our world. Now, Kevin synthesizes ancestral wisdom and decades of deep work in community in his new book, **The Five Elements**. It's a must read for leaders and organizations.
Deepa Iyer | activist, author of *Social Change Now: A Guide for Reflection and Connection*

Kevin John Fong provides light to help us navigate the struggles and confusion of our time. He calls us back to the essence of who we are by honoring and celebrating the ancient wisdom and power of our lineages. What he is offering is not some lofty, romantic custom from a far-away place and time; he has crafted an integrated, easy-to-apply approach to "technologies" that have proven to be effective for thousands of years. Just the very act of reading his words provides healing.
Joe Weston | facilitator, coach, advocate for lasting peace and author of *Fierce Civility: Transforming our Global Culture from Polarization to Lasting Peace*

The era of western depletion of spirit, connection and collective community is coming to an end. **The Five Elements** is an essential contribution to restoring our humanity, centered in ancient principles. Kevin teaches how to bring balance back into a personal practice and into the world.
La quen náay Elizabeth Medicine Crow | (Haida/Tlingit)

Kevin John Fong is a Wisdom Carrier who brings the teachings and practices of his lineage as an offering to the world. In this book, he has taken the ancestral knowledge of his people and made it available to all of us to integrate these practices towards a more balanced life of health and healing. This is a must read for everyone but especially for those working, teaching or serving others.
Maestro Jerry Tello | co-founder of the National Compadres Network and author of *Recovering Your Sacredness*

To my ancestors and teachers
who entrusted me
to bring this wisdom
to you.

CONTENTS

AUTHOR'S NOTE

Specifically defined terms and principles used in **The Five Elements** are capitalized and italicized to differentiate them from their common references; for example, any references to Water or the Philosopher refer to the element or archetype.

I use the gender-neutral pronouns "they", "their" and "them" instead of the gender-specific "he|she", "his|her" and "him|her."

PRONUNCIATION NOTE

Dit da jow is pronounced "Deet dah jiao"

Wu Xing is pronounced "Woo shing"

Qi is pronounced "Chee"

Yin Yang is pronounced "yin yahng"

Tao Te Ching is pronounced "Dow De Jing"

I-Ching is pronounced "Ee-Jing"

Huang-Di-Nei-Jing is pronounced "Hwang Dee Nay Jing"

Feng Shui is pronounced "Fehng Shway"

PREFACE

When I was a child, I would occasionally break out with red welts all over my body. My pediatrician attributed it to an allergic reaction from the foxtail that grew in the fields behind our house, but my grandmother had a different diagnosis.

"Wind burn," she called it, implying that there was too much fire in my system. She'd feed me seaweed soup and apply an herbal analgesic ointment of *Dit da jow* and camphor. These water properties, she claimed, calmed the wind and cooled the heat. Sure enough, my welts would disappear.

In high school, when I was hit in the face by an errant basketball and my right eye swelled shut, my grandmother smoothed a calming poultice of red clay on my eye and fed me turnip soup, allowing the earth properties to absorb and disperse the heat. By morning, the swelling had subsided and my eye was back to normal.

These cures, along with many others, have been passed down through my family for generations. They are based on principles developed and refined over four millennia, called *Wu Xing* (The Five Transformations Theory), to achieve and maintain health, balance and prosperity in our lives. I was formally reintroduced to these principles as a college student when I shared my childhood stories with Dr. K. C. Liu, my professor of Chinese philosophy at the University of California, Davis. Even though my grandmother did not have a day of formal education to her name, Dr. Liu praised her wisdom for applying foundational principles of healing that would rival any medical doctor's training.

"If you can understand and practice the power of the *Wu Xing*, like your grandmother did," Dr. Liu opined, "you can manifest harmony for yourself and for the world."

Thus began my journey with what I refer to in my work as **The Five Elements**, an East Asian philosophy that views the world through dynamic states, or phases, of constant change. **The Five Elements** describes the interaction between the more commonly known theory of *Yin Yang* and is based on the basic components of the material world: Water, Wood, Fire, Earth, and Metal.

For the past 25 years, this journey has led me down various paths with myriad teachers. Dr. Liu taught me how the concepts of *qi* and *Yin Yang* led to the development of the Chinese philosophies of Taoism, Confucianism and animism. These philosophies are the foundation of seminal texts such as the *Tao Te Ching* (The Virtuous Way), the *I-Ching* (Book of Changes) and the *Huang-Di Nei-Jing* (Yellow Emperor's Cannon of Internal Medicine). Written thousands of years ago, these profound teachings continue to be taught and practiced throughout the world.

While attending the University of California, Berkeley, earning a degree in East Asian Studies, I simultaneously studied under Professor Thomas Lin Yun Rinpoche, a Buddhist grandmaster and scholar. While my original intent was to learn about *Feng Shui* (the practice of adjusting one's environment to promote more constructive and balanced outcomes), Professor Lin and his senior student Katherine Metz immersed me in a deeper study of Buddhism and the Five Transformations Theory.

During that time, I met Robert Sachs, a licensed clinical social worker and author of *The Complete Guide to Nine Star Ki*. Through Bob, I learned how the Five Transformations manifest in our individual personalities and relationships with others.

A few years later, as the founder and administrator of the Clinical AIDS Program at Asian Health Services in Oakland, CA, I began to wonder if the Five Transformations would work with a collective of individuals, such as my hardworking and beleaguered staff. Might these practices and the philosophies that I had studied improve the health and well-being of organizations?

Up to that point, I had been employing conventional organizational development models that I had learned in classes, conferences and seminars through my work in the corporate sector and through my tenure as a W. K. Kellogg Fellow. While these frameworks were proven successful in the corporate, philanthropic and academic worlds, they did not translate well with my diverse and largely immigrant and refugee staff.

I realized that it was up to me to translate these frameworks in a way that my staff could understand and integrate into their daily lives and work routines with ease, harmony and balance. I chose two colleagues as my guideposts: Bounchanh, a limited-English-speaking refugee from Laos, and Julie, an American-born nursing student. If Bounchanh and Julie could understand my reasoning, I would know that I was in the ballpark.

After four years of trial and error, I found a way to blend the Five Transformations with Western organizational development models. This hybrid became the foundation for what you will read in this book. Drawing upon universal tenets of organization and change in both nature and the workplace, **The Five Elements** articulates a series of personal archetypes through the following components or "elements":

ELEMENT	ARCHETYPES
Water	The Philosopher
Wood	The Visionary, The Optimist
Fire	The Networker
Earth	The Caregiver, The Facilitator, The Rock
Metal	The Protector, The Achiever

Since we cannot see the air unless it is blowing through the trees, the characteristics of Air are included in the element of Wood.

This framework provides a means for us to identify the underlying patterns and threads that weave us together in ways that we can help ourselves and others.

Since 1998, I have been using the concept of **The Five Elements** as the foundation for my work as a consultant, trainer and facilitator in organizational design, transformative justice, and leadership development. Whether the client is comprised of two or 22,000 people, the concepts provided herein are relevant because they are embedded in the universal laws of nature, as well as in the quest that we all share in desiring to have healthy, balanced and prosperous lives and societies.

This book weaves together stories from hundreds of organizations and thousands of people who have experienced and applied **The Five Elements** into their personal and work lives. Here are a few encapsulations of the stories you will read:

⊙ As the CEO of a startup, Diane wanted to maintain a cohesive vision that was anchored in a clear mission and core values to attract potential investors and clients. She used **The Five Elements** as a guide to build a coordinated and integrated leadership team that aligned with and supported their work so that they could deliver high-quality products and services.

⊙ Sam and Terry, a recently engaged couple, wanted to find ways to build and sustain a healthy relationship. They used **The Five Elements** to first map out their individual profiles then create a combined profile to understand each other's personality and communication style. In doing so, Sam and Terry discovered ways to support their relationship and bring out the best in each other.

⊙ Ava and Carlos needed guidance on how to parent their three teenagers. "I don't know what happened," Carlos said of their children. "It's as if extraterrestrials came down and traded our kids for theirs!" **The Five Elements** helped to explain their teenagers' behaviors and provided healthy recommendations for Ava and Carlos to support their children as they grew into adulthood.

⊙ Laura, a school principal, wanted to understand the underlying patterns that drove her school's culture. Through **The Five Elements**, she learned about the individual and collective strengths of her staff, and how to develop the right teams for specific tasks and functions.

Similar to the individuals in these case studies, **The Five Elements** can guide you in developing generative and healthy practices and solutions in your own life.

The book is organized into three parts:

Part I: Overview of The Five Elements introduces you to the framework and how it operates in the supporting or restraining cycles. You will learn the language and methods to determine your own Five Elements profile.

Part II: The Five Elements Archetypes offers details on each of the personality and leadership archetypes.

Part III: The Five Elements as an Interpersonal Assessment Tool helps you understand how your Five Elements profile interfaces with others, and how to define the culture and group dynamics of a family, team, or organization from a Five Elements perspective.

The Appendix provides:

I.   The charts you will need to calculate your Five Elements profile.

II.   A summary of each of the 81 Five Elements profiles.

III.   A summary of recommendations to achieve and maintain balance for each profile

IV.   Frequently asked questions.

This book is designed to be used as guide where you can refer to the sections that appeal most to your interests and needs.

I recommend that you start with Part I to anchor yourself in the foundation of **The Five Elements**. Then you can skip to other sections that you find most engaging. Some of you may want to start by determining you own elemental profile (Chapter 3). Others might go straight to the section about how to navigate a conflict with a family member or colleague (Chapter 17).

The key to the success of **The Five Elements** is balance and nonjudgement. It does not label people or situations as good or bad. If the elements are working in harmony, there is health and well-being. If they aren't, we need only to diagnose which elements are out of balance and employ solutions to restore equilibrium.

My grandmother, who understood these principles and practiced them on a daily basis, spent only one night of her life in the hospital, and that was to have a pacemaker installed at the age of 90. She lived independently and never needed glasses, hearing aids or a walker. Grandmother retained her mental acuity and kept track of her many grandchildren and great-grandchildren. Most importantly, she lived a life of deep purpose and great joy until she died peacefully in her sleep at the age of 102.

On behalf of my grandmother, along with all of my teachers, elders and ancestors, I offer **The Five Elements** to you as a way to achieve balanced, healthy, harmonious and prosperous lives and communities.

Kevin John Fong | author

KEVIN JOHN FONG

PART ONE

OVERVIEW of
THE FIVE ELEMENTS

FACT

People create organizations and communities; therefore, the concepts and systems of any organization or community must reflect the diversity and complexity of the people who comprise it.

ISSUE

We are most healthy and productive when we achieve and maintain balance; however, balance is difficult to maintain in the context of constant change. In order to achieve this, we must:

⊙ Assess where we stand—first with ourselves, then with others—at any point in time;

⊙ Make sense of all the changes that are occurring in a way that everyone can understand; and

⊙ Create supportive and healthy responses so that people are happy, engaged and productive in meaningful ways.

Drawing upon universal tenets of development both in nature and business, **The Five Elements** builds upon the following personal archetypes:

ELEMENT	ARCHETYPES
Water	The Philosopher
Wood	The Visionary, The Optimist
Fire	The Networker
Earth	The Caregiver, The Facilitator, The Rock
Metal	The Protector, The Achiever

KEY

The key concept of **The Five Elements** lies in understanding how each element and archetype can support or restrain the other, and in determining how the balance between the elements and archetypes can foster constructive solutions in any situation.

PRONUNCIATION NOTE

Yin Yang is pronounced "yin yahng"
Qi or is pronounced "Chee"
Wu Xing is pronounced "Woo Shing"
Feng Shui is pronounced "Fehng Shway"

ORIGIN *and* OVERVIEW *of* THE FIVE ELEMENTS THEORY

Through the ages, people have turned to the natural world to unlock the mysteries of life, realizing that one of nature's fundamental laws is balance. For every action that occurs, there is a reaction of equal measure.

In East Asian philosophy, this dynamic is depicted in the *Yin Yang* symbol, where the actions and reactions are interconnected. Examples of these opposite but complementary relationships include:

FIGURE 1: YIN | YANG

YIN	YANG
Night	Day
Cold	Hot
Light	Heavy
Ascending	Descending
Dark	Bright
Psychological	Physical
Feminine	Masculine

WATER

WOOD

FIRE

EARTH

METAL

Nothing is completely *Yin* or *Yang*. The small circles or "eyes" (light within dark, and dark within light) reflect this interdependence. For example, daytime is always a part of the night with the presence of the stars (which are actual suns) in the sky. Nighttime is always a part of the day with the presence of the moon in the sky (although we may not see it because of the sun's brightness).

The force that interacts between *Yin* and *Yang* is defined by East Asian cultures as *qi*. Also known as *ch'i* or *ki*, this force flows among all living things. Because *qi* is invisible, it is impossible to quantify. One might feel the presence of *qi*—like a cool breeze against your face—but it cannot be seen or held. The study and cultivation of *qi* is the foundation of East Asian practices such as acupuncture, herbology, *feng shui*, divination, energetic healing and martial arts.

Around 2600 BCE, scholars developed a theory to express *qi* in the physical realm. The result is the *Wu Xing*, or the Five Elements Theory. Each element—Water, Wood, Fire, Earth, and Metal—represents hundreds of characteristics, including colors, seasons, tastes, parts of the body, lifecycles and directions.

An overview of each element is provided on the following pages, followed by an analysis of how each relates with the other through the Supporting and Restraining cycles.

WATER

Water implies a time of deep thinking, listening and reflection. Since water is the source of life, this phase marks the beginning of any process. It starts with people coming together with a common purpose or identified need. Patience and temperance are virtues of this stage as it may take time and negotiation for the greater truth to emerge.

The Water stage requires people to engage in "3S" thinking—Strategies, Systems and Synthesis—to assure that the group is continually anchored in its mission, values and rationale. Appropriate analysis and evaluation create a path for a smoother transition between stages, and assures high quality and efficiency of outcomes.

The drawback of this stage is that it is so powerful it can inundate a project with too much philosophy and data. This whirlpool effect can draw groups into a process that becomes so self-absorbed that nothing gets accomplished. The key lies in balancing "deep water" conversations (for example, purpose, philosophy, data analysis) with "moving water" conversations (like developing flow charts and turning strategies into action steps).

Outcomes of the Water stage include:

- ◉ developed or affirmed organizing principles and philosophies;

- ◉ analysis of lessons learned; and

- ◉ refinement of systems, processes and approaches.

With these outcomes in place, the group can proceed to the Wood stage, with an aligned perspective and deeper understanding toward the fulfillment of continued needs.

CHARACTERISTICS
of WATER

⊙ The group develops organizing principles and a philosophy (at the beginning of a process).

⊙ Analysis and refinement toward a deeper purpose or fulfillment of continued needs (at the end of a process).

Color	Blue, Black
Season	Winter
Physiognomy	Ears
Taste	Salty
Lifecycle	Consolidation
Direction	North
Skills	Analysis, Ethics, Perspective, Strategic Thinking

Archetype	The Philosopher
Motivation	Knowledge
Aspiration	Truth
Shadow	Cynicism

Supports	Wood
Is Supported By	Metal
Restrains	Fire
Is Restrained By	Earth

WOOD

Innovation and possibility are the primary factors of the Wood. Like the promise of spring, this stage provides a counterpoint to the contracting nature of Water by making way for expansive and bright visions of the future. The Wood stage is all about the big picture, as the group explores every option in fulfilling the mission and addressing the need.

Time becomes elastic in this stage, since creation rarely occurs in an orderly and sequential fashion. One good idea may lead to a surge of energy as people rush to explore new approaches to an issue. The generative nature of Wood becomes infectious, resulting in an infusion of enthusiasm; but just as quickly, that spark can fade and the group may fall into stasis. The consequence may be long periods of dormancy, even melancholy. The process may stall since creativity can't be rushed.

It is important to stay anchored in the facts and purpose of the project so that this phase does not experience mission drift. When a group is immersed in the creative process, it may often get lost amongst the trees and lose sight of the bigger picture. The Wood stage becomes a mission unto itself, and if not monitored, can result in a tangle of weeds.

Outcomes of the Wood stage include:

- ⊙ expansion of ideas and approaches to the fulfillment of a mission;

- ⊙ increased voices and commitment from the stakeholders; and

- ⊙ a sense of hope and inspiration for the journey.

This sets the stage for Fire to leverage Wood energy with focus and confidence.

CHARACTERISTICS
of WOOD

⊙ This sets the stage for Fire to leverage Wood energy with focus and confidence.

Colors	Green
Season	Spring
Physiognomy	Legs, Mouth
Taste	Sour
Lifecycle	Creation
Direction	East
Skills	Adaptability, Forecasting, Idealism, Innovation, Inquiry

Archetype	The Optimist, The Visionary
Motivation	Learning and Curiosity
Aspiration	Growth and Joy
Shadow	Instability and Melancholy

Supports	Fire
Is Supported By	Water
Restrains	Earth
Is Restrained By	Metal

FIRE

Transformational power is the hallmark of the Fire stage. Like a hearty soup that has been cooked to perfection, this stage has the potential of combining a disparate set of concepts and ideas into a cohesive, palatable story. The Fire stage is the intersection of the creative flair of Wood and the practical thinking of Earth.

Attaining the right strategic thinking to articulate the right message requires clarity, alignment and confidence; however, when playing with fire, one runs the risk of getting burned. Timing and temperature are crucial in delivering a perfect pitch that will attract the potential client, investor or partner. Much of this skill is reliant upon intuition and improvisation, and it is incumbent that the team trusts the torchbearer to carry and convey the right message. Fire works best when everyone is clear on their roles and responsibilities and focuses on the common task before them.

Because there is so much pressure to keep the fire burning, it takes considerable resources and support to stay in this stage. Upholding precise and transparent communication is paramount, as this phase requires constant and often subtle adjustments to find and maintain the right temperature.

Outcomes of the Fire stage include:

- prioritized goals and a clear strategic plan;

- branding and messaging; and

- networking, collaboration and partnerships.

With these outcomes in place, the group can create the conditions to take proper action.

CHARACTERISTICS
of FIRE

⊙ The group identifies specific strategies and attracts a larger community of supporters and investors.

Colors	Red, Purple
Season	Early Summer
Physiognomy	Eyes
Taste	Bitter
Lifecycle	Direction
Direction	South
Skills	Focus, Interconnection, Passion, Communication

Archetype	The Networker
Motivation	Opportunity
Aspiration	Connection
Shadow	Self-Absorption

Supports	Earth
Is Supported By	Wood
Restrains	Metal
Is Restrained By	Water

EARTH

One of the biggest factors for ensuring the success of an endeavor is establishing a healthy environment for people to thrive. Building and maintaining a culture of care and trust is the main objective of the Earth stage. This is accomplished by assembling the right people and supporting them with systems, policies, procedures and processes that are aligned with the organization's values.

The Earth stage is more pragmatic than the previous stages. It adheres to timelines and assures that everything is in its proper place in accordance with function and protocol. This stage works to bring order out of chaos through caring, consensus and community building.

While the tendency of Earth is to ensure the comfort and safety of the group, its risk-averse nature may paralyze the process and the group from moving on to implementation. People may become mired in the details, which will stress both the system and those involved. When this occurs, it is important to step back into Fire, shed some light on the situation and redirect.

Outcomes of the Earth stage include:

⊙ creating functional teams and operational systems that are in alignment with the organization's mission, strategies and goals;

⊙ establishing conditions where attitudes and behaviors reflect the organizations values; and

⊙ maintaining a culture of caring.

These outcomes will support a successful Metal phase.

CHARACTERISTICS
of EARTH

⊙ Establishing and maintaining healthy relationships and environments.

Colors	Yellow, Orange, Brown
Season	Late Summer
Physiognomy	Abdomen
Taste	Sweet
Lifecycle	Coordination
Direction	Center
Skills	Empathy, Facilitation, Fairness, Inclusion, Team building

Archetype	The Caregiver, The Facilitator, The Rock
Motivation	Service, Cooperation, Support
Aspiration	Harmony, Consensus, Stability
Shadow	Depletion, Manipulation, Stubbornness

Supports	Metal
Is Supported By	Fire
Restrains	Water
Is Restrained By	Wood

METAL

Metal implies maximum solidity, structure and efficiency. The team is now in full production mode. Strategic plans are put into action and tasks are executed with precision. There is no place in this stage for chaos and uncertainty.

As metal is a product of the earth, the attitudes and behaviors of the individuals exhibited in the Metal stage are manifested from the conditions established in the Earth stage. The quality of the processes and relationships built over the previous stages are put to the test in the tasks of Metal.

The Metal stage holds a "take no prisoners" approach to time. Relationships and even rules take a backseat if they do not serve accomplishing the task at hand. Discipline and order are required at all levels so that each part of the machine is ready to spring into action when needed. The success of any endeavor is based on efficiency and practical versus theoretical experience.

The pressure in this stage to deliver on the work from all of the prior stages is enormous. Because this is the last stage of the cycle, a mix of exhilaration and fatigue can arise. People may get moody and territorial, resulting in hurt feelings and grudges. For some, this stage becomes about more than just the work; it is also a statement about one's life and place in the world. Creating and finding moments of levity, appreciation and humor will go a long way in making this stage a more enjoyable experience.

Outcomes of the Metal stage include:

⊙ products and services produced and delivered;

⊙ the completion of the strategic or action plan; and

⊙ a deeper sense and commitment to team identity and bonding.

CHARACTERISTICS
of METAL

- Implementing a strategic or action plan.

- Achieving tasks in a time-sensitive manner.

Colors	White, Grey, Gold, Silver
Season	Autumn
Physiognomy	Head
Taste	Pungent
Lifecycle	Implementation
Direction	West
Skills	Strategy, Performance Orientation, Discipline

Archetype	The Protector, The Achiever
Motivation	Mastery, Competition
Aspiration	Order, Accomplishment
Shadow	Arrogance, Carelessness

Supports	Water
Is Supported By	Earth
Restrains	Wood
Is Restrained By	Fire

The Supporting and Restraining Cycles

Each of the elements interact in fluid and dynamic ways that support or restrain one another. When we look to nature, we see how these elements nurture each other in a Supporting cycle.

- ◉ Water nurtures Wood.

- ◉ Wood fuels Fire.

- ◉ Fire creates ash or Earth.

- ◉ Earth generates minerals or Metal.

- ◉ Metal condenses to form Water.

The Supporting cycle reveals itself as a circular formation, moving in a clockwise direction.

The concept of Metal condensing to form Water may be hard to grasp; but if you put a stainless-steel bowl in the freezer, the result will be condensation or water.

FIGURE 2
The Supporting Cycle

When it comes to conflict, the Law of Nature is stark and unquestionable, and **The Five Elements** affirm this through the Restraining cycle.

- Water extinguishes Fire.

- Fire tempers or melts Metal.

- Metal chops Wood.

- Wood depletes the nutrients from the Earth.

- Earth contains Water.

FIGURE 3
The Restraining Cycle

When combined, **The Five Elements** with the Supporting and Restraining cycles looks like this:

FIGURE 4
Five Elements Chart

It is important to note that the Supporting cycle does not automatically imply "good", nor does the Restraining cycle imply "bad." They are both part of the process of growth and decay that occurs in life. While it is preferable to operate within the Supporting cycle, it is sometimes strategic and necessary to utilize the Restraining cycle.

When the dynamics of the Restraining cycle are in full force, the results can be completely destructive; for example, water extinguishes fire. The conflict is uncompromising and only resolved when one element prevails over the other. Human behavior operates in a similar fashion. Conflict resolution often means two sides invoking their full power upon each other until one side prevails. Our military, legal, athletic and political systems confirm this win-lose dynamic.

Nature shows us that conflict transformation is possible under the right conditions. If we observe the subtleties among the elements in the Restraining cycle, we find that conflict can be not only resolved, but transformed into something good. For instance:

> ◉ When we apply Fire to Water in just the right degree, the result is the perfect bath temperature or a low simmer that produces a delicious pot of soup.

While it is preferable to operate within the Supporting cycle, it is sometimes strategic and necessary to utilize the Restraining cycle.

Nature shows us that conflict can not only be resolved, but transformed into something good.

Refer to Chapter 17 for more guidance on how to transform conflict from a Five Elements perspective on page 319.

⊙ The proper flame can temper Metal to a sharp and useful blade.

⊙ That blade, correctly applied, can prune a tree to maximize its growth.

⊙ Plants have the capacity to transform barren land into fertile soil.

⊙ Earth and Water, appropriately combined, produce clay that can be shaped into useful and beautiful objects.

By applying the principles of **The Five Elements** outlined in this chapter, you will learn how to identify and direct the nuances of each element to establish harmonious and productive outcomes.

CHAPTER ONE RECAP

◉ *Yin Yang* is the interpretation of the natural principle that for every action that occurs, there is a reaction of equal measure.

◉ *Qi is* the force that interacts between *Yin* and *Yang*. The study and cultivation of *qi* is the foundation of various East Asian practices such as acupuncture, herbology, *feng shui*, divination, energetic healing and martial arts.

◉ **The Five Elements** is the physical manifestation of *qi*, represented by the elements Water, Wood, Fire, Earth and Metal.

◉ The elements interact in a Supporting cycle (clockwise circular formation) and a Restraining cycle (star formation).

◉ A key concept of **The Five Elements** is learning how to balance the relative effects of the elements in their Supporting and Restraining cycles to maximize the positive effects that they bestow.

WATER

WOOD

FIRE

EARTH

METAL

Summary of each element:

⊙ **Water** implies a time of deep thinking, listening and reflection. Since water is the source of life, this phase marks the beginning of any process. This stage requires people to engage in "3S" thinking—Strategies, Systems and Synthesis—to assure that the group is continually anchored in its mission, values and rationale. Patience and temperance are virtues of this stage as it may take time and negotiation for the greater truth to emerge.

⊙ **Wood** is all about the big picture as the group explores every option in fulfilling its mission and addressing its needs. Innovation and possibility are the primary factors of the Wood stage.

⊙ **Fire** has the potential of combining a disparate set of concepts and ideas into a cohesive and palatable story. Attaining the right strategic thinking to clearly and concisely articulate the right message during this stage requires clarity, alignment and confidence.

⊙ **Earth** builds and maintains a culture of care and trust. This is accomplished by assembling the right people and supporting them with systems, policies, procedures and processes that are aligned with the organization's values. This stage works to bring order out of chaos through caring, consensus and community building.

⊙ **Metal** implies maximum solidity, structure and efficiency. In this stage, strategic plans are put into action and tasks are executed with precision. The quality of the processes and relationships built over the previous stages are now put to the test.

CHAPTER ONE KEY POINTS

I. There are five elements in East Asian philosophy: Water, Wood, Fire, Earth and Metal.

II. The elements interact in a Supporting cycle (clockwise circular formation) and a Restraining cycle (star formation).

III. The key concept of **The Five Elements** is learning how to balance the relative effects of the elements in their Supporting and Restraining cycles to maximize the positive effects that they bestow.

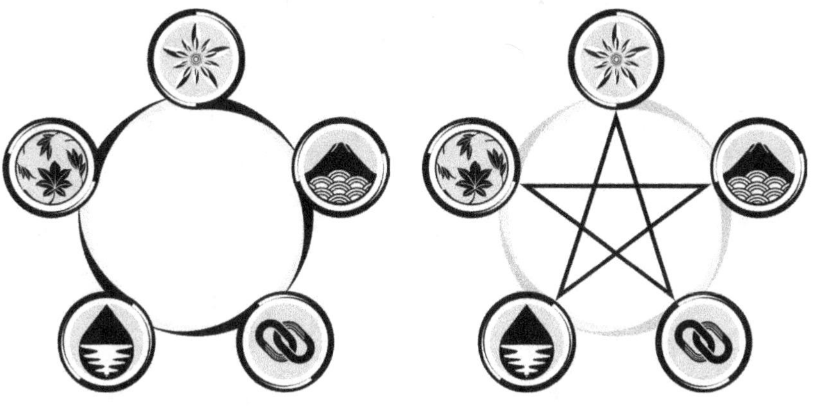

THE FIVE ELEMENTS
SUPPORTING CYCLE

THE FIVE ELEMENTS
RESTRAINING CYCLE

PRONUNCIATION NOTE

Xia is pronounced "sha"

Lo Shu is pronounced "Low shoo"

Tai Chi is pronounced "Tie Chee"

Chi Gong is pronounced "Chee Ghong"

Kung Fu is pronounced "Ghong Foo"

Chiu Kung Ming Li is pronounced "Chew ghong ming lee"

CHAPTER TWO

INTRODUCTION *to* THE FIVE ELEMENTS ARCHETYPES

Four thousand years ago during the Xia Dynasty in China, King Wen gathered the leading scholars of the time—philosophers, physicians, mathematicians, shamans, priests, architects, astronomers, astrologers, biologists, botanists, engineers, and artists—to formulate a deeper understanding and application of the laws of the universe. The foundation of their studies was the *Lo Square* (or, *Lo Shu*), a 3x3 formation of symbols comprised of solid and dashed lines called trigrams.

FIGURE 5: THE LO SQUARE

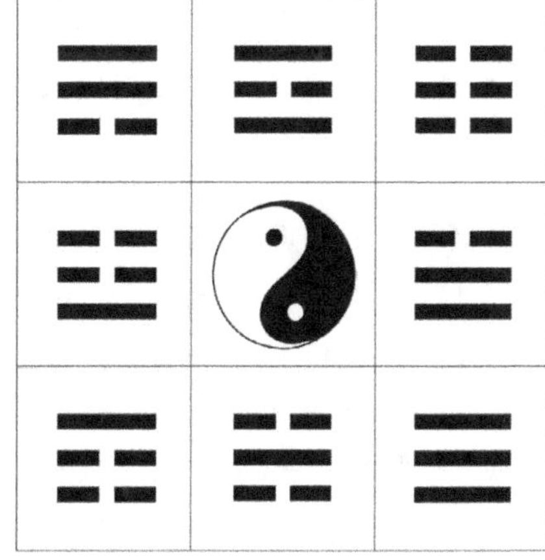

The *Lo Square* became the basis for modern practices of Traditional Chinese Medicine (acupuncture, herbology), architectural design (*feng shui*), martial arts (*tai chi, qi gong* and *kung fu*), divination (*I Ching*), and human development (*Chiu Kung Ming Li* and *Nine Star Ki*).

When the *Lo Square* is presented in a numerical format, the result is:

FIGURE 6
THE LO SQUARE AS APPLIED IN NUMBERS

4	9	2
3	5	7
8	1	6

The root formation is arranged with the number five in the center. The other numbers are arranged in a way that the sum of three numbers is 15, whether added vertically, horizontally, or diagonally.

The *Lo Square* functions as a map that tracks the movement of time in cycles of nine. With each succeeding timeframe (for example, minutes, hours, months and years), the square shifts so that another number occupies the central space.

If we consider yearly cycles, 2022 was the most recent year when the number five occupied the center of the *Lo Square*; therefore, 2022 is referenced as a five-year.

The numbers then rotate in descending order, so the next cycle of nine years is as indicated in the charts. 2031 is a five-year, at which point the cycle repeats itself.

In ancient times, each trigram and corresponding number was assigned a "family archetype" that served to categorize personality characteristics. The archetypes include, Father, Mother, Eldest Daughter, Youngest Son, and so on.

I've reassigned these family archetypes with the contemporary classifications listed below, followed by brief descriptions of each.

These updated classifications more appropriately apply in our current work and home settings. They are the nine archetypes featured in **The Five Elements** system.

4	9	2
3	**5**	7
8	1	6

2022
"A FIVE YEAR"

5	9	7
6	**4**	2
1	8	3

2023
"A FOUR YEAR"

4	8	6
5	**3**	1
9	7	2

2024
"A THREE YEAR"

3	7	5
4	**2**	9
8	6	1

2025
"A TWO YEAR"

2	6	4
3	**1**	8
7	5	9

2026
"A ONE YEAR"

1	5	3
2	**9**	7
6	4	8

2027
"A NINE YEAR"

9	4	2
1	**8**	6
5	3	7

2028
"AN EIGHT YEAR"

8	3	1
9	**7**	5
4	2	6

2029
"A SEVEN YEAR"

7	2	9
8	**6**	4
3	1	5

2030
"A SIX YEAR"

4	9	2
3	**5**	7
8	1	6

2031
"A FIVE YEAR"

#	ARCHETYPE	ELEMENT	CHARACTERISTICS
1	Philosopher	*Water*	Inquisitive, Insightful, Analytical
2	Caregiver	*Earth*	Nurturing, Humble, Compassionate
3	Visionary	*Wood*	Creative, Clever, Pioneering
4	Optimist	*Wood*	Affable, Inspiring, Empathetic
5	Facilitator	*Earth*	Inclusive, Sensible, Systematic
6	Protector	*Metal*	Orderly, Principled, Assertive
7	Achiever	*Metal*	Task-oriented, Driven, Conscientious
8	Rock	*Earth*	Solid, Dependable, Resourceful
9	Networker	*Fire*	Outgoing, Intuitive, Charismatic

1 | Philosopher ⊙ *Water*

Time and space take on a deep, cyclical quality for the Philosopher. Motivated by the continual quest for knowledge, this archetype aspires toward the Truth with a capital "T." Philosophers think from a perspective of "why" and have a keen interest in how disparate facts and figures can flow into bigger systems and strategies. They maintain a quiet, internal focus that makes them appear mysterious and even aloof.

2 | Caregiver ⊙ *Earth*

Like a warm blanket, Caregivers have the capacity to make others feel nurtured and comforted. Harmony is the Caregiver's highest aspiration and they attain it through service. They are skilled at simultaneously

meeting the needs of the group while tending to those of individuals. By nature, Caregivers are externally focused and seek fulfillment by celebrating the accomplishments of others. They are the most compassionate of the nine archetypes, always seeking to expand their circle of inclusion.

3 | **Visionary** ◉ *Wood*

The fast-thinking nature of the Visionary reflects the phenomenon of thunder. They thrive on change, always seeking new adventures and solutions to the situations that life offers. For the Visionary, there is never just one way to get from point A to point B. Their quest for learning feeds their aspiration for growth. The Visionary's outgoing and precocious nature makes them likeable companions. They view life as a series of synchronistic opportunities that simply need to be recognized

.

WOOD

4 | **Optimist** ◉ *Wood*

Optimists possess the capacity to bring a breath of fresh air to any situation. Their highest aspiration is joy, and if they can make the world a better place, their mission is fulfilled. People are attracted to Optimists because of their sunny disposition, intense curiosity and ability to empathize with others. Despite their joyful exterior, they can be tenacious advocates for the right cause.

WOOD

EARTH

5 | **Facilitator** ⊙ *Earth*

Facilitators hold the practical and spiritual core of a group. In this manner, they have the capacity to stand at the center and manage all components of any endeavor. They are the stage managers, chiefs of staff and COOs who are both invisible yet indispensable. Facilitators aspire toward consensus, allowing everyone to contribute their best selves.

METAL

6 | **Protector** ⊙ *Metal*

Protectors are charged with assuring the safety of those whom they identify as family, community and team. Order is their highest aspiration, as they believe that safety cannot be provided under chaotic conditions. Seen as natural born leaders, Protectors are caring but distant, always keeping an eye on their duty and mission. Integrity and loyalty are of the utmost importance to Protectors. Once that is assured, they will defend their people to the end.

METAL

7 | **Achiever** ⊙ *Metal*

"Let's do it!" This is the motto of the Achiever. The journey from here to there for the Achiever is a straight line, singular and direct. Their primary motivation is accomplishment. They derive satisfaction from checking off items on their list and seeing the fruits of their labors. Achievers have "work hard, play hard" personalities and will jump into any situation with full gusto. They are bold, daring and fun loving, which makes them popular companions.

8 | **Rock** ◉ *Earth*

Like a mountain, Rocks are solid, reliable and ever present. They are the most self-contained of the archetypes, possessing the wisdom and capacity to see what needs to be done and methodically accomplishing tasks without assistance. Rocks are loyal friends and trusted confidantes. They are resourceful and well versed in multiple skills, allowing them to respond to situations from many different perspectives. Their steadfast nature aligns with their aspiration for stability.

EARTH

9 | **Networker** ◉ *Fire*

Networkers possess a warmth and spark in their way of being. They are intellectually bright and intuitively gifted, giving them the ability to be good judges of people and situations. Networkers have a star quality and attract attention whether they want to or not. Perception and image are important to Networkers, thus they are both skilled and discerning with their words. Charming, affable, friendly and humorous, Networkers are excellent at connecting people and committing them to a cause.

FIRE

These numbers and their corresponding archetypes are used to determine a person's Primary, Secondary, Developmental and Relational attributes. The formulas for calculating one's personal archetypes are based upon a system called *Chiu Kung Ming Li*, developed in China 3,000 years ago, and its

Why are there 9 archetypes and 5 elements?

And why are they in this particular order?

Find the answer in Appendix IV.

modern manifestation, *Nine Star Ki* (*Kyu Sei Ki Gaku*), developed in the mid -20th century.

The charts and formulas provided in the next chapter will enable you to create your own Five Elements profile.

Taking an honest look at ourselves—whether it is our physical, emotional, mental or spiritual selves—is one of the hardest things for human beings to do. Like any assessment tool of this kind, it requires some suspension of doubt and a curiosity to see yourself through a different lens. I invite you to be open to this process of discovery.

CHAPTER TWO RECAP

⊙ The nine archetypes are based upon the Lo Square and its characteristics.

⊙ The archetypes were originally assigned family positions (Father, Mother, Eldest Daughter, Youngest Son, etc.) and have been updated for The Five Elements framework (Philosopher, Caregiver, Visionary, etc.)

The updated archetypes:

#	ARCHETYPE	ELEMENT	CHARACTERISTICS
1	Philosopher	*Water*	Inquisitive, Insightful, Analytical
2	Caregiver	*Earth*	Nurturing, Humble, Compassionate
3	Visionary	*Wood*	Creative, Clever, Pioneering
4	Optimist	*Wood*	Affable, Inspiring, Empathetic
5	Facilitator	*Earth*	Inclusive, Sensible, Systematic
6	Protector	*Metal*	Orderly, Principled, Assertive
7	Achiever	*Metal*	Task-oriented, Driven, Conscientious
8	Rock	*Earth*	Solid, Dependable, Resourceful
9	Networker	*Fire*	Outgoing, Intuitive, Charismatic

CHAPTER THREE

DETERMINING *your* FIVE ELEMENTS PROFILE

Although humans possess the capacity to draw upon the characteristics of all nine archetypes, between one and three elements and archetypes are predominant in any individual's Five Elements profile. These main elements and archetypes are calculated according to the following attributes:

PRIMARY ATTRIBUTE	SECONDARY AND DEVELOPMENTAL ATTRIBUTE	RELATIONAL ATTRIBUTE
Who you are when you are at your best. It is the foundation upon how you express yourself in the world when you are "in your element."	Characteristics that reflect the emotional patterns of your personality and typically arise when you are under stress. This attribute also reflects traits that manifested when you were a child, up until about the age of 18.	How you are viewed by others, especially upon first impression. This impression may be positive or negative.

The combination of these attributes describes your unique personal, leadership and communication styles. The keys to compiling your Five Elements profile involve the following steps.

I. Determine your Primary attribute and understand the characteristics of that attribute.

II. Determine your Secondary and Developmental attributes. (Note: these attributes are always identical.) Study the characteristics of these attributes, as well as the dynamics between the Primary, Secondary, and Developmental attributes.

III. Determine your Relational attribute. Study the relational characteristics of that attribute and how they align (or not) with the other attributes.

IV. Refer to the brief analysis of your Five Elements profile in Appendix II.

V. Once you have completed the above four steps, overlay your profile with that of other individuals to determine and understand interpersonal and group dynamics. (Refer to Part III for more information.)

Using your birthdate, you can determine your attributes within 60 seconds by either referring to the charts on pages 47, 50 and 52, or by using our mobile app - my5elements.life.

WHAT IS THE DIFFERENCE BETWEEN AN ARCHETYPE AND AN ATTRIBUTE?

For the purposes of **The Five Elements** system, An archetype refers to the nine personality and leadership profiles. The archetypes are:

#	ARCHETYPE
1	Philosopher
2	Caregiver
3	Visionary
4	Optimist
5	Facilitator
6	Protector
7	Achiever
8	Rock
9	Networker

An attribute refers to the lens by which the archetype is manifested. The attributes are:

ATTRIBUTES
Primary
Secondary
Developmental
Relational

STEP 1 | Determine your primary attribute

Your Primary attribute is an expression of who you are when you are "in your element."

Your Primary attribute represents the manifestation of that which you were born to become, and who you are at your best. The characteristics of your Primary attribute come through in your skills, gifts, talents and contributions. It is the foundation of how you express yourself in the world—particularly in your mannerisms, attitudes, behaviors and life's work.

The Primary attribute is based on the *Lo Square*, which rotates in nine-year cycles. Referring to the chart on page 47, the Primary attribute for Justin, who was born on June 10, 2015, is the 3|Visionary.

There is, however, a caveat. The cycles of the *Lo Square* are based upon a lunar year cycle.

Thus, if one is born between January 1 through mid-February of a given year, their Primary attribute may be determined by the Lo Square from the year *prior* to their birth year.

For example, if Justin was born on January 17, 2015, their Primary attribute would be the 4|Optimist (based on the 2014 *Lo Square*) since the 2015 lunar year did not begin until February 19, 2015.

2	7	9
1	**3**	5
6	8	4

2015
3|VISIONARY

3	8	1
2	**4**	6
7	9	5

2014
4|OPTIMIST

 If your birthday is between January 1 and mid-February, check the lunar year reference chart on page 363 to determine if your Primary attribute is calculated from your birthyear or the prior year.

PLEASE ENTER YOUR BIRTHDATE

Determine your Primary attribute by locating your year of birth in the chart below and matching it to the corresponding archetype.

9	8	7	6	5	4	3	2	1
Networker	Rock	Achiever	Protector	Facilitator	Optimist	Visionary	Caregiver	Philosopher
1910	1911	1912	1913	1914	1915	1916	1917	1918
1919	1920	1921	1922	1923	1924	1925	1926	1927
1928	1929	1930	1931	1932	1933	1934	1935	1936
1937	1938	1939	1940	1941	1942	1943	1944	1945
1946	1947	1948	1949	1950	1951	1952	1953	1954
1955	1956	1957	1958	1959	1960	1961	1962	1963
1964	1965	1966	1967	1968	1969	1970	1971	1972
1973	1974	1975	1976	1977	1978	1979	1980	1981
1982	1983	1984	1985	1986	1987	1988	1989	1990
1991	1992	1993	1994	1995	1996	1997	1998	1999
2000	2001	2002	2003	2004	2005	2006	2007	2008
2009	2010	2011	2012	2013	2014	2015	2016	2017
2018	2019	2020	2021	2022	2023	2024	2025	2026
2027	2028	2029	2030	2031	2032	2033	2034	2035

FIGURE 7:PRIMARY ATTRIBUTE CHART - 1910 - 2035

PLEASE ENTER YOUR PRIMARY ATTRIBUTE

NUMBER | ARCHETYPE

 If you are interested in knowing the mathematical formula behind calculating your Primary element, please reference Appendix IV.

EXAMPLE

SAM	TERRY
Sam's birthdate is January 25, 1986. According to Figure 7, Sam's Primary attribute is: **6**	Protector	Terry's birthdate is June 6, 1989. According to Figure 7, Terry's Primary attribute is: **2**	*Caregiver*

NOTE: Sam's birthdate falls before the 1986 lunar new year; therefore, his Primary attribute is calculated from 1985.

If your birthday falls on a cusp, check the archetype profiles on both sides of the cusp and determine which Secondary and Developmental attribute is the best fit.

STEP 2 | Determine your secondary and developmental attributes

Your Secondary and Developmental attributes embody your internal realm and describe the characteristics and patterns of:

- your childhood;

- your emotional state of being; and

- your attitudes and behaviors when you are under stress.

Like a drop of food coloring that infuses a glass of water, your Secondary and Developmental attributes influence your core being (Primary attribute) and your public image (Relational attribute).

The relationship between the Secondary and Developmental and Primary attributes are crucial in understanding the transition from childhood to adulthood. Many of us wonder why the teenage years can be so difficult. **The Five Elements** helps us gain a better understanding of the tensions and dynamics of this transition. In addition, **The Five Elements** provides solutions to make the transition easier, both for teenagers and those who live with them.

The Secondary and Developmental attributes are always identical.

 Read Chapter 15 for detailed information on the transition between the Developmental and Primary attributes.

You can determine your Secondary and Developmental attributes by locating the appropriate row of the month and day of your birthdate, along with the applicable column of your Primary attribute.

Primary Attribute	9	8	7	6	5	4	3	2	1
	Net	Rock	Ach	Pro	Fac	Opt	Vis	Care	Phil
Birthdate (MM|DD)									
4 Feb – 5 Mar	5	2	8	5	2	8	5	2	8
6 Mar – 4 Apr	4	1	7	4	1	7	4	1	7
5 Apr – 5 May	3	9	6	3	9	6	3	9	6
6 May – 5 Jun	2	8	5	2	8	5	2	8	5
6 Jun – 7 Jul	1	7	4	1	7	4	1	7	4
8 Jul – 7 Aug	9	6	3	9	6	3	9	6	3
8 Aug – 7 Sept	8	5	2	8	5	2	8	5	2
8 Sept – 8 Oct	7	4	1	7	4	1	7	4	1
9 Oct – 7 Nov	6	3	9	6	3	9	6	3	9
8 Nov – 7 Dec	5	2	8	5	2	8	5	2	8
8 Dec – 5 Jan	4	1	7	4	1	7	4	1	7
6 Jan – 3 Feb	3	9	6	3	9	6	3	9	6

FIGURE 8: SECONDARY AND DEVELOPMENTAL ATTRIBUTE CHART

PLEASE ENTER YOUR PRIMARY AND SECONDARY|DEVELOPMENTAL ATTRIBUTES

NUMBER | ARCHETYPE ⊙ ARCHETYPE

EXAMPLE

SAM	TERRY
Sam's birthdate is January 25 in a 6-year. According to Figure 8, Sam's Secondary and Developmental attribute is: 3 | *Visionary* Sam's profile so far is: **63** | Protector ⊙ *Visionary*	Terry's birthdate is June 6 in a 2-year. According to Figure 8, Terry's Secondary and Developmental attribute is: 7 | *Achiever* Terry's profile so far is: **27** | *Caregiver* ⊙ *Achiever*

Note: Since Terry's birthdate falls on a cusp (June 6), we checked both archetype profiles for the 8|Rock (June 5) and 7|Achiever (June 6). Terry determined that the 7|Achiever was a better fit.

STEP 3 | Determine your relational attribute

Your Relational attribute reflects your public persona and how you are viewed by others. It is often most evident upon your first impression. It is the attribute that we often aspire toward because it represents the qualities that we believe people want and expect from us. Use your Primary and Secondary and Developmental attribute numbers to identify your Relational attribute in the chart below.

914	813	712	611	519	418	317	216	115
923	822	721	629	528	427	326	225	124
932	831	739	638	537	436	335	234	133
941	849	748	647	546	445	344	243	142
959	858	757	656	555	454	353	252	151
968	867	766	665	564	463	362	261	169
977	876	775	674	573	472	371	279	178
986	885	784	683	582	481	389	288	187
995	894	793	692	591	499	398	297	196

FIGURE 9: RELATIONAL ATTRIBUTE CHART

PLEASE ENTER YOUR FIVE ELEMENTS PROFILE
NUMBER	ARCHETYPE ⊙ ARCHETYPE ⊙ ARCHETYPE

Coding provides you with a shorthand method of referring to a Five Elements profile by its numbers. The code is always listed with the attributes in the following order:

PRIMARY – SECONDARY AND DEVELOPMENTAL - RELATIONAL

Using Sam and Terry as an example, Sam's attributes are:

Primary - 6|Protector;
Secondary and Developmental - 3|Visionary; and
Relational - 8|Rock.

Thus, Sam's code is 638 (pronounced "six-three-eight").

Terry's attributes are:

Primary - 2|Caregiver;
Secondary and Development - 7|Achiever; and
Relational - 9|Networker.

Thus, Terry's code is 279 (pronounced "two-seven-nine").

These codes are used throughout the book in profiles describing a person's archetypes; for instance, Oprah Winfrey is a 297, Barack Obama is a 398, and Mark Zuckerberg is a 757.

For the purpose of clarity, I provide the archetypes along with the codes; for example, Sam's full Five Elements profile is: 638 - Protector|Visionary|Rock, and Terry's full profile is 279 – Caregiver|Achiever|Networker.

EXAMPLE

SAM	TERRY
Sam's Primary, Secondary, and Developmental numbers are 63.	Terry's Primary and Secondary, and Developmental numbers are 27.
According to Figure 9, Sam's Relational attribute is	According to Figure 9, Terry's Relational attribute is
8 | *Rock*	**9** | *Networker*
Sam's Five Elements profile is:	Terry's Five Elements profile is:
638 | *Protector ⊙ Visionary ⊙ Rock*	**279** | *Caregiver ⊙ Achiever ⊙ Networker*

Now that you know your Five Elements profile, you can assess the dynamics between your own Primary, Secondary, Developmental and Relational attributes to learn more about yourself and which elements you need to emphasize in order to achieve and maintain balance.

The result of your assessment could be harmonious or stressful, depending on the alignment of the Relational attribute with the Primary, Secondary and Developmental attributes. If the elements within the archetypes are in the Supporting cycle, the result will be harmonious. If they fall outside of the Supporting cycle, your life outside of the home can be more difficult.

Let's look at Sam as an example. Sam's Relational attribute is 8|Rock (Earth). Sam's Primary attribute is 6|Protector (Metal). Since Earth supports Metal, Sam's public persona of the solid and dependable Rock is aligned with the Primary Protector qualities of "take charge" leadership, loyalty and integrity.

But when Sam is in stress, the Secondary attribute of 3|Visionary (Wood) kicks in. The characteristics of being fun loving and noncommittal run against the grain of the solid and dependable Rock .

Thus, one's first impression of Sam might be very different if Sam is operating from a Primary or Secondary mode. Since first impressions last, Sam might be remembered as a solid and dependable leader (Relational|Rock supports Primary|Protector), or an overwhelmed and scattered leader (Relational| Rock is restrained by Secondary|Visionary)

Chapters 4 through 12 provide more information on each of the nine archetypes, including details on the:

To determine the formula for calculating the Relational attribute, consult Appendix IV.

⊙ Primary attribute;

⊙ Secondary attribute (characteristics under stress);

⊙ Developmental attribute (characteristics as a child);

- ⊙ Archetype in relationships;

- ⊙ Archetype in the workplace;

- ⊙ Advice for this archetype; and

- ⊙ Profiles of people who embody these archetypes.

They are presented in order from 1|Philosopher to 9|Networker. You may choose to read about each archetype or go straight to the chapters that correlate with your Five Elements profile.

Part III will guide you through the process of charting and analyzing your profile. This will help you understand the dynamics and nuances among the attributes and determine solutions, if needed. Once you have completed these steps, you can overlay your profile with that of other individuals to determine and understand interpersonal and group dynamics.

CHAPTER THREE RECAP

⊙ Although humans possess the capacity to draw upon the characteristics of all nine archetypes, between one and three archetypes are predominant in a person's Five Elements profile. These predominant archetypes are calculated according to the following attributes:

PRIMARY ATTRIBUTE	SECONDARY AND DEVELOPMENTAL ATTRIBUTE	RELATIONAL ATTRIBUTE
Who you are when you are at your best. It is the foundation upon how you express yourself in the world when you are "in your element."	Characteristics that reflect the emotional patterns of your personality and typically arise when you are under stress. This attribute also reflects traits that manifested when you were a child, up until about the age of 18.	How you are viewed by others, especially upon first impression. This impression may be positive or negative.

⊙ The combination of these attributes describes your unique personality, leadership and communication style. The key to determining your Five Elements profile involves the following four steps. All you need is a birthdate (mm|dd|yyyy) and the charts on pages 47-52.

I. Determine your Primary attribute and understand the characteristics of that attribute.

II. Determine your Secondary and Developmental attribute. (Note: these attributes are always identical.) Study the characteristics of that attribute, as well as the dynamics of the transition between the Primary, Secondary, and Developmental attributes.

III. Determine your Relational attribute. Study the relational characteristics of that attribute and how they align (or not) with the other attributes.

IV. Write down your numerical code (Primary, Secondary, Developmental and Relational) and match it with the corresponding archetypes.

#	ARCHETYPE
1	Philosopher
2	Caregiver
3	Visionary
4	Optimist
5	Facilitator
6	Protector
7	Achiever
8	Rock
9	Networker

PLEASE ENTER YOUR FIVE ELEMENTS PROFILE

NUMBER | ARCHETYPE ⊙ ARCHETYPE ⊙ ARCHETYPE

⊙ The combination of these attributes describes your unique personality, leadership and communication style.

⊙ Example: If your numerical code is 418, your Primary archetype is Optimist, your Secondary and Developmental archetype is Philosopher, and your Relational archetype is Rock.

⊙ Remember: If your birthday is between January 1 and mid-February, check the lunar year reference chart on page 363 to determine if your Primary attribute is calculated from the previous year.

PART TWO

THE NINE ARCHETYPES

PROFILE *of a* PHILOSOPHER

CHARLES
151

Philosopher ⊙ Facilitator ⊙ Philosopher

Charles is a solid man. At 6′4″ and 260 lbs., he can make a statement just by showing up. But as a Philosopher, that's not his style. Charles typically slips into a room unnoticed, sits in a corner and closes his eyes. In this quiet and secluded space, Charles listens intently, tuning in to the stillness and undercurrent in the room that, to him, speaks volumes. When he is ready, Charles raises his hand, and in a few words, articulates what has been said and unsaid with an uncanny degree of poetry and accuracy.

While quiet and reserved at most times, Charles also has a quick tongue that reveals a witty and humorous side when he is among close friends. He has an opinion on everything and will fully admit that he can't leave well enough alone. Nonetheless, not a day passes when friends and strangers won't call on Charles for his advice and counsel.

As a journalist and photographer, Charles often says things that are typical of a Philosopher:

- ⊙ *"How does this activity relate to your mission?"*

- ⊙ *"Do you have data to support that?"*

- ⊙ *"What are the facts? What do we know and what do we need to know?"*

- ⊙ *"I have one more question."*

Poised, enigmatic and perpetually cool, Charles keeps his family, friends and colleagues anchored by being an example of what it means to live a life with purpose and meaning.

Virtue	Wisdom
Skill	Analysis | Synthesis
Motivation	Knowledge
Aspiration	Truth
Element	Water
Preoccupation	Data
Fear	Exposure
Shadow	The Cynic
Tends to	Seek Sustainability
Needs to cultivate	Living in the present

CHAPTER FOUR

1 - THE PHILOSOPHER

"What does it all mean?" | "It'll never work."

Primary Attribute – Philosophers at Their Best

Philosophers are masters at balancing stillness and motion. Like a deep well, people are drawn to the Philosopher's ability to clearly shape and reflect a situation. Similar to a flowing stream, they seamlessly move from the abstract to the concrete, integrating purpose and values with data and results. Philosophers analyze situations with all five senses and exercise these skills to get beneath the surface and understand things as they really are. As leaders, they remind us of our true calling and help us determine our potential so that we can achieve our respective missions in an integrated fashion.

Philosophers, like water, have the capacity to find their own level in any situation. Grand entrances aren't their style. They prefer to quietly slip in, observe and assess. They will choose how and when to speak—and when they do, their words will likely have a deep impact.

As contemplative thinkers, Philosophers value their own space and independence. There is a quality of solitude in their being that makes them appear enigmatic. Their quiet nature gives people the perception that Philosophers are shy and aloof. On the contrary, they seek to merge thoughts, ideas and practices into a greater truth .

Secondary Attribute – The Cynic

Philosophers under stress can be prone to cynicism. They may find themselves stuck in a whirlpool that they cannot escape, leading to a sense of isolation and even depression. Under these conditions, they tend to retreat to their rooms, draw the drapes, and settle in with their favorite beverage and snacks to binge watch their favorite TV shows.

When Philosophers sink into a cynical mode, they become overly judgmental, worrisome, snippy, or just plain mean. Their energy can be so encompassing that they take everyone down with them. If a Philosopher says, "It'll never work," they are rarely challenged .

"When water starts boiling, it's foolish to turn off the heat."
NELSON MANDELA **133**

A Philosopher's biggest fear is being exposed. It is unacceptable for them to be wrong. Because of this, they can live in a state of anxiety and their level of mental chatter casts a pall of self-doubt which is difficult for them to dial down. Philosophers often manage this by using a device such as a camera, notepad or audio/video recorder to create a sense of separation and space from others so they can process information in their own way.

The best way to support a Philosopher is to give them time and space to reintegrate. When a sufficient amount of time has passed, gently provide structure for the Philosopher to reengage with the world. Meditation, quiet walks (especially by a lake or shoreline), music, and sunlight or firelight are helpful tools for engaging with Philosophers when they are in their cynical mode.

Relational Attribute – Philosophers in Public

At first impression, Philosophers can seem aloof and intimidating. Think about how children are warned to keep their distance from a swimming pool so that they don't fall in and drown. People take the same attitude toward Philosophers, tending to keep them at arm's length.

Because of their wise persona, people can also feel as if they are being constantly judged by Philosophers.

"If Plan A isn't working, I have a Plan B, Plan C, and even Plan D."
SERENA WILLIAMS 115

"I was a keen observer and listener. I picked up on clues. I figured things out logically, and I enjoyed puzzles. I loved the clear, focused feeling that came when I concentrated on solving a problem and everything else faded out."

SONIA SOTOMAYOR **142**

(Little do they know that the Philosopher is usually focused on judging themselves.) This sense of judgment reinforces the sense of formality and withholding that Philosophers experience when encountering others.

It is important to find a place of common interest and passion in order to connect with a Philosopher on a deeper level. Injecting humor and levity, as appropriate, will help in getting both of you into the flow of your relationship.

Developmental Attribute – The Young Philosopher

"Wise beyond their years" is a term that is often used to describe a young Philosopher. They seem to come into the world with a deep sense of knowing, as if it is not their first time on the planet. As children, Philosophers tend to be reserved and full of thoughts. Although they are well liked by their peers, young Philosophers do not tolerate fools and are selective with their choice of friends. They may befriend older peers or adults who can match their capacity to engage in their thirst for knowledge and intellectual conversation.

A young Philosopher will often open their sentences with "Why . . ." This leaves those around them with the difficult task of explaining why the sky is blue, why war exists, and why we have little toes. As they grow, Philosophers are studious and disciplined, typically latching onto a topic that grows into their passion. Whether it's robotics, ballet, badminton or drawing, this child will become an expert on the subject and it will likely influence their academic and career decisions later in life.

For those raising young Philosophers, it is important to provide them with a balance of space and structure. These children can entertain themselves for hours with the simplest things, as their minds engage in the minutest details of the book they are reading or the fort they are constructing. Allow them time and space to explore these nuances. Don't be tempted to put their project away before bedtime, as they might be on the verge of a new discovery.

At the same time, Philosophers need structure to keep them from sinking too deep into their own abyss. Engage them in activities, especially group or team pursuits, that stretch their comfort zone. They will likely find ways to tie their experiences back to their topic of primary interest.

Philosophers in Relationship

The moods and complexities that Philosophers bring into a relationship create multiple layers to explore

"I encourage people to find and use the power of their voices just as much when I do not agree with those voices as when I do agree with them."
NIKKI HALEY **169**

PROFILE *of a* YOUNG PHILOSOPHER

RAFAEL

611

Protector ⊙ *Philosopher* ⊙ *Philosopher*

As a child, Rafael was a keen observer of people and patterns. He took an interest in everything that moved, especially planes, trains, boats and buses. Throughout his childhood, Rafael constructed airports and ferry terminals with whatever was within his reach: blocks, books, sand, cardboard boxes, and even his stuffed animals.

When he was in the first grade, Rafael claimed a walk-in closet as his space. He stocked the shelves with his books, blocks, toy airplanes and boom box. Upon returning home from school, Rafael would grab a snack and head to his space to decompress. Forty-five minutes later, he'd emerge, ready to talk about his day.

Rafael graduated with a degree in urban planning with an emphasis on public transportation systems. While he was in college, he worked part time as a bus driver to gain a deep experience and appreciation for every aspect of the system. He is now the public information officer for a transportation authority in a major city.

When Rafael was born, the nurse looked at him and said, "His eyes are so big. It lets him understand more of the world than the rest of us." Indeed, he has.

and navigate. One day, the Philosopher might be in a light, go-with-the-flow attitude. The next day, they might be in a quieter, more reflective space.

Because of these unpredictable dynamics, it is helpful for partners to see themselves as a vessel that can be in sync with, but separate from, the water rather than being immersed in the water itself. This will prevent partners from falling into the ebbs and flows of the Philosopher's nature.

Because of their desire for solitude, Philosophers need to have the option and space to be alone. Their partners should not take this personally, as Philosophers do not measure success in a relationship through time spent together. Their need for alone time is not a rejection, but a way to recharge and reintegrate. It is important, however, for the partner to keep watch on the Philosopher in case they fall into an abysmal state. In this case, the Philosopher will feel isolated and trapped in their own whirlpool and the partner will feel adrift and powerless to reverse the vortex.

Philosophers are very loyal and choose their partners wisely. While their behaviors may indicate distance and formality, it does not reflect the depth of their love and affection. On the other hand, a Philosopher may become completely consumed with and defined by their partner, just as a container shapes and

"The less you talk, the more you're listened to."
ABIGAIL VAN BUREN 142

defines water. It is important to find the right balance of flow and containment with a Philosopher in order to maintain a healthy and harmonious relationship.

Philosophers in the Workplace

At work, Philosophers provide their organizations with "3S" thinking: Strategies, Systems and Synthesis. They are good at diving deep into questions of meaning and purpose, and connecting the dots between philosophy and operations. Philosophers can be relied upon to design and integrate values-based policies and processes within an organization.

Because of their skill at analysis and flow, Philosophers are gifted in areas such as finance, human resources, research, evaluation and strategy; however, their work has to have meaning. They need to find ways to connect directly with the mission and overall impact on their constituents. Thus, purely managerial or administrative duties are likely not enough to satisfy the Philosopher.

Philosophers prefer to operate independently. While they are good at supporting and nurturing others, they do it in a quiet, unassuming manner. When making a request of a Philosopher, be prepared to present a clear rationale, process and expected outcome. They will eventually have questions, and

"I think that policy matters. I'm a policy guy."
PETE BUTTIGIEG **169**

the questions will be valid. Give time and space for a response, as Philosophers may need to reflect on the matter.

Advice for Philosophers

Since Philosophers live for a deeper purpose, it is important to maintain a calm and clear disposition. Make time in your day to center yourself by closing your eyes and taking three deep breaths. If you sit for long periods of time, take an occasional walking break and get some fresh air. This will help center and align your body, thoughts, emotions and spirit so you can be wise and discerning.

Because Metal supports Water, Philosophers should identify small tasks that they can accomplish in a short period of time. Think daily or weekly tasks as opposed to monthly or annual tasks. By breaking down your big goals into small steps, you will be less prone to procrastination.

It is helpful for Philosophers to find ways to inject humor and spontaneity in their lives. By engaging with creative people, such as Optimists and Visionaries, you will not be tempted to take life so seriously and your insights can be used in a productive manner.

Since the primary body parts for the Philosopher are the ears, acquiring knowledge and information

"Don't gain the world and lose your soul; wisdom is better than silver or gold."
BOB MARLEY **187**

through auditory methods like podcasts and books on tape are preferred to visual methods such as books and videos. If a Philosopher needs to write a major report or book, try recording thoughts on tape then transcribing the notes. It will facilitate getting out of your head and prevent being fixated on editing the words on the paper or screen.

Add colors (grey, silver and green) and objects that symbolize Metal and Wood in your personal and work spaces. Keep building materials (modeling clay, building blocks, etc.) close by so you can construct ideas instead of just talking about them.

If a Philosopher is under stress or is required to speak in public, blue clothes (Water colors) with grey, silver or gold accents (Metal colors) such as a scarf, tie or jewelry is recommended in order to feel supported and in your element.

Philosophers would benefit by developing a meditation practice that can be done alone or with a group that involves the ears, eyes and body. Something that can be listened to and applied visually (like dance, *tai chi*, painting or a photography class) would be ideal.

Advice for Those Who Live and Work with Philosophers

⊙ Allow more time than you think for discussion and reflection. Do not expect a quick response.

⊙ Provide all significant data and use logic-based arguments.

⊙ Justify your position by providing historical precedence and alignment with ethics and values.

⊙ Find ways to interject humor and spontaneity to reverse the potential of cynicism.

⊙ Do not be offended if the Philosopher retreats and disengages. It is more about their need for time and space to rejuvenate.

"The world can become a very meaningless place if you don't really understand: 'Who am I? Why am I here? What am I doing?' To feel fulfillment and have a deeper level of understanding; personally, that is the most important thing."
ALICIA KEYS **169**

A Bit of Sage Guidance for Philosophers
FROM *THE BOOK OF CHANGES AND THE UNCHANGING TRUTH* BY HUA-CHING NI

"Be content with a "low" position. Like water, by
remaining low, one may be safe and free
from competition. Remain profound. A profound mind
is as quiet as the deep ocean. Therefore, it is
undisturbed by the waves on the surface.

Give generously. Water constantly gives without asking
to be repaid.

Speak faithfully. The flow of Water always faithfully
goes toward the sea.

Govern gently. Though Water moves with gentleness,
it can overcome even the hardest obstacles.

Work capably and adaptably. Water can fit what is
square or what is round. It keeps its true nature in any
containment or circumstance.

Take action opportunely. Water freezes in winter and
melts in spring. Its inflexibility in winter is like death.
Its softness in the spring generates new life.

Never fight. Water does not fight for itself; thus it is
beyond blame."

PROFILE *of a* NOTABLE PHILOSOPHER

BEYONCÉ

124

Philosopher ⊙ Caregiver ⊙ Optimist

Superstar. Icon. Legend. There is no doubt that Beyoncé can light up the world just by showing up. Yet beyond the spotlights, she is known to be a perfectionist who is deeply involved in all aspects of her work. "She cared about everything that was in the record," said one of her co-producers. "She cared about what piano we were going to use. Is there enough bass? She's got all the respect from me in the world that I can give."

> *"If you don't take the time to think about and analyze your life, you'll never realize all the dots that are all connected."*
>
> BEYONCÉ

In her groundbreaking album, "Lemonade" (accompanied by a 65-minute video), Beyoncé confronted her feelings around infidelity with larger societal issues of race, trauma and redemption. She wove in tributes to Black philosophers like Malcolm X, Audre Lorde, Octavia Butler, and Chimamanda Ngozi Adichie. The result was a testament to Black womanhood that influenced millions.

Beyoncé understands that she has as unique and powerful platform to be a social, political and cultural advocate for change. Peers such as Lizzo, Chloe X Halle, Rihanna, Adele, Sam Smith, and Lady Gaga all credit Beyoncé as an inspiration for their careers. She has shown us what it means to unapologetically live in one's truth—and no matter how much it might hurt, to find a path toward healing.

On the fifth anniversary of the release of "Lemonade," Beyoncé wrote:

I'm grateful that this body of work has resonated so deeply with so many people. I'm so thankful for all the beautiful souls involved in making one of my favorite pieces of art. As I celebrate five years of 'Lemonade', I encourage everyone to continue healing, loving, forgiving and uplifting. I hope you find joy today.

To which a fan commented, "'Lemonade' will continue bringing joy 500 years from now."

"When I'm not feeling my best, I ask myself, 'What are you gonna do about it'? I use the negativity to fuel the transformation into a better me."

BEYONCÉ

1 - THE PHILOSOPHER RECAP

⦿ Time and space take on a deep, cyclical quality for the Philosopher. Motivated by the continual quest for knowledge, they aspire toward the Truth with a capital "T."

⦿ Philosophers think from a perspective of "why" and have a keen interest in how disparate facts and figures can flow into bigger systems and strategies. They have a quiet, internal focus that makes them appear mysterious and even aloof.

⦿ Philosophers under stress can be prone to cynicism. They may find themselves stuck in a whirlpool that they cannot escape, leading to a sense of isolation and even depression. Their energy may be so encompassing that they can take everyone down with them.

⦿ Philosophers are very loyal and choose their partners wisely. They tend to be complex and moody, often needing time and space for themselves.

⦿ At work, Philosophers provide their organizations with "3S" thinking: Strategies, Systems and Synthesis. They are gifted in areas such as finance, human resources, research, evaluation and strategy.

⦿ Recommendations for Philosophers include finding a daily practice to stay anchored, and infusing humor and spontaneity into their routines.

PROFILE *of*
TWO CAREGIVERS

VON AND MELODY
225 and 225
Caregiver ◉ *Caregiver* ◉ *Facilitator*

Melody and Von are co-directors of a youth empowerment circle. Von, a former high school football player, and Melody, a half-marathon runner, still maintain healthy lifestyles, in part, because they believe that they need to set good examples of well-being for the young people they serve. They are like peas in a pod, working and communicating together as a team.

Their warmhearted and accommodating nature make them trusted confidantes among the youth. "It's all about serving the kids and surrounding them with as much love and opportunity as possible, " Von said.

"We let them know that we value our relationship with them, " continued Melody. "They are part of our community, and we will be here for them."

This devotion is reciprocated by their program's alumni, now young adults and parents themselves, who continue to volunteer as mentors. In walking through the circle, one will typically hear words like:

- ⊙ *"No matter what, the most important thing is for us stick together."*

- ⊙ *"How does everyone feel about this decision?"*

- ⊙ *"We haven't heard from some of you yet. What do you think?"*

- ⊙ *"Let's hug it out."*

This spirit of cooperation is a tribute to Melody and Von, who lead their lives with full hearts, open arms and kind spirits. They make all who are a part of their circle feel included, accepted and loved.

Virtue	Devotion
Skill	Perceiving others' needs
Motivation	Service
Aspiration	Harmony
Element	Earth
Preoccupation	Others
Fear	Conflict
Shadow	The Martyr
Tends to	Seek the perfect community
Needs to cultivate	Self-care

CHAPTER FIVE

2 - THE CAREGIVER

"How can I help?" | "No really, I don't mind."

Primary Attribute – Caregivers at Their Best

Dedicated, nurturing and forgiving are words used to describe Mother Earth. Such are the characteristics of the Caregiver.

Caregivers are viewed as a quiet force—the people behind the scenes who help others shine. Their devotion to community is an essential part of the Caregiver's existence. They derive their sense of purpose through service. True to their humble nature, they make others the center of attention.

Caregivers are skilled at creating a safe and welcoming environment for all, while maintaining a keen eye on individual needs. Imagine Von and Melody observing a reception that they coordinated. They might notice to their left that a table is out of place, or hear an elder coughing. To their right, they might note the need for more soft drinks, or see a young person searching for a pen. Von heads to the left, moves the table and hands the elder a glass of water. Melody walks to the right, asks the waitstaff to replenish the soft drinks, and hands the young person a pen. Two minutes later, these two Caregivers cross to the other side of the room, having established harmony without being noticed.

Caregivers are masters at establishing and maintaining a culture of care. They recognize the importance of ceremony as a means to ground a community and often organize birthdays, anniversaries and holiday celebrations. Likewise, they have the gift of gently reaching out to people who are experiencing difficult times, offering just the right gestures to bring comfort.

Secondary Attribute – The Martyr

It is 10 o'clock in the evening and the host committee is far from ready to receive 200 guests for the company's open house the next morning. The centerpieces are incomplete, programs need to be copied, and the registration table is not set up. The committee members are tired and frazzled. In the spirit of service, the Caregiver of the team tells everyone to go home and offers to stay late and finish up. Some folks wish to stay as well, but the Caregiver insists that they go, saying, "No really, I don't mind."

Our prime purpose in this life is to help others. And if you can't help them, at least don't hurt them."
HIS HOLINESS THE DALAI LAMA **279**

The Caregiver stays until one o'clock in the morning completing all the tasks at hand then returns an hour before the rest of the committee members arrive at the start of the event to make sure that all is well. Everything is taken care of with one exception: The committee did not thank the Caregiver, who upon receiving no acknowledgment, becomes a Martyr. The Caregiver won't say anything, preferring to wait until the opportune moment to seek their own form of justice.

Caregivers abhor conflict and will not advocate for their own needs. Because they are so accommodating, people tend to take advantage of them. When repeated, this results in a "doormat cycle" and the Caregiver becomes a perpetual victim. Self-sacrifice becomes an enduring pattern in their lives, which can manifest as co-dependent and passive-aggressive behavior.

Acknowledgment and appreciation are key factors in preventing this cycle. Simple gestures of gratitude (a short note, a pat on the back, flowers, or a cup of coffee) is all that a Caregiver needs to know that they are seen and valued. These small acts will bring the Caregiver back from martyrdom and ensure harmony and devotion.

"It's very important for us all to understand that we are interconnected and we need to hold hands together, especially when the going gets tough."
MICHELLE YEOH **261**

Relational Attribute – Caregivers in Public

The warmth and comfort that one feels after a good meal evokes the same feeling when encountering a Caregiver. People relax and let their guards down, knowing that they will be safe and nurtured under the Caregiver's stewardship.

Because of their service orientation, Caregivers are always occupied with a task, and if not, they appear to be busy. This may be a reflection of a Caregiver's general discomfort with being the center of attention. They tend to be withdrawn in the company of strangers, which people might take as a sign of unfriendliness. On the contrary, the Caregiver likely does not want to intrude if they are not requested.

The biggest compliment that a person can give to a Caregiver is offering a helping hand, or approaching them without a request but with a sincere interest in getting to know them. These gestures indicate a desire to build and sustain relationships, which is the lens by which Caregivers view the world.

Developmental Attribute – The Young Caregiver

"Sweet" is a word that is often used to describe a Caregiver child. Their quest for harmony contributes to their reputation as being agreeable, unassuming

"Who cares about winning? We should focus on serving."
JUSTIN TRUDEAU **216**

PROFILE *of a* YOUNG CAREGIVER

THERESA

225

Caregiver ◉ *Caregiver* ◉ *Facilitator*

Theresa's favorite childhood memory is peeling oranges for her grandmother while her father visited with his relatives. "My grandmother loved oranges," Theresa comments, "but her fingers weren't nimble enough to peel them. When I was four years old, I asked my mother if I could peel grandma an orange, and it became my duty. Seeing grandma's smile when she bit into an orange segment was the best part of my day."

Another of Theresa's favorite pastimes was to watch ants. She would lay out breadcrumbs and watch one ant pick up a crumb and pass it onto the next ant and the next until the ants made it home. She took those lessons and organized a food drive for her community. "I learned that if everyone does a little bit and helps each other, we're all better off for it."

A child of few words, Theresa was content in seeing others take the spotlight and would often shy away from being the center of attention. "Being in the background was fine with me," she recalls. "It kept me out of trouble."

Theresa is now the cultural preservationist for her tribe. She supports the council members in their daily work and manages major campaigns on behalf of her people. One of her most recent campaigns was advocating for the preservation of a mountain that her people consider sacred. The campaign was successful due primarily to Theresa's hard work and dedication. The tribal leadership insisted that Theresa be front and center in a photo that was featured in the local paper. It was their way of saying, "We see you and we honor you."

and appreciative. They say "please" and "thank you" without being prompted and will forego playing with the other children by running into the kitchen and asking, "How can I help?" or "What can I do?" If there isn't enough candy for everyone, Caregiver children will be the first to share theirs.

They may be referred to as "mom's favorite" or "teacher's pet" and people may read these intentions as self-serving. To the contrary, the Caregiver child gets deep satisfaction by simply helping others.

They are good students yet tend to downplay their accomplishments and even not realize their academic potential in order to not stand out amongst their friends. Their desire to help may lead to them being taken advantage of by their classmates, as they may be too generous with their help and participation, especially in group projects.

Caregiver children enjoy looking out for others and are good with animals, youngsters and elders. They are the ones who bring home stray animals and make sure that the elderly neighbor gets a handcrafted birthday card.

It is important for those who are raising young Caregivers to instill a sense of self-worth and confidence in them. They may tend to feel that no matter how much they try to save the world, it's not enough. Caregivers will need guidance in establishing boundaries and setting priorities. Make sure their basics are covered, including getting a proper diet, enough rest and ample relaxation.

Because they are the good and sweet ones, Caregiver children may be overlooked and even neglected. Try to schedule daily one-on-one time with them and listen to their accomplishments and concerns. This will provide an opportunity to see if they are being taken advantage of (for Caregivers always think the best of people) and lavish them with appreciation.

Caregivers in Relationship

Caregivers are desirable partners because their primary focus is on others. Their devotion and care are indicators that one has found the person of their dreams. Caregivers remember the little details of their partner's likes and dislikes (coffee with cream and no sugar, dogs versus cats, and orchids instead of roses), which is endearing. They are tender, affectionate, and sentimental, making Caregiver men an especially desirable catch.

Because the archetype of the Caregiver is fertile Earth, they tend to settle quickly into a relationship. A few dates are all that is needed for the Caregiver to determine whether their prospective partner is "the

"The fun for me in collaboration is working with other people; it just makes you smarter."
LIN-MANUEL MIRANDA **297**

one." Once that is determined, long-term plans can be made to secure the union.

Depending on the partner's element, this attribute may or may not serve the relationship well. If the partner feels overwhelmed by all the care and attention and responds with a harsh word or gesture, the Caregiver will remember that moment and often develop a grudge that can last for years. Caregivers will stick with the relationship out of devotion or suffering (if operating from the Martyr perspective), so it will be up to the partner to either take steps to repair the relationship or step away.

It is important for Caregivers to be acknowledged for their role in the primary relationship. Small and consistent gestures go a long way in maintaining a healthy and harmonious relationship with a Caregiver.

Caregivers in the Workplace

Many people would describe the Caregiver as the "glue" of their community, who somehow magically weaves individual and sometimes conflicting personalities into a harmonious and productive tapestry. Often thought of as the support people of the organization, Caregivers may occupy any title or position. While Caregiver deliverables might be hard to measure, they are no less essential to the health and productivity of any organization.

Caregivers are known to practice intrusive leadership, believing that it is important to understand what is happening in a colleague's personal life in order to make the best and most productive decisions for both the individual and the collective. A Caregiver who is an officer in the U.S. Navy describes it like this:

"We were prepping to conduct a drill at sea when I noticed one of my crew members was not as engaged as he normally is. I took him aside and asked him what was up, and he confided that his mother was receiving her first radiation therapy for cancer treatment that day. The young man apologized for being distracted, and for his own good and the good of the crew, I took him off the team that day. If I hadn't taken the time and care to connect with this crew member, our mission could have been compromised."

As quiet people of action, Caregivers embody the concept of servant leadership, keeping an eye on the bigger picture, as well as the nuances, to maintain a healthy, harmonious and prosperous workplace.

"Life is not a solo act. It's a huge collaboration, and we all need to assemble around us the people who care about us and support us in times of strife."

TIM GUNN **261**

Advice for Caregivers

The primary issue for Caregivers is the tendency to get stuck in process. They find it difficult to detach themselves from the minutiae and focus on outcomes. The primary recommendation is to shed some light on the dynamics at play that will support a plan of action.

Caregivers would be best served by developing a practical nature to all aspects of life, and by intentionally giving and seeking support every day—for example, having daily contact with different friends or loved ones, making a daily chore list, or cooking more often. It is important to find ways to express your wants and needs so others can acknowledge your contributions and support you. Practice saying "no" and "I need" and seeking clarity from trusted friends. This way, you are not giving people what they think they need but are paying attention to what people really need. When others do acknowledge a Caregiver, it is best for you to step into the spotlight—if only for a moment—and allow yourself to be seen and appreciated.

If you are a Caregiver, add colors (red, purple, grey, silver) and objects that symbolize Fire and Metal (candlesticks) to frame the elements that lead and follow Earth. Incorporate these elements into your wardrobe by wearing red, purple, grey or gold accents (a scarf or a tie) every day, and especially if you are under stress or speaking in public.

Caregivers would benefit by finding a way to connect directly to the earth, whether it is through gardening, going for a walk or working with modeling clay. Spiritual practices that involve community service are most appropriate for Caregivers, as your best spiritual food is helping others.

Advice for Those Who Live and Work with Caregivers

⊙ Acknowledge! Acknowledge! Acknowledge! Focus on the basics, such as when they last had a meal, how much sleep they've been getting, and when they last treated themselves to something they like. Even better, bring them lunch, coffee or a handwritten note of appreciation. Caregivers will long remember these kind gestures.

⊙ Be aware that Caregivers may have trouble saying no to you.

⊙ Caregivers aspire towards harmony. If you are giving a Caregiver critical feedback, choose your words carefully.

⊙ Process is important for Caregivers. Make sure that you establish terms of engagement at the outset of your relationship.

A Bit of Sage Guidance for Caregivers
FROM *YOUR TRUE HOME: THE EVERYDAY WISDOM OF THICH NHAT HANH* BY THICH NHAT HANH

"If we do not know how to take care of ourselves and to love ourselves, we cannot take care of the people we love. Loving oneself is the foundation for loving another person."

PROFILE *of a* NOTABLE CAREGIVER

OPRAH WINFREY
297
Caregiver ⊙ Networker ⊙ Achiever

Within months after Oprah Winfrey began hosting "AM Chicago" (later known as "The Oprah Winfrey Show"), the little-known morning program went from the lowest- to the highest-rated talk show in town, surpassing the established juggernaut, Phil Donohue. One reviewer wrote, "What she lacks in journalistic toughness, she makes up for in plainspoken curiosity, robust humor and, above all, empathy."

Oprah had a way of inviting us into her home and heart (and coming into ours) that made us feel safe, accepted and loved exactly as we are. She was warm, generous, gracious and humble enough to expose her struggles and imperfections. She wasn't afraid to shed a tear and give a supportive hug. For 25 years, "The Oprah Winfrey Show" and its eponymous host took care of us.

Considered to be among the most philanthropic individuals in the world, Oprah has donated more than $400 million to educational causes alone. She continues to produce and advocate for stories of love, compassion and acceptance through the Oxygen Channel, her publications and the OWN: Oprah Winfrey Network.

*"The best way to succeed is to discover what
you love and then find a way to offer it to
others in the form of service."*
OPRAH WINFREY

2 - THE CAREGIVER RECAP

⊙ Like a warm blanket, Caregivers have the capacity to make others feel nurtured and comforted. Harmony is the Caregiver's highest aspiration and they attain it through service. By nature, Caregivers are externally focused and seek fulfillment by celebrating the accomplishments of others. They are the most compassionate of the nine archetypes, always seeking to expand their circle of inclusion.

⊙ Because they are so accommodating, people tend to take advantage of Caregivers. When repeated, this results in a "doormat cycle" and they become martyrs. Self-sacrifice can manifest as co-dependent and passive-aggressive behavior.

⊙ Caregivers are desirable partners because their primary focus is on others. They are tender, affectionate and sentimental, making Caregiver men an especially desirable catch.

⊙ As quiet people of action, Caregivers embody the concept of servant leadership. They keep an eye on the bigger picture, as well as the nuances, to maintain a healthy, harmonious and prosperous workplace.

⊙ Acknowledgment and appreciation are key factors in preventing this cycle of martyrdom. Simple gestures of gratitude are all that a Caregiver needs to know that they are seen and valued.

KEVIN JOHN FONG

PROFILE *of a* VISIONARY

DANIEL
362

Visionary ⊙ Protector ⊙ Caregiver

Daniel has been the chief strategy officer for a tech company in Silicon Valley for four years. He calls himself an obsessive-compulsive learner, and despite his busy schedule, he finds time to read at least two books a month.

Because of the nature of both his job and the industry he works in, change and innovation are his driving forces. Daniel is constantly restructuring his team in an attempt to stay ahead of the needs of the organization. He encourages his team to be versatile, agile and flexible in order to meet the latest industry trends.

"I want us to lead from a place of 'yes', not a place of 'no'," Daniel recently told his co-workers. "We are a team of possibilities and we won't shut down any opportunity without fully vetting them."

An attentive listener, Daniel is always ready to take the time needed to explore possibilities; but as soon as he feels they have reached a dead end, he will jump in and say, "I'm not feeling this. Let's try something new."

Daniel creates a loyal following because he is so energetic and likeable. He is not afraid to dive deep in search of whatever pearls of wisdom might arise. Under his leadership, his team is ready and willing to follow him.

Virtue	Innovation
Skill	Creativity
Motivation	Learning
Aspiration	Growth
Element	Wood
Preoccupation	Change
Fear	Limits
Shadow	The Flake
Tends to	Seek the perfect vision
Needs to cultivate	Grounding

CHAPTER SIX

3 - THE VISIONARY

"I have a better idea!" | *"What was I supposed to do?"*

Primary Attribute – Visionaries at Their Best

Thunder possesses an explosive quality; its sound can be both exciting and terrifying. Such is the creative nature of the Visionary. They are fast thinkers who come up with fresh, innovative ways of looking at things. Their intense curiosity inspires others to see beyond the obvious. Just when we think a Visionary's reach exceeds their grasp, they step in and wow everyone. While others are asked to think outside the box, there is no box for the Visionary.

Visionaries thrive under changing conditions and are skilled at multitasking. They are known to be precocious, experimental, and drawn to a variety of activities and experiences. They are self-motivated, outspoken and humorous, and take ideas (but not themselves) seriously.

Like a startling crack of thunder, Visionaries serve as our teachers, guides, and prophets. Because they are future-oriented, their ways of thinking and being cannot be fully understood in present circumstances. Their sense of time is synchronistic, not sequential, so they are often late to meetings and are bad at maintaining deadlines.

At their best, outgoing Visionaries can be an innovative and positive influence. They know how to motivate people through their excitement and energy so that they come willingly and not forcefully. If they can focus their creativity from a sense of stillness and knowing, their forward-thinking contributions can result in a greater sense of alignment and understanding.

Secondary Attribute – The Flake

One can tell when the secondary attribute of the Visionary arises simply by observing their behavior. They talk faster, repeat themselves and gesticulate as if they are grasping at ideas in the air (called *porcupine qi*). They are edgy, irritated, and irritating. People around them generally become cautious as they don't want to be the target of their short temper.

When one's quills are up, people retreat and the Visionary withdraws. Deadlines are missed and they lose track of time. That is when the Flake emerges. They become impatient and hasty in their decisions and use of time. They will overcommit and double- or even triple-book their appointments. Where they were once skilled at multitasking, now they can only focus on one thing at a time.

Because Flakes always strive for innovation, they may not be aware of the inherent risks. At times, people will perceive them as being rash and impetuous. They become bored by routines and quickly turn to new interests. This results in a habitual lack of focus and follow-through. If things aren't moving at their preferred fast pace, they can get easily frustrated with others. They are open and honest with their opinions (often to a fault) and may alienate those around them.

Providing context and direction are the best remedies for *porcupine qi*. By anchoring the Visionary into a deeper purpose and greater value, they will more likely be able to link the past with the present and future. This will help them channel their energy in a focused direction that can improve both morale and outcomes.

Relational Attribute – Visionaries in Public

Upon first meeting a Visionary, one might get the impression that they are flirting. Their inquisitive

"I can't get no satisfaction."
MICK JAGGER **398**

nature, along with a desire to be in another's space, often sends the wrong message. They also have a cool, avant-garde affect about them, often keeping up with the latest fashions and trends.

Visionaries are well read and progressive in spirit. They always have something interesting and witty to say about current events. Their informal and approachable style makes them good companions at parties.

The best way to relate to Visionaries is to take them at face value. Because they are future oriented, they don't carry grudges. What's past is past and they move on. To them, it is perpetually springtime. The sun is shining and it is time to get out and play.

Developmental Attribute – The Young Visionary

Like trees in the late spring, young Visionaries reach for the sky in every possible way. Their focus is on growth and discovery, which makes them interesting to be around. While their natural curiosity can get them in trouble, they are able to manage their way through with their wit and charm.

Young Visionaries assert themselves at an early age and often test authority just to see how far they can push the limit. Tantrums are commonplace among

PROFILE *of a* YOUNG VISIONARY

JEFF
436

Optimist ⦿ Visionary ⦿ Protector

In class, Jeff was always the first to raise his hand. When called upon, he would spout out multiple solutions to a problem, amazing both his teachers and peers with his ability to think quickly. Jeff's mother called him her "great adventurer." She remarked on how he was always running off to explore around the next corner or in a crowd. "No one can keep track of that boy," she'd say.

Although Jeff was a bright student, he was often caught daydreaming in class. Popular among his peers, Jeff was often the center of attention, given his natural charm and pluck.

Jeff loved to figure out how things work. He took apart radios, clocks and toys, but didn't put them back together. He'd rarely make his bed or hang up his jacket, and would only brush his teeth or comb his hair when he was reminded. Despite his inattention to his appearance, Jeff never appeared dirty. It was as if he was purposely unkempt, and his friends followed suit with his hip look.

To Jeff, and to those in his presence, the world was full of wonder and possibility. He excelled in the classes he enjoyed and built a successful career in industrial design. At the peak of his career, Jeff quit his job and opened SoleSpace, an innovative combination shoe store and community arts space.

these children, but they don't last long. Once a limit is set, they will find a way to create within it.

Visionaries are voracious learners and will choose reading over sleep any day. They typically have a stack of books on a variety of topics by their bedside, even though it is unlikely that they will finish any of them. Young Visionaries enjoy a good debate and games that involve "what if" scenarios.

For those raising young Visionaries, it is important to anchor them in good values and be consistent. At the same time, try not to be too restrictive of their behaviors. They need to explore these values and make mistakes on their own. If the values are well rooted, they will thrive.

Visionaries in Relationship

Relationships are always an adventure with a Visionary. They thrive on filling their lives with intense "wow" moments of spending entire paychecks on a scrumptious meal or pair of shoes. Spontaneous and fun loving, Visionaries can be great friends and partners if one doesn't mind living on the edge and leaving the stack of dirty dishes behind to chase that perfect sunset.

Visionaries are social creatures and because of their love for learning, they are conversant in many

It sounds obvious, but I think you only learn to love again when you fall in love again."
ADELE **335**

things. This can be intimidating and overwhelming for some people, as Visionaries are not very mindful of maintaining personal space and confidentiality. They are sometimes too honest with their opinions; they often share their thoughts before thinking them through. To their credit, Visionaries are open to learning and being corrected.

If there is a match in a common mission and a quest for growth, change and adventure, Visionaries can be exciting and fun partners. Given the right mix of stability and structure, the partnership will be successful in all ways.

Visionaries in the Workplace

Visionaries play a key role in motivating teams to stay engaged with their work. Their enthusiasm reminds people that even the most mundane tasks can be accomplished in innovative ways. For the Visionary, it's all about the experience. While a task may not be completed in a timely manner, people will have a good time doing it.

Inhabiting the realm of possibilities, Visionaries "think forward" and are best used to develop big-picture concepts; however, they are also good at working on complex situations and finding new ways to approach them. It is helpful for a Visionary to

"I don't go by the rule book. I lead from the heart, not the head."
PRINCESS DIANA 317

work with ideas that are concrete. This keeps them focused and productive.

Visionaries are well suited to areas such as development, strategic thinking, public relations, marketing and the arts. They need time, space and materials to try things out. Visionaries see failure as a necessary component of success. While they enjoy the camaraderie and energy of collaborating, their independent nature often requires that they work on their own.

Visionaries operate on an assumption of time that is synchronistic rather than sequential. In situations where matters are time-sensitive, they will not likely thrive. Visionaries often say, "How strict is that deadline?" and "I just haven't gotten to that email yet." They are habitually late for meetings because they tend to double- or triple-book their schedules.

Leaders and executives who are Visionaries need to be mindful of how they communicate their ideas to their organization, as people may not be able to discern whether the leader is serious about an idea or just testing it. Without that clarity, staff may be confused, and may invest time and resources into ideas that the executive had no intention of pursuing. They need to be clear on discerning between "thinking out loud" versus "serious idea" conversations so their co-workers will understand their intentions.

Advice for Visionaries

If you are a Visionary, it is important to develop patience and perspective so you don't bite off more than you can chew. Visionaries would be well served to seek out others, especially Philosophers, to help you link your creative energy to practical and realistic concepts; and Networkers, to support you in being focused and action oriented.

Because Visionaries thrive best on the edge of innovation, it is also helpful for you to find people to assist you with life's practical tasks, such as managing your finances and changing the oil in your vehicle—not because you will not or cannot do them, but because they are not areas in which your time is best spent.

Clarity is an essential trait for the Visionary to cultivate so that your ideas can be understood. It is important to anchor your thoughts and actions with your life mission. Maintaining a daily practice of quiet meditation or prayer is recommended.

Access all of your five senses to communicate and convey concepts. Multimedia presentations, the spoken word, group participation and interactive activities are some ways for Visionaries to express ideas. This will help to concretize spoken ideas before they dissipate. If you have to invest the time

"You can't let fear paralyze you. The worse that can happen is you fail, but guess what: You get up and try again. Feel that pain, get over it, get up, dust yourself off and keep it moving."
QUEEN LATIFAH **344**

to develop a concept in a multifaceted way, you will be more thoughtful about your process.

Add colors (red, purple, blue) that symbolize Water and Fire. Keep a variety of materials like colored marker pens, a white board, and an audio/video recorder close by. Visionaries would do well to wear something with red, purple or blue accents (a scarf or a tie) every day, but especially when under stress or speaking in public.

Look to Water for support. Stay hydrated, take a walk near a lake, install a fountain in your work or living space, or have a sound recording of ocean waves playing for inspiration.

Advice for Those Who Live and Work with Visionaries

⊙ Provide a context and container for them to work. Instead of asking them for ideas to solve world hunger, ask them how a neighborhood or school might address the issue of hunger locally.

⊙ Support their divergent thinking. What might seem illogical in the moment will take shape if the Visionary has time to think their ideas through.

⊙ Provide practical and logistical support. Mundane tasks and follow-through are not the strengths of a Visionary.

⊙ Schedule time for fun and adventure, even if it's a five-minute break to search for a new song on the internet or enjoy a funny video.

⊙ Have materials on hand to engage in the creative process, such as paper, markers, molding clay and building blocks. Visionaries create and communicate by constructing ideas.

A Bit of Sage Guidance for Visionaries
FROM *THE BOOK OF CHANGES AND THE UNCHANGING TRUTH* BY HUA-CHING NI

*"In the midst of all changes, remain undisturbed.
Whether the days are good or bad, whether dealing
with virtuous or unvirtuous ones, do not leave the
wholeness of your spirit."*

PROFILE *of a* NOTABLE VISIONARY

BARACK OBAMA
398
Visionary ⦿ *Networker* ⦿ *Rock*

In July 2004, then-Senator Barack Obama took the stage at the Democratic National Convention and spoke about his vision of a country where one's name, race and heritage are not barriers to success. He spoke of hope as "... the bedrock of this nation, a belief in things not seen, a belief that there are better days ahead."

Senator Obama affirmed this theme in his book, The Audacity of Hope, and in his 2008 presidential campaign slogan, "Yes we can."

As President of the United States, Barack Obama became an icon of hope, change and possibility. As the first Black U.S. president, the nation could imagine a future that, for many, was beyond their wildest dreams.

President Obama faced his challenges with a sense of inquiry, always searching for creative and innovative solutions to sometimes deeply entrenched issues. While he possessed the ability to be formal and pragmatic, his reputation as an affable and accessible president who was unafraid to sing, dance and be playful is an important part of his legacy.

Despite what we might feel about his politics and accomplishments,
we can all agree that President Obama made groundbreaking history,
instilling us with a sense of new possibilities for a new century.

*"Change will not come if we wait for
some other person or some other time.
We are the ones we've been waiting for.
We are the change that we seek."*
PRESIDENT BARACK OBAMA

3 – THE VISIONARY RECAP

⊙ The fast-thinking nature of the Visionary reflects the phenomenon of thunder. They thrive on change, always seeking new adventures and solutions to the situations that life offers.

⊙ For Visionaries, there is never just one way to get from point A to point B. Their quest for learning feeds their aspiration for growth. Their outgoing and precocious nature makes them likeable companions because they view life as a series of synchronistic opportunities that simply need to be recognized.

⊙ When under stress, Visionaries suffer from a condition called *porcupine qi*. They can be edgy, irritated and irritating, becoming impatient and hasty in their decisions and use of time.

⊙ Visionaries thrive on filling their lives with intense "wow" moments. They can be great friends and partners if one doesn't mind living on the edge and leaving the stack of dirty dishes behind to chase that perfect sunset.

⊙ Inhabiting the realm of possibilities, Visionaries are future oriented and are well suited in areas such as development, strategic thinking, public relations, marketing and the arts.

⊙ Providing context can anchor the Visionary into a deeper purpose and greater value. This will help them channel their energies in a focused direction.

PROFILE *of an* OPTIMIST

SYLVIA
463
Optimist ⊙ *Protector* ⊙ *Visionary*

Sylvia doesn't believe in handshakes. Whether she is greeting a friend or a stranger, she offers them a big hug and smile.

As an executive for a community foundation, Sylvia knows that she has the capacity to transform people's lives, and it is something that she takes very personally. She encounters a lot of people in unfortunate circumstances and strives to maintain a lighthearted spirit.

Sylvia is keenly aware of the value of time and timing, and isn't afraid to exercise patience until the moment is right. She is humble enough to know that she cannot do her job alone and has surrounded herself with a strong support team. People trust her because she has worked to build a good rapport and reputation as kindhearted, transparent and always positive.

Despite the many demands of her work, Sylvia remains both positive and determined, carrying a belief that it will all work out in the end. "I wake up every day and say to myself, 'It's a new beginning. Let's make a difference'."

Virtue	Empathy
Skill	Inspiration
Motivation	Curiosity
Aspiration	Joy
Element	Wood
Preoccupation	Success
Fear	Authority
Shadow	The Innocent
Tends to	Seek the perfect cause
Needs to cultivate	Discipline

CHAPTER SEVEN
4 - THE OPTIMIST

"It's all good!" | Oops!"

Primary Attribute – Optimists at Their Best

The wind is nature's representation of the Optimist, as their free spirit is always looking for ways to make life better for others. Optimists view the world through a poet's eye, noticing the exceptional within the ordinary. Where most of us see a dead end, they imagine opportunities. While they understand hardship and injustice, Optimists choose not to dwell on these things, instead devoting their time and energy toward envisioning a better world.

Like the wind, the Optimist acts as an invisible force that has a big influence on our lives. Without a word or gesture, they have the power to change the tenor of a room, most often for the better. Empathy is their greatest virtue, and they possess an uncanny power to take away the blues with little effort on their part.

Optimists lead with their emotions and engage the world with open arms and a smile. Their positive energy easily wins hearts and people are immediately captivated by their cheerfulness. Their courteous and sensitive nature makes them good friends and counselors. As leaders, they motivate and inspire others to look on the bright side and to constantly find ways to improve themselves.

Just because Optimists possess light and airy characteristics does not mean they aren't tough. They also represent early spring and the potential of hope and abundance that accompany it. Like a seedling that breaks ground for the first time, Optimists are tenacious and patient. They know all about the importance of timing and how each day brings an opportunity to begin anew.

Secondary Attribute – The Innocent

There is a particular tarot card that depicts a young traveler who is so focused on the blue sky and the birds that he doesn't realize he is stepping off a cliff. Such is the peril of the Innocent. Optimists have such faith in people that they at times might be gullible to those who may take advantage of them. They will give their grocery money to a person in need and come home empty handed to a hungry and not-so-happy family.

Because of their strong sense of empathy, Optimists tend to take responsibility for injustice even if they are not directly impacted. They get overwhelmed by the realities of the world—poverty, war, violence, injustice, etc.—that are beyond their control to fix. A sense of melancholy can overtake them, which can manifest in an emotional outburst or withdrawal. Thus, listening to the news can create a hardship for them.

When the shadow side emerges, the Innocent can become moody and fickle, with a "why is the world such a bad place" attitude. They may exhibit self-indulgent behavior in an attempt to claim a piece of joy for themselves. Innocents may also be evasive with those closest to them and feel that if they cannot bring joy to their loved ones, they have no purpose.

It helps to provide context and direction to bring the Innocents out of their doldrums. Reminding them of the good deeds they have done will reconnect them to their deeper purpose and greater value. They will soon spring back into form. If all else fails, playing their favorite feel-good music or movie will cheer them up in no time.

"Love isn't about what we did yesterday. It's about what we do today, tomorrow and the day after."
GRACE LEE BOGGS **445**

Relational Attribute – Optimists in Public

Optimists bring a breath of fresh air to any setting and find ways to bring smiles to others' faces. Their gentle nature reflects tenderness and affection. People are drawn to Optimists because they see others for who they are without judgment. They are genuinely interested and will not hesitate to ask complete strangers, "What's exciting in your life?" This is their way of finding out what brings people joy and what the Optimist can do to maintain that joy.

Because of their desire to bring joy, Optimists can sometimes be overbearing, especially if one is not in a good mood. They may try to fix that person with simple gestures and feel-good attempts. In these situations, exercise diplomacy and try not to hurt the Optimist. Instead of a direct confrontation, ask another person to speak to the Optimist on your behalf. In all other instances, open your arms and prepare yourself to be greeted with a big hug.

Developmental Attribute – The Young Optimist

To the young Optimist, the world is an open book where everything is good and anything is possible. They are able to traverse real and imaginary worlds with ease and often spend their time in fantasy play. The bubble they inhabit does not burst even as they

PROFILE *of a* YOUNG OPTIMIST

MALIKA
243
Caregiver ⊙ *Optimist* ⊙ *Visionary*

When 10-year-old Malika, the daughter of a good friend, came home from school in tears, it nearly broke my heart. I recall holding her as an infant and marveling at the joy that she emanated through her smile. That same sweet disposition carried her through her toddler and pre-school years.

Now that she was on the verge of her teenage years, her mother confided that she was worried and a bit sad that Malika would lose that sense of joy as she grew older. Perhaps, I thought, these tears were the start of that journey.

- "What's wrong, Malika?" I asked. "Didn't you have a good day at school?"
- "I had a great day at school," she sobbed.
- "Then why are you crying?" her mother asked.
- "Because," Malika cried, "Carmen had a bad day at school and I couldn't do anything to make her feel better."

I smiled at the obvious fact that Malika was still very much an Optimist, with her empathy intact. For in her attempt to comfort her best friend, Malika herself got the blues.

- "You're a great friend to Carmen," I expressed, giving Malika a big hug. "Things will be better tomorrow."

Indeed they were. Malika is now in middle school and she still retains her sunny disposition. She and Carmen are still best friends.

engage in the real world of school. Depending on which element they transition to as an adult, that bubble may never burst.

Because of their capacity for empathy, Optimist children relate well with adults, especially the elderly. They have a keen sense of the power of stories and are not bored by tales from the past. To them, it is another world to explore and integrate onto their storyboards.

The best way to support a young Optimist is to not judge or make light of their view of the world. For some, it may seem saccharine or Pollyanna, eliciting chuckles and eye rolls; but to the Optimist child, this way of being is their desired state, not only for them but for everyone. Be mindful of melancholy moments and trust that the best way to "fix" the situation is to be present. In due time, the Optimist child will have the capacity to re-establish balance.

Optimists in Relationship

Because they aspire to joy, Optimists are affectionate, tender and eager-to-please partners. They are the most romantic of the nine archetypes, aspiring to make their partner's wishes come true. Because of their whimsical nature, they can also be fun and spontaneous.

"When you become the image of your own imagination, it's the most powerful thing you could ever do."
RUPAUL CHARLES **481**

Like the wind that changes directions, Optimists are known to change their minds and life paths frequently, often creating problems of commitment and dependability. Their sense of curiosity and wonder can get them into trouble, however, as they tend to be too trustful of others and vulnerable to exploitation. Because they don't want to disappoint others, they may procrastinate in making decisions, thereby creating doubt and confusion.

A partner who enjoys attention and spontaneity while also being able to provide support and structure would be well matched with an Optimist.

Optimists in the Workplace

While Optimists have not been traditionally valued in the workplace, their role is being acknowledged more frequently as organizations in the 21st century are emphasizing happiness at work. Who is better equipped to take the lead on this than the Optimist? By their nature, Optimists believe that a positive future is possible and that they have the means to achieve it. Time and timing are important qualities of an Optimist and, like a seedling enduring the winter to break ground in the spring, Optimists can be deliberate and strategic in maximizing resources and opportunities. Through their goodwill and reputations, they can also call upon others to help.

"You can do what you have to do, and sometimes you can do it even better than you think you can."
JIMMY CARTER 418

For Optimists in leadership positions, it is important that they anchor themselves and their organizations in values-based practices so there is alignment between their leadership style and the organization. People who are attracted to the organization will line up to the vision of the Optimist, thus creating a work culture that is centered on hope and optimism.

Advice for Optimists

If you are an Optimist, your strong outward and adaptable nature can best be supported by anchoring yourself in your own sense of purpose and values. By possessing a deeper self-awareness, you will be less prone to the whims of the environment around you and can assert your own direction in ways that benefit you in the longer term.

Realize that you cannot save the world on your own. Seek trusted friends and colleagues to provide clarity and guidance, especially in more concrete aspects such as career and financial management.

Continue to find ways to celebrate life and share happiness. Know that generosity creates joy and from joy comes reciprocity. In order to stay engaged, you need to be nurtured. It is important that, for every act of generosity given to others, you provide an act of generosity to yourself.

"Every day is a gift."
ARETHA FRANKLIN 472

Advice for Those Who Live and Work with Optimists

⊙ Support them in maintaining a healthy exercise regimen that involves movement with a destination. Jogging, walking, cycling and swimming are all good activities for an Optimist.

⊙ Maintain a serene atmosphere. Too much information or many distractions can easily overwhelm an Optimist.

⊙ Provide practical and logistical support. Mundane tasks and follow-through are not the strengths of an Optimist.

⊙ Schedule time for fun and adventure, even if it's a five-minute break to search for a new song on the internet or enjoy a funny video.

A Bit of Sage Guidance for Optimists
FROM *THE BOOK OF CHANGES AND THE UNCHANGING TRUTH* BY HUA-CHING NI

"Terrifying thunder keeps people alert, but this
is all right. There is an undisturbed joyful meeting
among those who follow the correct way of conduct.
Although a loud thunderclap brings shock, ceremony is
still kept in good order."

PROFILE *of a* NOTABLE OPTIMIST

ROBIN WILLIAMS
436
Optimist ◉ Visionary ◉ Protector

Whenever Robin Williams stepped onto the stage, the room would explode with a burst of energy. His gift was filling peoples' hearts with love, light and laughter.

The late Christopher Reeve, Robin's longtime friend and college roommate, said of him: "He was like an untied balloon that had been inflated and immediately released. To say that he was 'on' would be a major understatement."

Robin was my neighbor in the late-1980s and I would often see him and his family around our San Francisco neighborhood. Every time we interacted, I felt a sense of quiet delight in his presence, as if he couldn't help but emanate joy. We later discovered that underneath that joy was a deep sense of melancholy.

"Do I perform sometimes in a manic style? Yes," Robin said. "Am I manic all the time? No. Do I get sad? Oh yeah. Does it hit me hard? Oh yeah."

Robin Williams epitomized the characteristics of the Optimist, both in light and in shadow. Thankfully, his gift of joy will continue to uplift our spirits for generations to come.

"Spring is nature's way of saying,
'Let's party'!"

ROBIN WILLIAMS

4 – THE OPTIMIST RECAP

⊙ Optimists possess the capacity to bring a breath of fresh air to any situation. Their highest aspiration is joy, and if they can make the world a better place, their mission is fulfilled.

⊙ People are attracted to Optimists because of their sunny disposition, intense curiosity and ability to empathize. Despite their joyful exterior, they can be tenacious advocates for the -right cause.

⊙ The Optimist can become melancholy and fickle, overwhelmed by the problems of the world. They may also be evasive with those closest to them, feeling that if they cannot bring joy to their loved ones, they have no purpose.

⊙ Optimists are the most romantic of the nine attributes, as they aspire to make their partner's wishes come true. Because of their whimsical nature, they can be fun and spontaneous.

⊙ At work, Optimists are deliberate and strategic on maximizing resources and opportunities. Through their goodwill and reputation, they can also call upon others to help.

⊙ Optimists thrive in serene environments with regular routines. Providing a sense of the bigger picture will reconnect them to their deeper purpose and greater value.

⊙ If all else fails, play their favorite uplifting movie or song and they will cheer up in no time.

PROFILE *of a* FACILITATOR

PEGGY
519
Facilitator ⊙ Philosopher ⊙ Networker

As the third of five children, Peggy was the bridge between her older and younger siblings. She negotiated the bathroom schedule and made sure everyone had equal time. She set up a magnet system to track chores, and she carried her younger siblings' lunch money until they were old enough to carry it themselves.

Peggy didn't mind these duties because they came naturally to her. As a teenager, she performed in a dance company, but discovered that her real passion was offstage as a choreographer.

"It was so satisfying to work with my dancers and see the joy on their faces as they performed my dances," she shared. "I knew that my days as a performer were numbered, but as a choreographer, anything was possible."

She continued to work as a dancer, teacher and choreographer until she was asked by the mayor to direct a new citywide initiative to bring dance into classrooms and community centers. Peggy collaborated with the school district, performing artists, and local community centers. The program launched with a waiting list of 400 kids.

"No problem," Peggy said, as she picked up the phone to organize more classes.

Virtue	Wholeness
Skill	Organizing
Motivation	Cooperation
Aspiration	Consensus
Element	Earth
Preoccupation	Pleasing everyone
Fear	Irrelevance
Shadow	The Manipulator
Tends to	Seek the right team
Needs to cultivate	Self-care

CHAPTER EIGHT

5 - THE FACILITATOR

"Let's get organized!" | *"Let me tell you how it really happened."*

Primary Attribute – Facilitators at Their Best

Five is the central number of the archetypes; thus, the Facilitator plays a pivotal role in relationships, keeping in touch with and coordinating all other archetypes. As a central figure, they have the ability to control situations well. Facilitators enjoy being in the spotlight, as it allows them to link ideas and bring people together. Skilled at organizing chaos, they tune into the emotional tenor of the group, as well as the needs and motivations of the individuals. They strive for harmony through connecting, creating and telling stories. Facilitators listen, build consensus and calmly get things done.

Warmhearted, conscientious and cooperative, Facilitators work hard to establish and maintain balance. People often seek them out as confidantes and will share their deepest secrets with them. Facilitators are entrusted to hold those secrets and handle situations in a sensitive manner. Because of this, Facilitators possess the power to control and manipulate narratives and events. People will turn to Facilitators for "the real story", which is theirs to weave.

The primary aspiration of the Facilitator is consensus. Like the hub of a wheel, they make sure each spoke is aligned so the wheel turns smoothly. Facilitators strive to work toward an agreeable outcome that works for all.

The downfall of the Facilitator is a reflection of their primary role as the hub. They feel that they can never let go of their role, lest things fall apart. Facilitators believe themselves to be indispensable in all situations and feel left out if this is not the case. They are so focused on holding things together for others that their own life can be unbalanced and chaotic. It is important for Facilitators to pace themselves, seek council and stay centered so they can navigate a clear path forward.

Secondary Attribute – The Manipulator

The worst thing a Facilitator can hear is, "Thanks for your help, but we've got this handled. We don't need you anymore." What? To the Facilitator, that is like the planets no longer needing the sun. It makes no sense and reveals the Facilitator's biggest fear: irrelevance.

Like the Caregiver, the Facilitator has no meaning without others. In fact, they tend to become so focused on others that their own lives are a mess. They have trouble maintaining relationships, keeping their pantry stocked and taking any time for themselves. Self-care is not a term that exists in their vocabulary.

Because of their need to be needed, Facilitators can take on the traits of a Manipulator. Their anxiety and mental noise begin to weave stories from the secrets that people have shared with them to start rumors, sabotage relationships and dismantle trust. In no time, people can come running back to the Facilitator, saying, "We need you back!" The Facilitator retakes their place in the center and all is well once again.

Or is it?

The issue of self-care remains unaddressed. It is important for the Facilitator to not sink back into complacency but to continue advocating for themselves and accept help from others.

Relational Attribute – Facilitators in Public

Whether they actually do or not, Facilitators always seem to have an entourage with them. Their gravitational force draws people to them and holds them in orbit so everything works in harmony. When a

Facilitator is on and present, people know what to do and that their contribution matters .

They are often well put together—smartly dressed but not too flamboyant. Everything about them is centered and refined. Their gestures and speech are open but careful. They have the capacity to exude warmth and distance at the same time. People aspire to want to be strong and confident like the Facilitator, but wouldn't want their job.

Facilitators can also be potentially intimidating. They are capable of wearing many masks and are difficult to read. They care less about overriding values of good or bad, and more about establishing a process that moves forward. Like the Hindu deity Kali, they use their power for both creation and destruction.

Their tough exterior is a front for a tender heart. If a person can exercise patience and find a way to connect at the heart level with a Facilitator, they will have a loyal friend.

Developmental Attribute – The Young Facilitator

Young Facilitators are the kids that everyone turns to when group assignments are given out in class. "Can I be on your team? How are we going to do this? You've got this figured out, right?" The young

"What we all need to do is find the wellspring that keeps us going, that gives us the strength and patience to keep up this struggle for a long time."
WINONA LADUKE **555**

PROFILE *of a* YOUNG FACILITATOR

KAIPO
757
Achiever ◉ Facilitator ◉ Achiever

Kaipo was everyone's best friend in grade school.

"Of course he's my best friend," his classmates would say. "I can go to him for anything and he'll take care of it."

In high school, Kaipo was referred to as the glue of the soccer team.

"We never would have made it to state championships without him," his teammates acknowledged.

While Kaipo was not the most skilled player, his teammates turned to him as their reference point on the field. He never scored a goal throughout the season, yet he held the school record in assists. He was an average student who never had ambitious career goals. Kaipo currently works as a coordinator for an organization that serves homeless youth.

"As long as I'm part of a bigger effort to make the world a better place, I'm good," he shared.

While Kaipo dated throughout high school and college, he hasn't expressed any desire to settle into a long-term relationship. He admits that he's always had more of a group orientation rather than a focus on individual relationships. He lives alone and enjoys having a degree of control over his environment. Kaipo still plays soccer with his high-school friends, who continue to report that he's an all-around nice guy who brings out the best in people.

Facilitator has already thought this project through, developed a list and matched the tasks with potential teammates. Once the Facilitator gives the word, everyone falls into place and the project unfolds in an organized manner.

These children are popular not because they are natural born leaders or class clowns, but because they bring a sense of calm to the chaos. It is the young Facilitator who resolves conflicts on the playground or comes up with a solution on how to split a pizza with too many people and too few slices. They provide a balancing force when things get rough.

Young Facilitators enjoy being in a group but always separate themselves from the crowd, as if they are peacekeeping monitors. They are respected, even revered, among their peers.

Advice for those who are raising young Facilitators is to ensure that they have a place to relax and be themselves. They carry a big burden on behalf of their peers and likely feel that they are "on" every time they step out of their front door. Teach them how to set boundaries and advocate for themselves, as self-care is a challenge for Facilitators.

"I'd rather lose an argument than get into a long discussion in order to win it."

RAFAEL NADAL 582

Facilitators in Relationship

Facilitators are constant and devoted partners. They prefer quiet, intimate gatherings over large parties, which feel like work to them. They can be tender, even delicate, in their demeanor. Facilitators exercise great discernment in choosing their partners as a means to provide assurance that the partner wants to be in a relationship with both the private and public person.

Facilitators have a natural charisma and, when in their element, move through life with ease. Being the central number, they are able to bridge the masculine and feminine realms, and often have androgynous quality about them.

They lead complex lives, as people call on them often with requests. Thus, Facilitators rarely keep a regular schedule, which can be taxing on a relationship, not to mention their own well-being. A partner who understands this dynamic and doesn't mind sharing their Facilitator with the world will do well in this relationship.

Facilitators in the Workplace

Facilitators like to approach their work as "being of it, but not in it." While they thrive in playing central roles, they do so from behind the scenes. Facilitators would

"The ultimate goal is to be an interesting, useful, wholesome person. If you're successful on top of that, then you're way ahead of everybody."
MARTHA STEWART **564**

rather be the director than the star, the campaign manager instead of the candidate, and the COO rather than the CEO. In many ways, they know that the true power lies in the person behind the scenes calling the shots.

They are great problem solvers, especially with complex issues that involve diverse stakeholders. Under those conditions, Facilitators will step into the center stage and shine. As a true Earth, they will do so in the spirit of service to the collective, not as an ego-boosting exercise.

Because of the conflict-related nature of their work, Facilitators rarely keep a regular schedule. Their routines ebb and flow, depending the needs and cycles of the organization at large. Through it all, they maintain their primary purpose and contribution to aligning values, roles and responsibilities and working toward consensus.

Advice for Facilitators

As the peacemakers of the world, you would do well to invite peace into your own body and spirit. Because you feel that you are essential in holding it all together (the hub), there isn't a moment's rest. Simple practices of breathwork, stretches and

"Ya gots to work with what you gots to work with."
STEVIE WONDER **582**

quieting the mind that can be employed throughout the day are preferred to taking longer periods of time to meditate.

You would be best served by developing a practical nature to all aspects of your life and intentionally giving and seeking support every day; for example, having daily contact with a friend or loved one, making a daily to-do list, or cooking at home more often. It is important to find ways to express your wants and needs so others can acknowledge your contributions and support them. Practice saying "no" and "I need"; and seek clarity from trusted friends who have no requests or agendas.

Add colors (red, purple, grey, silver) and objects that symbolize fire and metal (candlesticks) to frame the elements that lead and follow. Incorporate these elements into your wardrobe by wearing red, purple, grey or gold accents (a scarf or a tie) every day, but especially if you are under stress or speaking in public.

You would benefit by finding a way to connect directly to the earth, whether through gardening, going for walks or working with modeling clay. Spiritual practices that involve community service are most appropriate, as your best spiritual food is helping others.

Advice for Those Who Live and Work with Facilitators

⊙ Because Facilitators so often hold the center for others, they have difficulty holding it for themselves. Self-care is often an issue, so it is important to check in with Facilitators regularly to make sure they are attending to their basic needs like eating, sleeping and keeping their medical appointments.

⊙ Facilitators also benefit from the emotional grounding and stability of others. Because so many people look to Facilitators to fix situations, they may feel overwhelmed by the responsibility. Being a good listener or lending a helping hand makes a big difference.

⊙ Be prepared for extremes in engagement from Facilitators. There will be times when you are in daily contact with them, then they may disappear for months. Maintain respectful communication and let them know that you're available when they are ready.

A Bit of Sage Guidance for Facilitators
FROM *THE BOOK OF CHANGES AND THE UNCHANGING TRUTH* BY HUA-CHING NI

"T'ai represents a time of peace, harmony and prosperity. The literal translation of the word 'T'ai' means 'best order' or 'perfect condition.' During such times, the wise take the reins and correctly utilize the resources that benefit all."

"In helping people and caring for life, our own lives will be very rewarding."

PROFILE *of a* NOTABLE FACILITATOR

TAMMY DUCKWORTH
519
Facilitator ⊙ Philosopher ⊙ Networker

Long before she was elected to the U. S. Senate, Tammy Duckworth was adept at finding solutions through adversity. As a teenager, she prevented her family from experiencing homelessness by selling flowers out of a plastic bucket on Waikiki Beach.

"I never worked as hard as when we were at our poorest ... so I felt if we could end up there, anyone could."

Tammy continued working low-paying jobs and joining the ROTC to support herself through college. She chose to be trained as a helicopter pilot because it was the closest a woman could get to the combat lines at the time. While deployed in Iraq in 2004, the Blackhawk helicopter that Ms. Duckworth was piloting was hit by enemy fire. As a result, she was in a coma for over a week, and lost both her legs and partial use of her right arm.

During her long recovery, Ms. Duckworth began organizing and advocating for veterans' rights, eventually becoming the U.S. Assistant Secretary of Veterans Affairs, where she created programs to address veteran homelessness and serve the specific needs of female veterans.

Elected to the U.S. Senate in 2016, Senator Duckworth continues to be a fierce facilitator for veterans, including co-founding the Senate Environmental Justice Caucus. In 2018, she became the first senator to give birth while serving in office, and takes pride in bringing her daughters to the halls of Congress.

"Sometimes it takes dealing with a disability – the trauma, the relearning, the months of rehabilitation therapy – to uncover our true abilities and how we can put them to work for us in ways we may have never imagined."

TAMMY DUCKWORTH

5 - THE FACILITATOR RECAP

⊙ Facilitators hold the practical and spiritual core of a group. They aspire toward consensus, allowing everyone to contribute their best selves.

⊙ They have the capacity to stand at the center and manage all of the components of any endeavor. They are the stage managers, chiefs of staff and COOs who are invisible yet indispensable.

⊙ The Facilitator's biggest fear is irrelevance. When under stress, they have a tendency to manipulate situations by starting rumors, sabotaging relationships and dismantling trust. If they know they have a central role, this can be avoided.

⊙ Facilitators are constant and devoted partners. Being a central number, they are able to bridge the masculine and feminine realms, and often have an androgynous quality about them.

⊙ They are great mediators and problem solvers, especially with complex issues that involve diverse groups.

⊙ Because Facilitators so often hold the center for others, they have difficulty doing so for themselves. Self-care is often an issue, so it is important to check in with Facilitators regularly to make sure they are attending to their basic needs.

PROFILE *of a* PROTECTOR

GREG
638
Protector ◉ Visionary ◉ Rock

It is 8:40 in the morning and the bell has just rung. At 8:42, Greg, an elementary school principal, begins canvassing the school, making sure the students are lined up and heading to class, the facilities are secure, and the teachers have what they need.

Although Greg makes several sweeps of the school throughout the day, he always has his cell phone in hand, ready to respond to any situation—from a scraped knee to a distressed parent or an overflowing toilet. In the event of a crisis or emergency, Greg is trained and prepared to risk his own safety to protect his students and staff.

Without a doubt, his favorite time of day is recess.

"At any point, I can see hundreds of children on the playground running, yelling, laughing and crying—living life at its fullest," Greg comments. "They may not see me, but it's important that they know I'm here to keep watch and tend to their needs."

While he may not be in the classroom educating children, Greg's role as the school's guardian and protector is essential for its mission to be achieved.

Virtue	Morality
Skill	Strategy
Motivation	Mastery
Aspiration	Order
Element	Metal
Preoccupation	Rules
Fear	Chaos
Shadow	The Dictator
Tends to	Choose the highest road
Needs to cultivate	Compassion

CHAPTER NINE

6 - THE PROTECTOR

"I've got your back." | "It's my way or the highway."

Primary Attribute – Protectors at Their Best

Consistency, strength and boldness are standard characteristics of the Protector. They are seen as the leader of the pack. People follow them because they know who they are, what they stand for, and that they are committed to those they protect. Protectors love a challenge and excel in providing solutions to complex situations.

Integrity is a Protector's middle name. To them, work isn't just work, but a statement about their lives and their places in the world. As Protectors, they provide order and assurance for those in their care so everyone can prosper. In return, Protectors expect loyalty and a standard of excellence.

Protectors strive to do the right thing because it's the right thing to do. They stick up for the underdog and will not agree with the majority simply because it's easy or practical. For the people in their care, they will fight to defend and protect them.

At the same time, a good Protector is mindful of the allure of ego; therefore, compromise and accommodation of the other is always a noble option if it fulfills the mission

It is important for Protectors to find ways to unwind in order to bring out their warmer, gentler nature. They consider other people's needs as well as their own, particularly if there is a conflict between what the people want and what the Protector thinks they need. Protectors would be wise to seek counsel from others who can provide clarity and direction on achieving a win-win for all.

Secondary Attribute – The Dictator

The shadow of the Protector—the Dictator—is a common archetype in our society. The Dictator emerges if a Protector starts acting out of personal gain or self-preservation, and they lose sight of the people in their care. Once that happens, order descends to chaos.

Whether one is a Protector or a Dictator also depends on the will of the followers. If the followers are safe and prosperous, their leader is their protector. If they feel oppressed, or if they are banished, that same

"Bigger than life is not difficult for me. I am bigger than life."
RITA MORENO **647**

person is a dictator. It is a unique challenge for some leaders to be both a Protector and Dictator at the same time, depending on the circumstance and point of view.

When the shadow of the Dictator emerges, the "icebox effect" takes over. In their attempt to preserve order, they build walls and shut themselves and their people inside. They won't ask for help or return calls. They become rigid and disagreeable. If they close themselves off for too long, they will suffocate in their own fear and ego.

It is important for Dictators to realize that asking for help can be a sign of strength, not weakness. They would do well to seek trusted advisors—especially Philosophers, Rocks and Caregivers—to separate the ego and draw them back to their greater mission of service and compassion.

Relational Attribute – Protectors in Public

It is always evident when a Protector walks into a room because the mood shifts. People stand a little taller, speak in hushed tones and are mindful of their appearance. It doesn't matter if the Protector is in a suit or sweats—until they give an "at ease" signal, people will hold their positions of attention and deference.

"Knowledge will give you power, but character, respect."
BRUCE LEE 656

PROFILE *of a* YOUNG PROTECTOR

MEREDITH
564
Facilitator ⦿ Protector ⦿ Optimist

Being a Protector was both a blessing and a curse for Meredith. As the oldest daughter, she was responsible for the care of her younger siblings. It was a role that she enjoyed, as it gave her a purpose and a sense of duty. Besides, she couldn't tolerate child's play and was more focused on growing up and getting on with her life. In caring for her younger brothers, Meredith honed her skills at diplomacy. Each of them reported that she was strict, but fair. "There was definitely a line you didn't cross," one chuckled.

"It's all about respect," Meredith added. "If you respect my rules, I'll be nice to you."

While Meredith was the undisputed authority at home, it was a different story at school. When she ran for class president, she was chided for daring to run against a boy.

"They thought that I wasn't up for the job because, as a girl, I wasn't presidential material. Who says that to a 14-year-old girl?"

Meredith ran anyway. She lost, but it taught her a lesson.

"I ran against that boy out of spite," she commented, "and I realized it was all for the wrong reasons. If I was going to do something with my life, it was going to be for the good of the people I care about."

Meredith eventually went onto law school and ran a successful public interest firm in her hometown. She was recently appointed to the bench as a judge.

Protectors have a dignified presence. They typically have a consistent look about them in what they wear, how they style their hair, the cars they drive, and the tone and tenor of their voices. It is their outward manifestation of confidence, control and order.

Unless one is in their inner circle, Protectors will be seen as Protectors first and average people second. Even so, there may be an air of formality in relating to the Protector, as if one wouldn't want to disturb them with casual conversation. Thus, many people have an arms-length relationship with Protectors.

Aware of this dynamic, a mindful Protector has the skills to be fun-loving and carefree while also maintaining their duty and keeping an eye on the horizon. It is helpful when relating to Protectors to respect their position and not take offense when duty calls.

Developmental Attribute – The Young Protector

From an early age, Protectors are either given or claim authority. Before they have anyone to boss around in their youth, they might arrange their stuffed animals in orderly formations. As they grow older, Protectors will become leaders of their packs, taking initiative in forming teams or clubs and determining who is in and who is out. They are not short on expressing

"The price of freedom is eternal vigilance."
DESMOND TUTU **674**

their opinions and judgments, and people are in the least impressed by their self-assurance and swagger.

Yet underneath that swagger lies a person who can easily crack under the pressure. The young Protector may have developed a persona that is not easy to extricate from and just be a child.

The best way to support young Protectors is to give them permission to take off their armor once in a while. Create a safe environment where there is safety and order, but it is not up to the young Protector to maintain it.

Protectors in Relationship

To be in a relationship with a Protector is to take comfort in knowing that they are in charge. Protectors do not shy away from making decisions, whether big or small. In their households, their word is the law. They strive for an orderly home with clearly laid out schedules to avoid unnecessary conflicts and crises. Abide by the rules and all will be well.

Protectors demand open and honest communication, so they aren't waiting up at four o'clock in the morning for a child to come home.

"I don't care if my 19-year-old stays out past midnight," one Protector mom remarked, "but as long as they are living under my roof, they need to tell me when and if they will be back so I can get a good night's sleep."

If those conditions are met, one can be assured of a peaceful home environment. People in the care of a Protector can be certain that their needs will be met. "I've got your back" is their motto, and they will do anything in their power to assure that their loved ones are safe and happy.

Because of their judgmental "my way or the highway" mindset, Protectors can also create alienation within families, communities and relationships. Depending on their tolerance level and where they draw the line, there may be a number of people whom the Protector has disowned, causing tension and tough choices for those around them.

Protectors would be best served by having a couple of close people in their circle who can advise them and call them out if their egos get in the way. It is also helpful if Protectors can allow themselves to remove their mantle of responsibility on occasion and let things be.

Protectors in the Workplace

Of the nine archetypes, we lift up the Protector as the natural born leader. They possess the qualities of an effective head of state, CEO, military leader and minister. Whether they have the formal title or not, the Protector is the primary mover and initiator in the workplace. Nothing happens without their nod of approval.

At their best, Protectors are stimulating and transformational. They demonstrate the wisdom to call upon the skills and contributions of all nine archetypes before establishing a strategy. They call on the past to inform their decisions for the present and future. They know when to move forward or step back, keeping their focus on the welfare of those they are entrusted to protect.

Protectors can also become tyrants, especially when they allow their pride to get in the way and lose sight of their mission and duty. They will miss opportunities if they are too cautious and alienate others in the process.

Because they are so influential, it is important to keep Protectors (regardless of their actual title and position) happy. In order to do so, 1) establish a set of operating principles and stick to them, 2) maintain a high standard of integrity and accountability throughout the organization;, 3) have an established plan with clearly stated rationale, and 4) create an environment where everyone can bring their best to the job.

"We have so much room for improvement. Every aspect of our lives must be subjected to an inventory . . . of how we are taking responsibility."

NANCY PELOSI **647**

Advice for Protectors

As a Protector, you may often feel as if you carry the weight of the world on your shoulders and cannot let down your guard. Our society has conditioned us to believe that Protectors are the one and only type of leader when, in fact, there are myriad ways in which the other attributes can assume leadership roles. When you find ways to reconnect with your own humanity and understand that you are not in this alone, a greater spirit of shared leadership can emerge.

You would do well to seek counsel from others—especially Caregivers, Rocks and Philosophers—who can provide support in achieving a win-win for all. Endeavor to seek connection in every interaction so your intentions can be understood.

As a Protector, you would benefit from adding colors (blue, black and earth tones) and objects (a fountain, bowl of water with stones in them, like soapstone) that reflect earth and water in your personal and work spaces. Wear something with earth tones and blue or black accents (a scarf or a tie) daily, but especially if you are under stress or speaking in public.

"Integrate what you believe in every single area of your life. Take your heart to work and ask the most and best of everybody else, too."
MERYL STREEP **611**

Develop a practice or activity that involves listening, such as music, podcasts, audiobooks, storytelling or spoken word. Spend less time with visual activities like videos and reading.

Do something that builds your community every day; for example, connect with a friend and cook at home with loved ones more often Engage in community service such as working in a community garden or serving people in need. Your best spiritual food is helping others.

Advice for Those Who Live and Work with Protector

- ⊙ Communicate clearly, concisely and with confidence, providing solid, evidence-based rationales.

- ⊙ Protectors aspire toward order. Adhere and appeal to protocols, traditions and procedures.

- ⊙ Respect established timelines.

- ⊙ Protectors can be brusque with their language and mannerisms. Don't take it personally.

- ⊙ Find ways to help the Protector unwind in order to bring out their warmer and gentler nature.

A Bit of Sage Guidance for Protectors
FROM *THE BOOK OF CHANGES AND THE UNCHANGING TRUTH* BY HUA-CHING NI

"For a human to express 'Dragon' energy, they must have the four Yang virtues of being positive, creative, progressive, and persevering, all of which build a strong foundation for a universal life."

PROFILE *of a* NOTABLE PROTECTOR

RUPERT MURDOCH
647
Protector ⊙ *Optimist* ⊙ *Achiever*

Rupert Murdoch's opportunity to pursue the path of a Protector came at the age of 22, when he took the reins of his father's newspaper business in Adelaide, Australia. He established a plan to publish a respectable newspaper with the highest standards of integrity and excellence. Over time, he acquired Australia's first national newspaper.

Murdoch moved to London, where he continued to acquire newspapers and build his now global corporation. "I sensed the excitement and the power," he said. "Not raw power, but the ability to influence at least the agenda of what was going on."

In 1985, he expanded his media empire into television and entertainment by founding FOX, Inc. through a series of acquisitions. Both FOX Entertainment and FOX News have become major influences in the global culture.

In more recent years, Murdoch's parent company, News Corporation, has continued to acquire newspapers, magazines, television stations and movie studios to become one of the biggest and most powerful media conglomerates in the world. Murdoch is not shy in proclaiming his conservative political views and, depending on where one falls on the political spectrum, he is seen by some as a Protector and by others as a Dictator.

Political views aside, Rupert Murdoch is a take-charge leader who protects those who are loyal to him and destroys those who are not. While well into his 80s, and despite the fact that he is one of the world's richest men, Rupert Murdoch is still intimately involved in what he referred to as "the family business."

> *"If the head man in a company is not working 12 hours a day, doing things, taking risks, but also standing with his people in the trenches at the most difficult of times, then the company loses something."*
>
> RUPERT MURDOCH

6 - THE PROTECTOR RECAP

⊙ Protectors are charged with assuring the safety of those whom they identify as family, community, tribe and team. Order is their highest aspiration.

⊙ Seen as natural born leaders, Protectors are caring but distant, always keeping an eye on their duty and mission. Integrity and loyalty are of utmost importance to Protectors.

⊙ In stress, the Dictator emerges. In their attempt to preserve order, they build walls and shut themselves and their people inside. If they close themselves off for too long, they will suffocate in their own fear and ego.

⊙ Protectors are the take-charge types in relationships. People in the care of a Protector can be assured that their needs will be met, and they will do anything in their power to assure that their loved ones are safe and happy.

⊙ Protectors possess the qualities of an effective head of state, CEO, military leader and minister.

⊙ At their best, Protectors are wise enough to call in the skills and contributions of all. Protectors can also become tyrants, especially when they allow their pride to get in the way and lose sight of their mission.

⊙ Protectors would do well to seek counsel from others—especially Caregivers, Rocks and Philosophers—who can provide support on achieving a win-win for all.

PROFILE *of an* ACHIEVER

JACQUELINE
757
Achiever ⊙ Facilitator ⊙ Achiever

Jacqueline was always on! No matter the circumstance, she found herself generating check lists and driving toward attaining the goal. Even later when she was diagnosed with cancer and went through multiple surgeries, she continued working. Managing her affairs in this way energized her.

As the creative director of a national retail home furnishing company, it was a mystery, even to Jacqueline, how she kept on going. From her meticulous attention to her appearance to her ability to shine affirming light on the accomplishments of those around her, she kept moving forward so that others would as well. "I can't" was not a part of her vocabulary.

Still, Jacqueline wasn't so serious about life that she didn't know how to have a good time. She took pleasure in hosting parties at her beautifully appointed home, often cooking sumptuous meals and weaving rich stories to keep everyone entertained.

An avid sportsperson, Jacqueline was a triathlete, skier, cyclist, paddler and hiker. She organized trips around the world with friends and family, often being the first to dive into new adventures. And she didn't think twice about accepting a last-minute invitation for a weekend getaway with her friends.

Jacqueline made every day count. Her mantra up until her final day was, "I can rest later. For now, there is too much living to do."

Virtue	Accomplishment
Skill	Persistence
Motivation	Competition
Aspiration	To win
Element	Metal
Preoccupation	Tasks
Fear	Stasis
Shadow	The Hustler
Tends to	Seek the perfect project
Needs to cultivate	Reflection

CHAPTER TEN

7 - THE ACHIEVER

"Let's do it!" | "Win at all costs."

Primary Attribute – Achievers at Their Best

Achievers are action-oriented, work-hard-play-hard people. If there is something to be done, the Achiever will be the first to volunteer. Fearless and driven, they attack every opportunity with gusto. One might find an Achiever saying, "Somebody had to do it first."

This type of fun-loving gusto for life makes them a great motivator for others. They are outgoing and make great hosts because they have a capacity to listen and sense what others are thinking. People will often comment that Achievers are a step ahead of everyone else. That said, they don't waste time with pleasantries. If someone is not here to work, then they'd better get out of the way. Achievers are sharp, calculating, and speak their minds without much editing. If there is a way to maximize gain and minimize effort, they will find it.

The archetype of the Achiever is the lake, which often presents a calm surface, but there's always a lot of activity churning underneath. They may present a calm, cool exterior but their minds are always alert and engaged. The quest for excitement and the next thing to do is ever present, and their lives are far from dull.

As a lake is the embodiment of the accumulation of water and resources, the Achiever values pleasure and material success. The world is a place of abundance, and the harvest awaits. This outlook feeds their robust and ambitious personalities as they seek to accomplish the next task.

Secondary Attribute – The Hustler

When Achievers go into their shadow, they tend to be hypercompetitive and won't hesitate to throw somebody under the bus in order to win. Their biggest satisfaction lies in the afterglow of successfully accomplishing a task, and the Hustler will accomplish that task by any means necessary.

Hustlers are vague, distracted and undisciplined— qualities they abhor in others. They bite off more than they can chew and become frustrated at the demands that are placed upon them (even though they place the demands on themselves). Their drive toward personal advancement alienates others, although they are often not aware of the hardships they cause in their wake. To the Hustler, they are fine. It's everyone else who has the problem.

Hustlers become obsessed with seeking pleasure, likely through impulsive and addictive behaviors. They are never completely satisfied, however, and feel as if something better is just beyond the horizon. Those around them will note that Hustlers always seem to be on the verge of a meltdown.

It is important for Hustlers to take an honest look in the mirror and understand the destruction they are causing themselves and others by engaging in this behavior. Finding a place to ground themselves (likely somewhere in nature) can provide understanding of the greater perspective.

Relational Attribute – Achievers in Public

Charming, polished, stylish and cool are accurate descriptors of the first impressions of an Achiever. With a playful smile and a twinkle in their eye, they will step into a situation asking what needs to be done and be ready to dive in with their sleeves rolled up.

Underneath the polish and style lies some grit and bite. With their straightforward communication style, Achievers may say things that seem offensive or insincere. They often don't think about the

"The first rule is not to lose. The second rule is not to forget the first rule."
WARREN BUFFETT 721

consequences of their words and actions but are dismissed by friends and family, who might say something like, "Just ignore them. Sometimes they just get carried away."

Despite their missteps, people like to be around Achievers because they are such movers and shakers. Their energetic and playful outlook gets people up and moving. They know how to celebrate and enjoy the richness of life. It is helpful for those who relate to Achievers to communicate with them in the context of a project or task. If they can understand how the bigger picture relates to the task at hand, they will find common ground.

Developmental Attribute – The Young Achiever

"Are we done yet?" is a common phrase that comes from young Achievers. Always seeking the next opportunity and adventure, they have little patience to see things through. They navigate the world with all of their senses and limbs, wanting to experience as much as life has to offer.

Young Achievers thrive on change and have the capacity of a chameleon to adjust themselves to fit any situation. They are skilled in relating with multiple groups, entertaining both adults and children with their stories. They appear to be worldly

PROFILE *of a* YOUNG ACHIEVER

GRETA THUNBERG
775
Achiever ◉ Achiever ◉ Facilitator

On August 20, 2018, 15-year-old Greta Thunberg sat alone in front of the Swedish Parliament with this handmade sign:

"My name is Greta, I am in ninth grade, and I am school-striking for the climate."

The following day, a stranger joined her. By the end of 2018, thousands of students across Europe had begun school-striking for the climate. Within a year, an estimated four million people around the world were protesting against climate change, citing Greta's example of taking action as their inspiration. The "Greta effect" has taken hold since then, with her no-holds-barred calls for action on social media and in front of the United Nations.

While only 20 years old as of this writing, Greta's achievements are many. She was the youngest person to be named Person of the Year by *Time Magazine* (2019), and was nominated for the Nobel Peace Prize from 2019 to 2022. A person whose actions match her words, Greta refuses to travel by air and famously sailed in a catamaran across the Atlantic Ocean to address the United Nations General Assembly in New York. "We are in the beginning of a mass extinction, and all you can talk about is money and fairy tales of eternal economic growth," she told these world leaders. "How dare you."

As a double Achiever (Primary and Developmental), Greta will continue to manifest her "what you see is what you get" leadership approach, inspiring allies and clapping back at detractors. Nothing and no one is going to get in her way.

and sophisticated beyond their years and often associate with peers who are older than them.

Young Achievers aspire to be where the action is and seek to be a major influencer in that action. They are savvy and typically seek out the most powerful person in the room to build an alliance with. In this manner, they are protected.

"I'm not a quitter. Never have been."
LISA MURKOWSKI **757**

The best way to support a young Achiever is to create spaces and places where they can slow down and reflect on the bigger picture. Getting them out in nature is a great way to decrease the "buzz" that surrounds them. Make their bedroom an electronics-free sanctuary, which will allow them to find that off switch where their mind and body can rest.

Achievers in Relationship

The gregarious, *bon vivant* charm of the Achiever gives them an irresistible quality. They don't do things halfheartedly and will dive into a relationship without hesitation. There is an adventurous, even dangerous, side to the Achiever that will ensure that the relationship is full of action and excitement.

Achievers like the finer things in life and know how to stretch their resources to make the best of their situations. They are prone to exaggerate and even resort to little lies to maintain an air of status and popularity. They keep up with the latest trends and styles, and assure that everything they touch is polished and refined.

Because they see life is a cornucopia, Achievers tend to collect experiences instead of savoring moments. Even if they remain true to one person, they may have many relationships that fulfill different needs. It is difficult for an Achiever to set boundaries and say no. Their work ethic may also impact relationships.

Partners who can channel and manage the energy of the Achiever in a way that serves the relationship and their community would be ideal. In return, they will receive a life filled with fun and adventure.

Achievers in the Workplace

When there is a time-sensitive project to be done, the Achiever will be the first to volunteer the extra time and energy needed. "Let's get it out the door," they will say as they roll up their sleeves.

They take pleasure in completing tasks and sometimes create mundane or even counter-productive tasks for the satisfaction of checking things off of their task lists; but when the need arises, Achievers will step forward and do what it takes.

"I'm good at working, but I'm very good at playing."
SALMA HAYEK **721**

Achievers have quick minds that can adjust to whatever a situation requires. Rather than plan things out, they would rather dive in and see what happens. They persist in spite of obstacles and can act as agents of innovation as they discover new ways of doing things. Their focus on quantity over quality might lead them to cut corners and deliver sub-standard products.

Achievers are not very good team players, especially if their partners aren't skilled in accomplishing the tasks at hand. They can get impatient with coworkers, telling them to "Step aside, I'll just do it myself." Afterward they will issue an apology in the manner of "Nothing personal. This is just business."

A good way to support Achievers in the workplace is to provide clear, short-term action plans and a schedule to regularly check in for quality assurance. Provide professional development opportunities for them to build their skills and infuse a sense of fun and brevity into the work environment.

Advice for Archievers

If you are an Achiever, your work-hard-play-hard nature could result in a life that is not integrated in a way that connects to a deeper purpose—thus leading to a life that is rather shallow. It is important to bring your skills and gifts to pursuits that have a greater

"Burst down those closet doors once and for all, and stand up and start to fight."
HARVEY MILK **757**

meaning and impact in the world. This will allow you to broaden your definition of success to more than material wealth.

While Achievers bring a common sense and realistic approach to work, your task orientation can be exclusionary. It would help to be open to new approaches that are more inclusive and fun. This will test your assumptions about developing the power of both process and relationships in ways that contribute to the bottom line.

You would do well to seek counsel from others—especially Caregivers, Rocks and Philosophers—who can provide support and clarity on achieving a win-win for all.

Achievers would benefit from adding colors (blue, black and earth tones) and objects (a fountain, bowl of water with stones in them, like soapstone) that reflect earth and water in your personal and work spaces. Wear something with earth tones and blue or black accents (a scarf or a tie) every day, but especially if you are under stress or speaking in public.

Develop a practice or activity that you can do alone or with a group that involves hearing and listening, like music, podcasts, audiobooks, storytelling or spoken word. Spend less time with visual activities such as

"Every night on the court I give my all, and if I'm not giving 100 percent, I criticize myself."
LEBRON JAMES **775**

videos and reading. Take up pottery or gardening. It would be great if these practices and activities can also engage the spirit of community service.

Advice for Those Who Live and Work with Achievers

- ⊙ Be action-oriented and ready to talk about the "challenge" of the task.

- ⊙ Clearly define the Achiever's role; otherwise, they will start inventing tasks, which may be counterproductive.

- ⊙ Provide an established timeline, then step back and let them do their work.

- ⊙ Double check their work, as Achievers may tend to cut corners.

- ⊙ Remind them of the bigger picture to help them maintain a sense of balance and perspective.

A Bit of Sage Guidance for Achievers
FROM *THE BOOK OF CHANGES AND THE UNCHANGING TRUTH* BY HUA-CHING NI

> *"The Lake guides us to develop and inner, constant peace of mind that is not upset by external circumstances. People who seek happiness from others, or who seek only to please others, will never discover the fountain of joy within."*

PROFILE *of a* NOTABLE ACHIEVER

DOLORES HUERTA
647
Achiever ◉ Protector ◉ Protector

Labor leader and human rights activist Dolores Huerta was never known for shying away from good arguments and hard work. Her work ethic and demand for justice was instilled in her by her father, a farmworker and state legislator; and her mother, who owned a hotel and restaurant. As a young teacher, Dolores couldn't tolerate seeing her students coming to school hungry. So she left teaching and became an organizer, eventually co-founding the United Farm Workers Union (UFW) in 1965 with César Chávez, and serving as vice president until 1999.

> *"If you don't get out there and*
> *try to solve your own problems,*
> *it's never going to change."*

DOLORES HUERTA

From 1965 to 1970, Dolores served as the director for the National Boycott for California Table Grapes, where she gained national attention and began to inspire countless women, including Gloria Steinem, to step into their power. For 70 years, she organized workers, negotiated contracts, advocated for safer working conditions, fought for unemployment and healthcare benefits, and campaigned for candidates.

Robert Kennedy credited Dolores for securing his California presidential nomination in 1968, and Barack Obama's campaign slogan ¡Sí se puede! (Yes we can!) was first coined by Dolores. These roles came with great sacrifice, as Dolores spent large stretches of time away from her children. In 1988, Dolores was brutally beaten by policemen in San Francisco. Through it all, she never gave up.

In 2022, I had the honor of working with Dolores. After one of our meetings in Bakersfield, California, Dolores casually mentioned that she was embarking on a five-day, five-city trip that evening, which would take her to financial institutions on Wall Street, to the U.S. Capitol, and to a community center in Los Angeles—all of this in spite of the fact that she was 93 years old and the country was just emerging from a pandemic. As we parted, she gave me a warm hug and said, "I'm off to work."

> *"Every moment is an organiz-*
> *ing opportunity, every person a*
> *potential activist, every minute*
> *a chance to change the world."*
>
> DOLORES HUERTA

7 - THE ACHIEVER RECAP

⊙ "Let's do it" is the motto of the Achiever, whose journey from point A to point B is singular and straight-lined. Their primary motivation is accomplishment.

⊙ They have work-hard-play-hard personalities and will jump into any situation with full engagement. Achievers are bold, daring and fun-loving, making them popular companions.

⊙ Achievers in shadow tend to be hypercompetitive and won't hesitate to throw somebody under the bus in order to win. They will accomplish that task by any means and people will see them as insincere, unkind and unreliable.

⊙ Achievers don't do things halfheartedly and will dive into a relationship without hesitation. There is an adventurous, even dangerous, side to the Achiever that will ensure their relationships are full of action and excitement.

⊙ At work, Achievers will step forward and do what it takes to get the job done. They take pleasure in completing tasks and may create counter-productive tasks for the satisfaction of checking things off of their task lists.

⊙ Because of their task-orientation, Achievers can benefit from approaches that are fun and inclusive. This will allow them to integrate the power of process and relationships in ways that contribute to the bottom line.

PROFILE *of a* ROCK

AUNTY PUA
813
Rock ⊙ *Philosopher* ⊙ *Visionary*

Aunty Pua lives at her family's homestead in the Lualualei valley at the foot of Mt. Ka'ala in Oahu, Hawai'i. "This mountain has given me strength for over 70 years," she says.

Considered to be the friend that everyone can depend on, Aunty Pua's approach is to listen, absorb and wait for the answers to emerge. She leads from her na'au, the core of her body, in a way that calms and grounds people. Aunty Pua's many visitors claim that her presence alone makes them feel better.

She is not one to be rushed, and prefers the stability of home and hearth to the adventure of travel. That said, if she has a friend in need, Aunty Pua will be there.

"To refer to her as our rock would be an understatement," say her family and friends. "She is kind and loving—until you get her angry. Then she'll cut you down with a single glance."

Thankfully, Aunty Pua doesn't invoke this power often. Instead, she goes about her days quietly and persistently as a storyteller, cultural translator, poet, advisor and aunty, healing families and communities one peace at a time.

Virtue	Patience
Skill	Cultivation
Motivation	Support
Aspiration	Stability
Element	Earth
Preoccupation	Details
Fear	Change
Shadow	The Volcano
Tends to	Seek the perfect project
Needs to cultivate	Spontaneity

CHAPTER ELEVEN

8 - THE ROCK

"You can count on me!" | "Grrr."

Primary Attribute – Rocks at Their Best

The stability of the Rock refers to a dependable, grounded and self-reliant person. They are pragmatic and responsible, deciding in a logical manner what needs to be done and accomplishing their task with steady focus, regardless of distractions. They take pride in assuring that everything is in its proper place in accordance with tradition and function.

Rocks are the friend that everyone can rely on. While they may tend to be reserved and cool in most situations, people may perceive this as uncaring. In actuality, they are quietly listening and observing, as they find ways to support their friends.

Unlike the Visionaries and Optimists, Rocks view life as less of an opportunity and more as a struggle. Their journey is an uphill climb, where challenges are invitations to work around or through. Still, they have their goal of reaching the mountaintop and are in no hurry to get there. Rocks know that slow and steady wins the race.

This outlook results in Rocks having a series of mountaintop experiences throughout their lives. This advancement may manifest through academic degrees, military service, traditional practices (like martial arts) or work promotions.

It is important for Rocks to call upon their greater sensibilities of service and nurturing to maintain balance. They should engage in ways that keep their minds and bodies flexible and adaptable. They can practice saying "yes" to invitations to try something new. Exposing themselves to new ways of being will refresh their habits and skills.

Secondary Attribute – The Volcano

Even though a Rock's exterior might be calm, there could be a rumbling below the surface that explodes unexpectedly when under stress. While volcanoes don't often erupt, they can cause lasting harm. Such is the wake of the Rock's temper.

It is important for the Rock, and for those around them, to monitor any given situation. If a Rock is doing their own thing, are they productively focused on it? Or are they tamping down their emotions by stewing and simmering? If the latter is the case, it is important for Rocks to find their release valves to let off some of the pressure.

Rocks are also prone to become stubborn and inscrutable under stressful conditions. The sense that they do not depend on anyone for anything may be perceived as obstinate and evasive. They can give mixed signals, such as being shut down and reactive, or irritated and emotionless. This behavior is a means of alienating people so that Rocks can retreat into their caves. Separation is their path to self-preservation.

Rocks—especially those who have had mountaintop experiences—have a strong sense of justice and fairness, which can easily turn into self-righteousness. While Rocks do not tolerate fools, they also believe that they are immune from being foolish themselves. They can be haughty and defiant, challenging others' commitments and loyalty because no one is more committed and loyal than a Rock.

Relational Attribute – Rocks in Public

Like a mountain, Rocks can overwhelm. Their presence can be felt from a distance and their reputations

"Trust, but verify."
RONALD REAGAN **822**

often precede them. People may feel intimidated at first and not know how to approach a Rock. In these circumstances, it is helpful to have an intermediary introduce one to the Rock. It's as if the intermediary serves as a guide who advises, "Here are the safe approaches to the mountain."

Once a person has access and meets with the Rock's approval (again citing the importance of an intermediary), the Rock is easygoing, relatable and warm. When a person can have an authentic experience with a Rock, they will have a steadfast ally.

Developmental Attribute – The Young Rock

As children, Rocks are self-contained and low maintenance. They are content to sit with their books, homework, projects or hobbies for long stretches of time without interruption.

Visitors might ask if the Rock child is okay. Those who know the Rock will say, "They're just fine. They'll let us know if they need anything. Otherwise, it's best to leave them alone."

Rock children possess a quiet predictability. They are reserved and understated in their dress and mannerisms, and prefer to let their accomplishments speak for themselves. While they would rather be

PROFILE *of a* YOUNG ROCK

ALEX
683
Protector ◉ *Rock* ◉ *Visionary*

From an early age, Alex was a keen observer of nature and was fascinated at how things came together to form something new. He started reading books on chemistry, which were well beyond his grade level. He struggled to understand the concepts, yet he persisted.

Alex discovered the science of cooking by watching his mother prepare meals as he read his chemistry books at the kitchen table.

"The thing I was so interested in," he said, "that process of alchemy, was happening right in front of me."

Alex found his calling and decided he was going to be a chef. He switched from chemistry books to cookbooks, studying menus and following them precisely. He worked and saved to purchase the best tools he could afford, and sought out mentors who could guide him on his path. At age 14, Alex got his first restaurant job. He kept his head down, did what he was told and observed, knowing that with patience and perseverance, he would reach his goal.

Alex eventually became a renowned chef with a reputation for impeccable flavors and an eye on every detail. In the spirit of service, Alex is now devoting his time as an advocate for training young people of color to be chefs and bringing nutritious and delicious meal programs into public schools.

alone, Rocks are good team players who will stop at nothing to defend their teammates. Their loyalty can run so deep that they might get too involved in the lives of others. Supporting young Rocks to maintain boundaries in such situations is helpful.

Young Rocks will likely have a number of mountaintop experiences that serve as rites of passage. For them, childhood is not an innocent walk in the park, but a treacherous journey through a forest. Nonetheless, they are prepared and ready for the challenge, as they know that the wisdom they gain from the experience will be worth the hardship.

It is important to bring a sense of lightness and humor into a young Rock's life. Encourage them to try something new, which to them might be taking the bold step of tasting chocolate chip ice cream instead of vanilla. Celebrate those brave steps, as it isn't easy to move a mountain.

Rocks in Relationship

When it comes to partnerships, Rocks are the most stable of all of the archetypes. As creatures of habit, they can provide a warm, safe environment for the partnership to settle in for a long and comfortable journey. Rocks prefer deep friendships with a few people whom they can spend their days sitting in

"If it wasn't hard, everyone would do it. It's the hard that makes it great."
TOM HANKS **867**

quiet reflection, as if they have all the time in the world. They are slow and deliberate in choosing their partners but tend to know it when they see it. They will commit to a person long before they admit it, as there is no need to rush into a relationship.

A Rock's emotional reserve can lead to a sense of detachment, as if the partner doesn't really know what is going on. Rocks can demonstrate multiple emotions at once—both tender and spiteful, calm and explosive—as a reflection of their inability to communicate their feelings. They are also very possessive and prone to jealousy, which can explode on occasion.

It is wise for the partner of a Rock to be calm and deliberate in their actions and communication. Stay away from surprise announcements and parties, and trust that slow and steady wins the race.

Rocks in the Workplace

When it comes to work, Rocks are pragmatic, diligent and loyal. Their combined qualities of persistence and contemplation are well matched for jobs that require attention to detail. Because they are so level-headed, they are also well suited to bring balance and perspective in high pressure situations.

> "Sometimes you see how humanity can rise above any kind of cultural ills and hate, that a person's capacity to love and communicate and forgive can be bigger than anything else."
> VIOLA DAVIS **858**

While Rocks value family, friends and loyalty above accolades and accomplishments, they typically feel more comfortable working in solitude at their own pace. They may bring their work home on a regular basis or may have home offices for such situations. They may keep their home and work lives completely separate. Whatever their choice, they crave a sense of stability and predictability.

Rocks can be relied upon to deliver a high-quality product, but not necessarily in a timely manner. In fact, the more pressure one puts onto a Rock, the longer they will take. If a workplace can avoid surprises and last-minute requests, they will get a good and loyal employee in a Rock.

Advice for Rocks

Because Rocks are the most grounded of all attributes, it is important to cultivate a sense of lightness. You would be well served by adopting daily practices to keep your body flexible and adaptable. Yoga, *tai chi*, martial arts and other forms of movement that have a deeper meaning and philosophy are well aligned with the Rock's sensibilities.

In addition, it would be wise for you to stay mentally nimble. Be open to seeing, hearing and trying something new. Call upon your greater sensibilities of service and explore community work with a group that you would not normally associate. This will open you up to a different way of looking at life and perhaps provide you with an added mountaintop experience.

You would be best served by developing a practical nature to all aspects of your life, and intentionally giving and seeking support every day; for example, having daily contact with a friend or loved one, making a daily to-do list and cooking at home more often. It is important for Rocks to find ways to express your wants and needs so others can acknowledge your contributions and support. Practice saying "no" and "I need" and seek clarity from trusted friends who have no requests or agendas.

Add colors (red, purple, grey, silver) and objects that symbolize fire and metal (candlesticks) to frame the elements that lead and follow. Incorporate these elements into your wardrobe by wearing red, purple, grey or gold accents (a scarf or a tie) every day, but especially if you are under stress or speaking in public. Rocks would benefit from finding a way to connect directly to the earth, whether through gardening, going for a walk or working with modeling clay. Spiritual practices that involve community service are most appropriate for Rocks, as your best spiritual food is helping others.

> *"People can judge me for what I've done. And I think when somebody's out in the public eye, that's what they do. So, I'm fully comfortable with who I am, what I stand for, and what I've always stood for."*
> HILLARY CLINTON **831**

Advice for Those Who Live and Work with Rocks

- ⊙ If you have changes to present, plan ahead. Rocks aspire to stability and need ample time to adjust to change.

- ⊙ Provide plenty of space. Rocks are both self-aware and self-contained. They will ask for assistance if needed. Otherwise, they will likely not want to be disturbed.

- ⊙ If you are meeting a Rock for the first time, it's helpful to have an intermediary to create a safe path.

- ⊙ If you have a close relationship with a Rock, don't be afraid to introduce small changes to their routine. Trying chocolate chip instead of vanilla ice cream might be a big risk for a Rock. Celebrate those courageous adventures.

- ⊙ Since Rocks are so used to fulfilling requests and agendas, contact them with no expectation other than the pleasure of their company.

A Bit of Sage Guidance for Rocks
FROM *THE BOOK OF CHANGES AND THE UNCHANGING TRUTH* BY HUA-CHING NI

"The virtue of Mountain is its stillness. Growth is generated and maintained with strength. With calm and inward focus, one can clear the mind of selfish thoughts and desires and maintain the tranquility of a Mountain."

PROFILE *of a* NOTABLE ROCK

BARBARA WALTERS
849

Rock ⊙ Optimist ⊙ Networker

When Barbara Walters died in 2022, phrases like "fearless trailblazer, unwavering journalist, towering figure, and icon" were posted by her colleagues. "She paved the way for so many," wrote David Muir. "We learned from her and remain in awe of her to this day."

These accolades were well deserved and earned. Walters spent half a century honing her reputation as a consummate professional and dogged journalist, building trust with both those she interviewed and with the general public.

When Walters began her career in 1961 as a writer for "The Today Show", she was viewed as the token woman in a sea of men. She soon moved to the front of the camera as a "Today girl." While her predecessors were given stories about fashion, cooking, and other matters of the home, Walters wrote and produced her own material on socially significant topics.

Fifteen years later, in 1976, she became the first female news anchor and the highest-paid anchor – male or female – in history. While her male colleagues and many of the viewers dismissed her as a gimmick, she paved the way for future female network anchors like Jane Pauley, Katie Couric and Diane Sawyer.

That same year, Walters began her iconic "Barbara Walters Specials", where she further honed her skills as a journalist to secure interviews with U.S. presidents from Carter to Biden; world leaders, including Boris Yeltsin, Fidel Castro, and Yasir Arafat; and celebrities like Michael Jackson, Barbra Streisand, and Katherine Hepburn. Her interview with Monica Lewinsky garnered 50 million viewers, and her proclivity to make people cry, including Gen. Norman Schwarzkopf, was famous.

In 1997, Walters created "The View", featuring a racially diverse panel of all-female hosts—once again, creating opportunities for countless women to build their careers in journalism. Oprah Winfrey wrote, "Without Barbara Walters, there wouldn't have been me—nor any other woman you see on evening, morning, and daily news." She will continue to be a rock and an inspiration for generations to come.

"Life sometimes brings enormous difficulties and challenges that seem just too hard to bear. But bear them you can, and bear them you will, and your life can have a purpose."

BARBARA WALTERS

8 - THE ROCK RECAP

⊙ Rocks are solid, reliable and ever-present. They are the most self-contained of the archetypes, possessing the wisdom and capacity to see what needs to be done and accomplishing the task.

⊙ Rocks are loyal friends and trusted confidantes. They are well versed in multiple skills, allowing them to respond to situations from many different perspectives. Their steadfast nature aligns with their aspiration for stability.

⊙ Rocks are prone to become stubborn and inscrutable under stressful conditions. They can give mixed signals and be shut down and reactive, or irritated and emotionless.

⊙ As creatures of habit, Rocks can provide a warm and safe environment for the partnership to settle in. They can be possessive and prone to jealousy, which can explode on occasion.

⊙ When it comes to work, Rocks are pragmatic, diligent and loyal. Their qualities of persistence and contemplation are well matched for jobs that require attention to detail. Because they are so level-headed, they are also well suited to bringing balance and perspective into high pressure situations.

⊙ It is important for Rocks to find ways to express their wants and needs. They should practice saying "no" and "I need" and seek clarity from trusted friends who have no requests or agendas.

PROFILE *of a* NETWORKER

MS. JACKIE
932
Networker ⊙ Visionary ⊙ Caregiver

Ms. Jackie can never slip into a room. Whether she intends to or not, she makes an entrance to the degree that people stop what they are doing and bask in her warmth. She is a people person and is never short on company, conversation or compliments.

Ms. Jackie appreciates beauty and excellence in a variety of domains—from nature and art to science and everyday experiences. That said, she won't hesitate to adjust your collar or dust some lint off of your lapel. Nothing gets by Ms. Jackie.

While Ms. Jackie certainly has style, she backs it up with substance. As a teenager in the deep South, she risked being thrown in jail and worse by participating in a walkout at her school. That was the first of many courageous acts Ms. Jackie took as a lifelong civil rights activist and leader. Having gone through the fire of the civil rights era, Ms. Jackie's ability to observe a situation and articulate it is uncanny. She is never short on opinions and seems to know exactly what one needs to hear.

Many of us collect her sayings, which we commonly refer to as "Jackie-isms":

⊙ You don't recognize transformation when it's happening to you.

⊙ I don't have to get people in a room to be a teacher.

⊙ Be careful of people who don't see color because they don't see you.

⊙ It's only when we have the capacity to love ourselves into healing that we can change the world.

There's no doubt that Ms. Jackie not only lets her light shine, but instills light in others, too.

Virtue	Intuition
Skill	Communication
Motivation	Opportunity
Aspiration	Connection
Element	Fire
Preoccupation	Pleasure
Fear	Isolation
Shadow	The Diva
Tends to	Seek the perfect relationship
Needs to cultivate	Moderation

CHAPTER TWELVE

9 - THE NETWORKER

"Spread the love!" | *"Why is this happening to me?"*

Primary Attribute – Networkers at Their Best

The archetype of the Networker represents the midday sun when everything is at its brightest. When a Networker comes into your presence, they are not easily forgotten. Their warm, passionate nature commands attention and when the spotlight is on them, they are never tongue-tied.

Networkers have an innate sense of perception. Like fire, they not only cast light on things, but reveal the shadows as well. In this manner, Networkers have good judgment regarding people and situations. Their intuition, combined with their flair for creativity, gives them the talent and ingenuity to set the world on fire.

Networkers love to be in the center of the action. Their ability to speak well and connect people makes the Networker a perfect diplomat and spokesperson.

Like fire, Networkers need a steady amount of fuel to keep them going, or they will likely burn out. It is helpful for Networkers to surround themselves with creative people and engage in activities for continual learning. They need to seek support in staying grounded and managing the practical matters of their lives.

Secondary Attribute – The Diva

When Networkers invoke their shadow, the Diva arrives and everything comes to a halt. Divas have a way of sucking the air out of a room and consuming everything in their paths. If someone crosses them, they will read people like a book and have the vocabulary to do a thorough job at it.

The Diva can be demanding, fussy and needy. Some of their moods might be justified; after all, the Networker is the initial point person for all things good and bad. If a situation turns for the worse when they are at the podium or on stage, the spotlight is on them and the Networker will get the blame and criticism, whether they are responsible for it or not. Still, they lean towards drama and tend to make mountains out of molehills.

If Divas don't get their needs met, they can descend into a deeper pool of self-pity. A "don't you know

"I'm a big old egotistical baby and that's okay. I can accept it."
WHOOPI GOLDBERG **959**

who I am" attitude might develop and they may find themselves abandoned without any support.

It is important for Divas to show gratitude and compassion for those around them. When things go wrong, everyone suffers because they are but a part of a larger team. For those who hope to keep the Diva archetype at bay, they can provide grounding, support and inspiration for the Networker by including them in new ideas and endeavors.

Relational Attribute – Networkers in Public

Many people may experience a push/pull dynamic with Networkers. Individuals may be attracted to a Networker at first, but may later become afraid of getting too close for fear of being burned. This is reinforced by the Networker's self-confidence, which may make them appear vain and inconsiderate.

Their expressive and sociable approach may draw admiration from some, while others may view them as shallow. A person encountering the Diva will likely pick up on their air of superiority and self-centeredness. Whatever their reactions, people typically do not have a neutral opinion about the Networker.

Even so, Networkers are affable and gregarious most of the time. Since they seek connection, they have an

"My job is to make sure that whatever happens in a performance lives in somebody else, that it's memorable . . . If you forget tomorrow what you heard yesterday, there's really not much point in you having been there—or me, for that matter."

YO-YO MA **977**

almost magical way of making people around them feel special. For that reason, they are loved, or at least tolerated, in a group.

Developmental Attribute – The Young Networker

Brilliant, intuitive and never short on words—these are common ways to describe a young Networker. As fire has the ability to shed light on objects, these children can reveal people and situations for what they are; and although they can be thoughtful and articulate, they are usually not shy in sharing their opinions.

Young Networkers are sharp students who tend to learn less through books and lectures, and more by discussion, debate and experiential learning. When working in groups, young Networkers are often called upon to be the spokesperson. Their communication skills often result in them getting more credit than they deserve. Some children might be drawn to their warmth and star quality, while other children might resent it.

Life tends to come easily for young Networkers because they can see their paths so clearly. They are natural problem solvers and their keen insights can often quickly result in multiple ways to address an issue. When they run into a pinch, Networkers can also call upon their natural charm to work their way

"If you are going to achieve excellence in big things, you develop the habit in little matters. Excellence is not an exception; it is a prevailing attitude."
COLIN POWELL **932**

PROFILE *of a* YOUNG NETWORKER

MALALA YOUSAFZAI
398
Visionary ⊙ Networker ⊙ Rock

When she was 11 years old, Malala Yousafzai took to the stage at a conference in Peshawar, Pakistan. Her speech, "How Dare the Taliban Take Away my Basic Right to Education", garnered international attention, along with death threats in her native country.

The following year, Malala began blogging for the BBC (under a pseudonym) about what it was like to live as a young woman under Taliban rule. When she was 15 years old, Taliban soldiers boarded Malala's school bus and shot her in the head. She and two of her classmates, who were also shot, miraculously survived.

Since then, Malala has become a global advocate for girls and education. At age 16, she spoke before the United Nations and wrote her bestselling autobiography, *I Am Malala: The Girl Who Stood Up for Education and Was Shot by the Taliban*. At 17, Malala became the youngest person in history to receive the Nobel Peace Prize.

To celebrate her 18th birthday, Malala, through proceeds raised by the Malala Fund, opened a school for Syrian refugee girls living in Lebanon.

"Today, on my first day as an adult, on behalf of the world's children, I demand of leaders we must invest in books instead of bullets," she proclaimed while speaking in one of the school's classrooms.

As a young Networker, Malala has already become the torchbearer for a global movement. As she transitions into her adult Visionary role, she will no doubt continue to be a voice of hope and possibilities for generations to come.

out of a situation. Because of this, they have little empathy for others who might struggle.

It is important to provide the young Networker with the right balance of praise and humility. Be mindful of their need for connection by giving them some uninterrupted time each day. This will keep them grounded and inspired to continue exploring their potential in a positive light.

Networkers in Relationship

If one likes to be seen in the right places with the right people, they would be wise to choose a Networker for a partner. In whatever circles Networkers associate, they are the local celebrity and life of the party. Most people would consider themselves lucky to be in the presence of a Networker.

Because of their bedazzling and brilliant persona, Networkers can choose any partner they wish and charm their potential catch into anything they want them to do. Fortunately, Networkers have the far-sighted intelligence to choose partners who can provide them with balance (Philosophers), stability (Rocks) and inspiration (Visionaries).

Romantic by nature, Networkers can make someone believe that, whether the encounter is 30 seconds or 30 years, they are the only person that matters.

"I don't want to be thought of as the girl who was shot by the Taliban, but the girl who fought for education. This is the cause to which I want to devote my life."
MALALA YOUSAFZAI **398**

This seductive quality that Networkers possess can lead to dalliances, but their hearts remain loyal to their partners.

In their Diva mode, Networkers can be fickle, arrogant and demanding. They have little patience for pain and suffering, unless it is their own. Supporters need to give them space and time, but also call on their greater capacity for generosity and benevolence. Networkers strive for connection, to give and receive pleasure. In their efforts to "spread the love", it is important for Networkers to be reminded of who their family is, and their allegiance to their greater purpose and deeper values.

Through their intuitive powers, they know what others need, especially their partners. If they can remain focused on that, Networkers will have a long and happy partnership.

Networkers in the Workplace

The Networker's role of providing inspiration and clarity gives them the power to navigate others through troubled waters. "Here's how I see it" is a common phrase that Networkers use in the workplace, and because of their track record of success, their co-workers often give them the floor. Once Networkers share their observations, the group

"Stay hungry. Stay foolish."
STEVE JOBS **959**

often sees things more clearly and is willing to adjust their plans.

Networkers are skilled orators. They can prove well suited to roles such as spokesperson, minister, politician or salesperson. However, just because they are good with words does not mean that they are well versed on the topics they are representing. Networkers sometimes have more style than substance, so they need a team of researchers and fact checkers to back them up.

The Diva in them can give Networkers the sense that they are the best and brightest people in the organization . They assume more authority than they can handle and may make promises and decisions without going through the appropriate channels. For this reason, they need to be consistently checked and handled, and are thus considered high maintenance.

Advice for Networkers

Networkers, like fire, cannot exist in a vacuum. You need fuel and air through the constant flow of creativity and inspiration to keep going. It is helpful for you to surround yourself with Visionaries and Optimists. At the same time, you would be wise to seek guidance from Philosophers and Caregivers to prevent burnout.

"Be strong, be fearless, be beautiful. And believe that anything is possible when you have the right people there to support you."
MISTY COPELAND **977**

Because Networkers have a bit of a star quality about them, people may often place you on a pedestal. For better or worse, you become role models and social influencers. As a Networker, you must be vigilant about your behaviors, since you are being watched at all times. Focusing on others versus yourself is a good practice for Networkers to cultivate.

While Networkers may be suitable for senior leadership positions, they need to have the support necessary to deliver with all of their pistons firing. Give them time and space to both prepare for their "performance" and to cool down. Hold compassion for the amount of energy that they carry and be empathetic during periods of burnout. Like a phoenix, they will rise again.

The primary issue for Networkers is to maintain a healthy and sustained sense of fire so you don't burn out or run too hot . In everything that you do, it would be helpful to seek clarity and alignment so your messages and intentions are understood. Listen intently before speaking and find multiple ways to communicate. In addition to speaking, write, draw or act things out.

In your office and personal spaces, add colors (greens and blue) and objects (plants, fountains) that symbolize wood and water. Try to wear something

"I intend to live life, not just exist."
GEORGE TAKEI **932**

with green or blue accents (a scarf or a tie) every day, but especially if you are under stress or speaking in public. If you need to ponder or talk about something serious, take a walk in a wooded area or near water.

Develop a meditation or reflection practice that you can do alone or with a group that involves the ears and eyes—something you can listen to and apply visually, like dance, *tai chi*, painting or photography.

Advice for Those Who Live and Work with Networkers

⊙ Networkers need to seek support in staying grounded and managing the practical matters of their lives.

⊙ To keep the Diva at bay, provide grounding for the Networker through practical support and inspiration. Include them in new ideas and endeavors.

⊙ It is important to provide the young Networker with the right balance of praise and humility. Be mindful of their need for connection by giving them some uninterrupted time each day. This will keep the Networker grounded and inspired to explore their potential in a positive light.

⊙ Make sure they have the support necessary to deliver with all of their pistons firing. Give them time and space to both prepare for their "performance" and to cool down.

⊙ In everything that you do with a Networker, seek clarity and alignment so their messages and intentions are understood. Encourage them to listen intently before speaking and to find multiple ways to communicate, such as writing, drawing or acting things out.

A Bit of Sage Guidance for Networkers
FROM *THE BOOK OF CHANGES AND THE UNCHANGING TRUTH* BY HUA-CHING NI

"The mind and the heart represent the Fire energy in our bodies. Only when they are harmonized with the body, which represents Water energy, can one achieve the correct goal of fundamental cultivation: good health."

PROFILE *of a* NOTABLE NETWORKER

BILL CLINTON
986
Networker ⊙ *Rock* ⊙ *Protector*

After reporter Charlise Lyles met with President Bill Clinton in 1995, she wrote:

> ⊙ He exudes a sincere charisma so potent it can lull you into loving him.

> ⊙ His boyish truthfulness made it harder for me to believe he could repeatedly cheat on his wife or dodge a draft.

> ⊙ Although he showed no signs of a sense of humor, how could I not love a guy leaning back and snapping down cookies while surrounded by assertive journalists braced to crumble him?

One might think that Bill Clinton's charisma would be a substitute for his intelligence. Not so. This man, born in rural Hope, Arkansas to a single mother, honed his gifts to become the most powerful man on the planet.

As a teenager, Mr. Clinton chose to pursue a life of public service when he shook hands with President John F. Kennedy. He is the only

U.S. President who was named as a Rhodes Scholar. At age 32, he was elected Governor of Arkansas and, at 46, Mr. Clinton was elected President of the United States, marking a new era in American politics.

Like fire, when President Clinton shined, his light was bright; but he could also diminish into a heap of ashes. In 1998, he was impeached by the House of Representatives for sexual indiscretions with Monica Lewinsky, then an intern. Despite this scandal, for which he was found not guilty, President Clinton sustained popular approval ratings.

After he left the White House in 2001, Mr. Clinton enjoyed immense popularity wherever he went. During the 2016 Democratic National Convention, where his wife won the nomination for President, The Washington Post touted Mr. Clinton's skill as his ability to "leave a room completely at his attention." And at a more recent star-studded fundraiser, a reporter noted that "the room stopped … and then everyone freaked out" when Mr. Clinton entered.

His brilliance and charisma have not dimmed.

"All my life I've been interested in other people's stories. I wanted to know them, understand them, feel them. When I grew up into politics, I always felt the main point of my work was to give people a chance to have better stories."

PRESIDENT BILL CLINTON

9 – THE NETWORKER RECAP

⊙ Networkers possess a warmth and spark in their way of being. They are intellectually bright and intuitively gifted, which gives them the ability to be good judges of people and situations. Networkers possess a star quality and attract attention whether they want to or not .

⊙ Perception and image are important to Networkers; thus, they are both skilled and discerning with their words. Charming and affable, Networkers are gifted at connecting people and motivating them to commit to a cause.

⊙ When in stress, the Diva arrives. They will be demanding, fussy and needy. If Divas don't get their needs met, they can descend into self-pity.

⊙ Networkers strive for connection and intimacy. Romantic by nature, Networkers can be flirtatious, but if they are in love, their hearts remain loyal to their partners.

⊙ The Networker's role in providing inspiration and clarity give them the power to navigate people through troubled waters. They would be well suited in roles such as spokesperson, minister, politician and salesperson.

⊙ The primary issue for Networkers is maintaining a healthy and sustained sense of Fire so they don't burn out or run too hot. In everything that they do, it would be helpful for them to seek clarity and alignment so their messages and intentions are understood.

KEVIN JOHN FONG

THE ARCHETYPES
AT A PARTY

- ⊙ **The Philosopher** sits in a corner and watches everyone. They may bring a camera or a notepad to record the interactions for later reflection.

- ⊙ **The Caregiver** heads straight for the kitchen to help with food prep or wash the dishes.

- ⊙ **The Visionary** brings the latest party game, music and recipes to spice things up.

- ⊙ **The Optimist** hangs out at the door, greeting everyone with a hug and making them feel welcome before passing them onto the Caregivers and Networkers.

- ⊙ **The Facilitator** is in the middle of the crowd, directing conversations but not really participating in them.

- ⊙ **The Protector** is quietly critiquing the party with an "if I were in charge" point of view, and keeping an eye out for people who are misbehaving.

- ⊙ **The Achiever** is busy working the room for opportunities and trying to win the party game that the Visionary brought.

- ⊙ **The Rock i**s sitting in a corner with someone who sought them out for advice.

- ⊙ **The Networker** would be the life of the party - cutting jokes, singing songs, and spreading the love.

Each relationship asks us to be clear on who we are, how we are,
what we are doing, where we are headed, and how we are going to
be together in a balanced, healthy and generative way.

PART THREE

THE FIVE ELEMENTS
as an INTERPERSONAL ASSESSMENT TOOL

Clarity and alignment are key factors for any relationship to prosper. Whether two people have just met or have known each other for a lifetime, each relationship asks us to be clear on who we are, how we are, what we are doing, where we are headed, and how we are going to be together in a balanced, healthy and generative way.

In this section, you will acquire the tools to analyze relationships through **The Five Elements**.

◉ **Chapter 13** guides you in assessing your own Five Elements profile, giving you a deeper understanding of how the attributes manifest in you.

◉ **Chapter 14** focuses on analyzing interpersonal dynamics between two people. Although I am featuring a couple who is engaged to be married, this process can be applied to any two people in a relationship—be they friends, relatives, co-workers or partners.

◉ **Chapter 15** looks at the specific period of adolescence, when young people are transitioning from their Developmental to their

Primary attributes. Depending on the elemental relationship between the two attributes, the transition may be smooth or rough. Teens, as well as their often-beleaguered parents, teachers, mentors and family members, typically strive for some explanation and relief. **The Five Elements** may provide some perspective.

⊙ **Chapter 16** explores using **The Five Elements** as a tool to assess leadership and communication dynamics in larger groups. While a work situation will be featured, the tool applies to any group situation of any size, including families, community groups, teams, and social groups.

⊙ **Chapter 17** outlines how **The Five Elements** can confront and transform conflict in a generative way to achieve healthy outcomes.

⊙ **Chapter 18** provides advice on integrating **The Five Elements** into your daily routines and practices.

"**The Five Elements** present themselves without bias or judgment. They simply say, "this is what needs to be done to bring you back to balance in a good way."

If you are coding and charting a profile for a person under the age of 15, please use their Secondary and Developmental attribute as your main reference point. They will not manifest their Primary attribute until adulthood.

If you are coding and charting a profile for a person between ages 15 and 20, use both the Secondary and Developmental and Primary attributes as main reference points, since they are transitioning from one to the other.

CHAPTER THIRTEEN

ANALYZING *your* FIVE ELEMENTS PROFILE

Now that you have calculated your Five Elements profile and discovered more about your archetypes, you can explore the dynamics and nuances of the attributes—both for yourself and for the groups and communities in which you belong. The easiest place to start is by analyzing your individual chart. This chapter guides you through that process.

Step 1 | Charting

The first step is charting your profile. Take your code and apply each attribute to the chart in Figure 11 on pg. 240 in the following manner -

Primary attribute	**BOLD UPPERCASE**
Secondary and Developmental attribute	lowercase letters
Relational attribute	*Italics*

Once the attributes are applied to the chart, it is easier to see the dynamics For example, here is how Sam's Five Elements profile looks when it is mapped out on a chart

NAME	CODE	ARCHETYPES
Sam	638	**PROTECTOR** ⊙ visionary ⊙ *Rock*

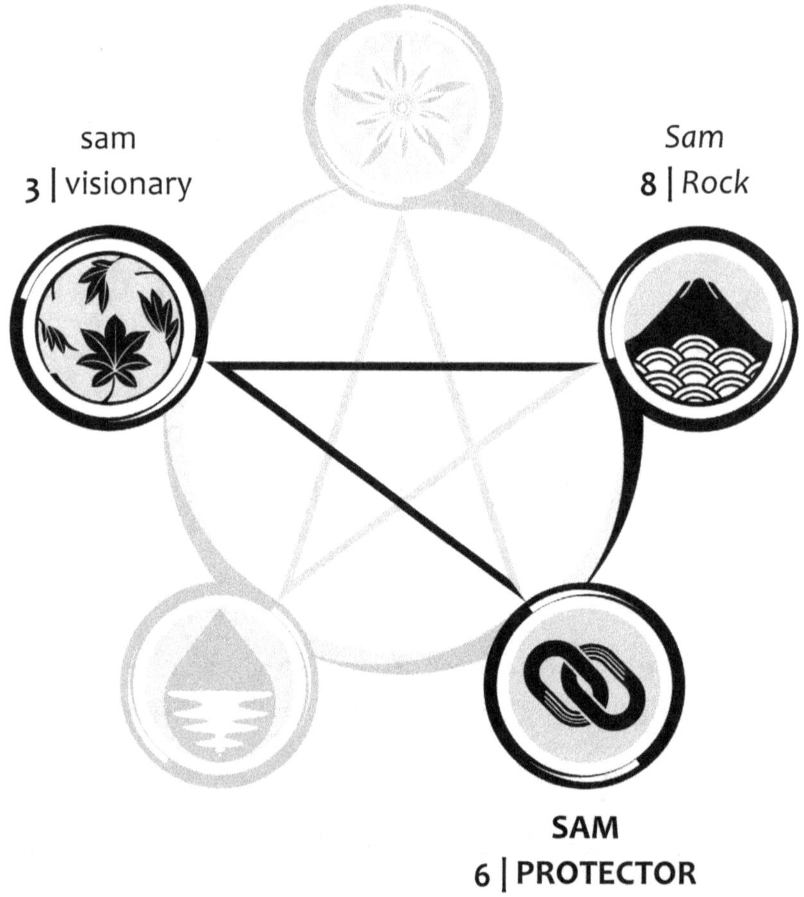

Once the attributes are applied to the chart, it is easier to see the dynamics among the elements and analyze the tensions and considerations.

Step 2 | Analysis

The next step is to map out the dynamics among the elements in the Supporting and Restraining cycles. Upon initial review, Sam's chart indicates the following:

I.   Of the five elements, three (Metal, Wood and Earth) are present in Sam's profile.

II.   Since Earth supports Metal, there is a good relationship between Sam's Relational|Rock and Primary|Protector attributes.

III.   Since Metal restrains Wood there is tension between Sam's Primary|Protector and Secondary|Developmental| Visionary attributes.

IV.   Since Wood restrains Earth, there is tension between Sam's Secondary Developmental|Visionary and Relational|Rock.

From this quick review of the elemental dynamics, we can make the following observations about Sam's personal, leadership and communication styles:

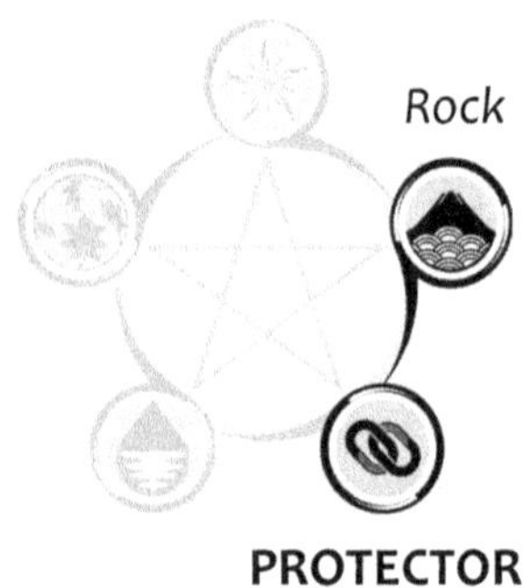

I. When Sam is operating from the Primary|Protector attribute, his attitudes and behaviors align well with peoples' perceptions of a Relational|Rock (Earth supports Metal). Sam's public persona is that of a dependable leader who will keep things safe and orderly.

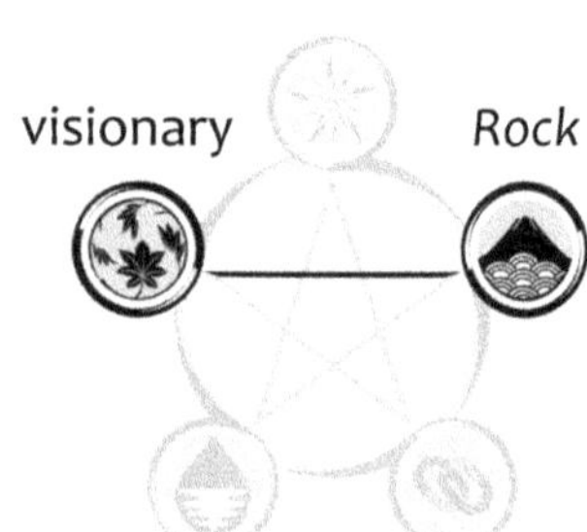

II. However, when Sam is operating from the Secondary|Visionary mode, there is conflict with the Relational|Rock attribute (Wood restrains Earth). Sam's forgetful and flaky stress behavior runs counter to the reliable Rock that people expect. People may get confused by Sam's attitudes and actions, as they don't match up with their perceptions.

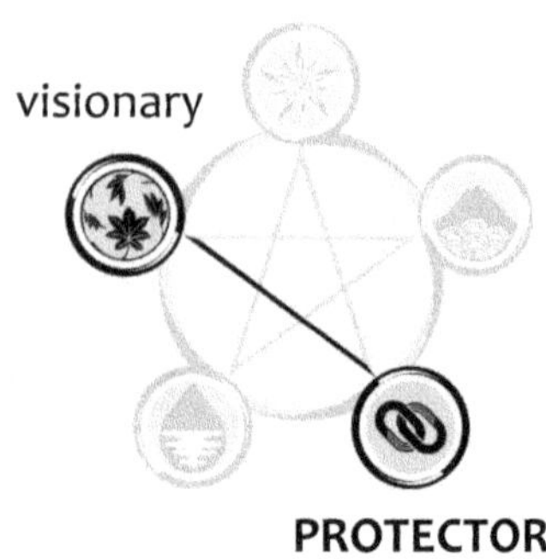

III. When Sam goes into stress, it is a forward motion from Metal to Wood, so it is easy for Sam go there. Once Sam is in the Secondary|Visionary mode, it is difficult to break out of it and return to the Primary|Protector mode. Thus, Sam can remain flaky and forgetful (instead of protective and orderly) for a long time.

A deeper review of Sam's chart indicates more:

IV. Sam's transition from Developmental|Visionary to Primary|Protector (mid-teens and early twenties) was likely difficult, as the journey was going from Wood to Metal, against the flow of the Restraining cycle.

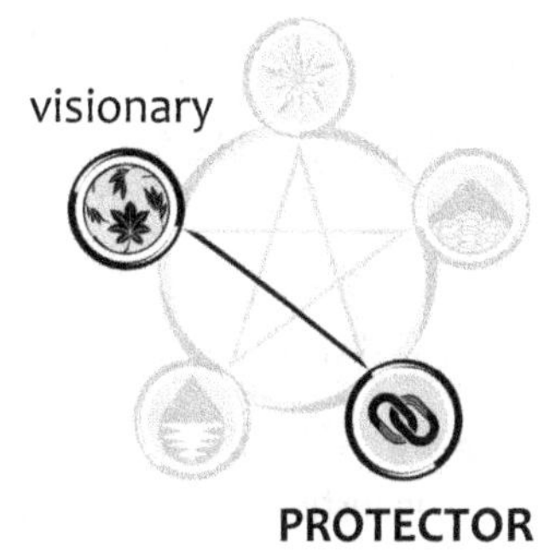

For Sam, the teenage years were like walking on the edge of a knife. The pressure to be responsible, accountable and duty bound (Protector traits), whether from internal or external sources, meant that Sam had to likely cut out parts of his life that brought him joy. There was probably a long, painful cleaving or metamorphosis that allowed Sam to assume the Primary|Protector role.

As an adult, when Sam began to move out of the Secondary|Stress attribute (Wood|Visionary) and back to the Primary attribute (Metal

|Protector), memories from his late teens may have arisen, making the journey more difficult.

The dynamic creates an internal tension that could be confusing in the least and at times paralyzing for Sam There is some degree of self-sabotage present as Sam creates obstacles that result in feeling depleted. What can Sam do to attain balance and harmony?

Step 3 | Recommendations

The next step is to determine recommendations for Sam to attain and maintain balance and harmony.

The dynamics only manifest when Sam goes into Secondary | Stress mode. Relief comes if Sam is able to stay in Primary | Protector mode. If he can avoid slipping into the Secondary | Visionary state, things will remain balanced and orderly.

The first thing to do is circle the elements that are not represented in the profile. In Sam's case, the elements are Water and Fire; therefore, Sam needs to bring in recommendations from these two elements in order to maintain balance.

Basic knowledge of The Five Elements means:

Reading and understanding the concepts of the Supporting and Restraining cycles, but not necessarily the transitions;

and

Familiarizing yourself with your own elemental attributes.

If Sam has a basic knowledge of **The Five Elements**, I would recommend focusing on two elements: Water and Fire.

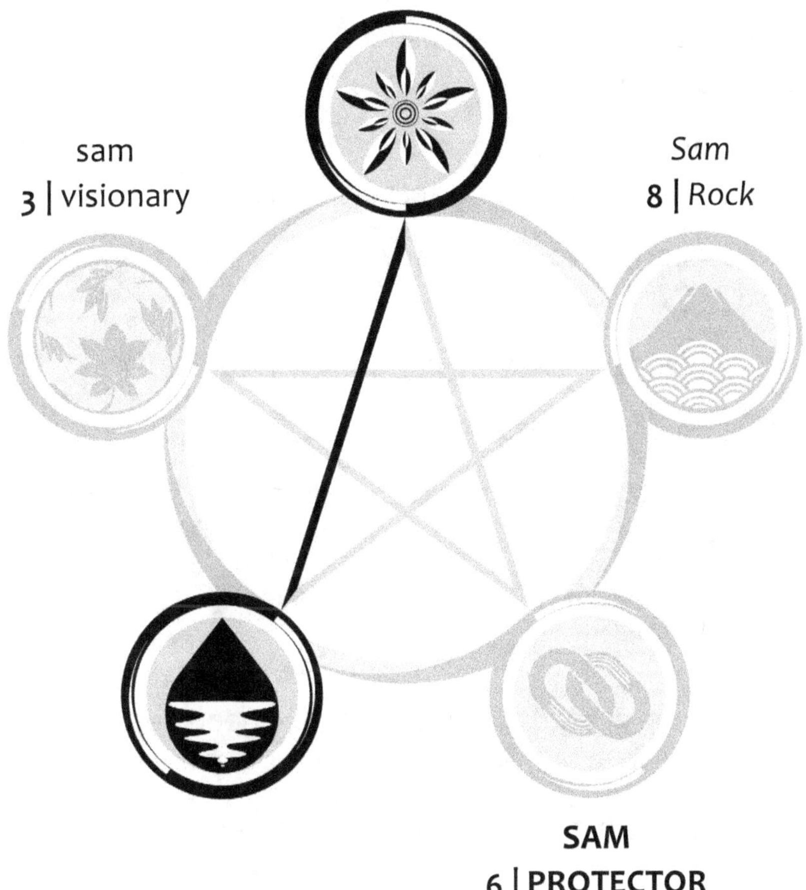

NAME	CODE	ARCHETYPES
Sam	638	**PROTECTOR** ⊙ visionary ⊙ *Rock*

Follow Goldilocks

⊙ By "Following Goldilocks", Sam can attain that perfect balance of not too little, not too much, but just right. This manifests in the balance of listening and visualizing, along with inward and outward alignment.

⊙ Sam can be an advocate for Water and Fire through language that leads to a balance between listening and visualizing.

⊙ "Let's recap the main points we want to convey and make sure we're clear."

⊙ "What is the best way we can communicate our mission?"

⊙ "What would success look like in a story?"

⊙ "Are we good with each other? Or do we need to take a step back and reflect?"

In addition, Sam can:

⊙ Spend time every day reflecting on the good deeds that have been or need to be fulfilled.

⊙ Go for walks near water or have a cup of tea.

⊙ Express appreciation on a regular basis.

⊙ Cultivate a daily meditation practice.

With these practices, Sam can manifest positive seeds of innovation and creativity in ways that support a healthy balance between the Primary|Protector and Secondary|Visionary attributes.

The next few pages will assist you in coding and charting your own Five Elements profile.

STEP 1 | Coding and Charting

Enter your Five Elements code in the box and label your chart on pg. 240 as follows:

Primary attribute	**BOLD UPPERCASE**
Secondary and Developmental attribute	lowercase letters
Relational attribute	*Italics*

STEP 2 | Analysis

Draw arrows on your chart to indicate the dynamics between your elements according to the Supporting and Restraining cycles. Consider the following questions:

- Which elements are represented in your chart?

- What dynamics are occurring between the elements and attributes?

- What is the relationship between your Primary and Relational attributes (when you are seen at your very best)?

- What is the relationship between your Secondary and Relational Attributes (when you are stressed or at your worst, or if the person you are assessing is under age 18)?

⊙ What is the relationship between your Primary and Secondary attributes (the transition from feeling strong to feeling stressed)?

⊙ What is the relationship between your Primary and Developmental attributes (the transition from adolescence to adulthood)?

⊙ What observations can you make about how these dynamics relate to your personality, leadership and communication styles?

STEP 3 | Recommendations

Circle the elements that are not represented on your chart. Consider the following questions:

⊙ Which of these elements would support you in staying in your Primary attribute?

⊙ Which of these elements would prevent you from moving into your Secondary attribute (stress mode)?

⊙ Which of these elements would alleviate the tension points in your chart? (Hint: look at the relationships from Step 2 in the Restraining cycle).

⊙ Of all the elements that are circled, what is the best element that you can invoke to keep you healthy, balanced and productive?

⊙ What are some practices that you can employ that are aligned with this element? (Refer to Appendix III for recommendations.)

CHAPTER THIRTEEN RECAP

⊙ In this chapter, you learned how to identify and understand the dynamics and nuances of your own profile. Here is a recap of the steps:

I.   Code and chart your profile.

II.   Analyze the elemental tensions and dynamics that occur between the following attributes: Primary and Relational, Secondary and Relational, Primary and Secondary, and Developmental and Primary.

III.   Identify the element(s) that would support balance. Determine practices and solutions related to those elements.

⊙ Brief assessments of all 81 Five Elements profiles are listed in Appendix II. The page numbers of each profile are referenced in Figure 11 on page 241.

⊙ These assessments will provide a general guide on the dynamics that manifest in your profile; however, they do not offer recommendations that might be specific to your situation and needs. Please consult a Five Elements practitioner for more detailed information.

FIVE ELEMENTS CHART WITH CODING TABLE

NAME	CODE	ARCHETYPES

FIGURE 11
WITH REFERENCE PAGES TO INDIVIDUAL ASSESSMENTS
RELATIONAL ATTRIBUTE CHART

914 (pg. 403)	813 (pg. 398)	712 (pg. 393)	611 (pg. 389)	519 (pg. 384)	418 (pg. 379)	317 (pg. 374)	216 (pg. 370)	115 (pg. 365)
923 (pg. 403)	822 (pg. 399)	721 (pg. 394)	629 (pg. 389)	528 (pg. 384)	427 (pg. 379)	326 (pg. 375)	225 (pg. 370)	124 (pg. 365)
932 (pg. 403)	831 (pg. 399)	739 (pg. 394)	638 (pg. 390)	537 (pg. 385)	436 (pg. 380)	335 (pg. 375)	234 (pg. 371)	133 (pg. 366)
941 (pg. 404)	849 (pg. 400)	748 (pg. 395)	647 (pg. 390)	546 (pg. 385)	445 (pg. 380)	344 (pg. 376)	243 (pg. 371)	142 (pg. 367)
959 (pg. 404)	858 (pg. 400)	757 (pg. 395)	656 (pg. 391)	555 (pg. 386)	454 (pg. 381)	353 (pg. 377)	252 (pg. 372)	151 (pg. 367)
968 (pg. 405)	867 (pg. 401)	766 (pg. 396)	665 (pg. 391)	564 (pg. 386)	463 (pg. 381)	362 (pg. 377)	261 (pg. 372)	169 (pg. 368)
977 (pg. 405)	876 (pg. 401)	775 (pg. 397)	674 (pg. 392)	573 (pg. 387)	472 (pg. 382)	371 (pg. 377)	279 (pg. 373)	178 (pg. 368)
986 (pg. 406)	885 (pg. 402)	784 (pg. 397)	683 (pg. 392)	582 (pg. 387)	481 (pg. 383)	389 (pg. 378)	288 (pg. 373)	187 (pg. 369)
995 (pg. 407)	894 (pg. 402)	793 (pg. 398)	692 (pg. 393)	591 (pg. 388)	499 (pg. 383)	398 (pg. 378)	297 (pg. 374)	196 (pg. 369)

NOTE REGARDING CHILDREN AND TEENS:

If you are coding and charting a profile for a person under the age of 15, please use their Secondary and Developmental attribute as your main reference point. They will not manifest their Primary attribute until adulthood.

If you are coding and charting a profile for a person between ages 15 and 20, use both the Secondary and Developmental and Primary attributes as main reference points, since they are transitioning from one to the other.

CHAPTER FOURTEEN

THE FIVE ELEMENTS
for COUPLES

Several months after Sam and Terry started dating, they decided to get a Five Elements analysis of their relationship.

"We thought it would be fun," Terry commented, "but we had no idea how much we would learn about ourselves and each other."

"The Five Elements came at a good time for me," Sam added. "I was getting pretty serious about our relationship. And while I had no doubt that Terry would be up for it, I was questioning my own readiness. The assessment gave me the confidence that I could handle whatever came up because I would be clear on what to do to get ourselves back into alignment."

243

 Refer to Chapter 13 to learn how to code and chart an individual Five Elements profile. Refer Chapter 16 Title Page for note regarding coding for children and teens.

Developing a Five Elements Assessment Between Two People

Analyzing interpersonal dynamics between two people requires the following steps.

I. Code and chart the individual Five Elements profiles and lay the charts side by side.

II. Code and chart a Five Elements pairs profile by combining the information from the two individual profiles.

III. Look for overall patterns and dynamics. Which elements are present and which are not? What are the dynamics at play regarding the Supporting and Restraining cycles? Do not make any conclusions or recommendations yet; simply note the patterns.

IV. Code and chart for possible scenarios that can occur between these two people. The scenarios are:

⊙ Both are operating from their Primary attributes.

⊙ Both are operating from their Secondary attributes.

⊙ Person "A" is operating from their Primary attribute while Person "B" is operating from their Secondary attribute.

⊙ Person "B" is operating from their Primary attribute while Person "A" is operating from their Secondary attribute.

V. Overlay the Relational attributes on each scenario.

VI. Look for overall elemental patterns and dynamics. Which elements are present and which are not? What are the dynamics at play regarding the Supporting and Restraining cycles?

⊙ What dynamics are occurring between the elements and attributes?

⊙ What is the relationship between your Primary and Relational attributes (when you both are seen at your very best)?

⊙ What is the relationship between your Secondary and Relational attributes (how you are seen when you both are stressed or at your worst)?

⊙ What is the relationship if Person "A" is operating from their Primary attribute and Person "B" is operating from their Secondary attribute?

⊙ What is the relationship if Person "A" is operating from their Secondary attribute and Person "B" is operating from their Primary attribute?

⊙ What happens when the Relational attributes are overlayed on all four scenarios?

Refer to Chapter 13 to learn how to code and chart an individual Five Elements profile.

⊙ What observations can you make as these dynamics relate to your individual and collective personality, leadership and communication styles?

VII. If an overall pattern or trend becomes evident in step 6, congratulations! You can now determine what element(s) would contribute to supporting your relationship and develop practices and solutions aligned with that element(s). If no overall pattern or trend appears, you may need to develop several solutions to respond to situations as they present themselves.

Let's walk through an example of an analysis between Sam and Terry. We charted their profiles as individuals in Chapter 3; now let's look at their profiles as a couple.

To Review,

Sam's profile is 638 - Protector|Visionary|Rock. Terry's profile is 279 - Caregiver|Achiever|Philosopher.

Step 1 | Code and chart the individual profiles and lay them out side by side.

Here are Sam's and Terry's individual charts:

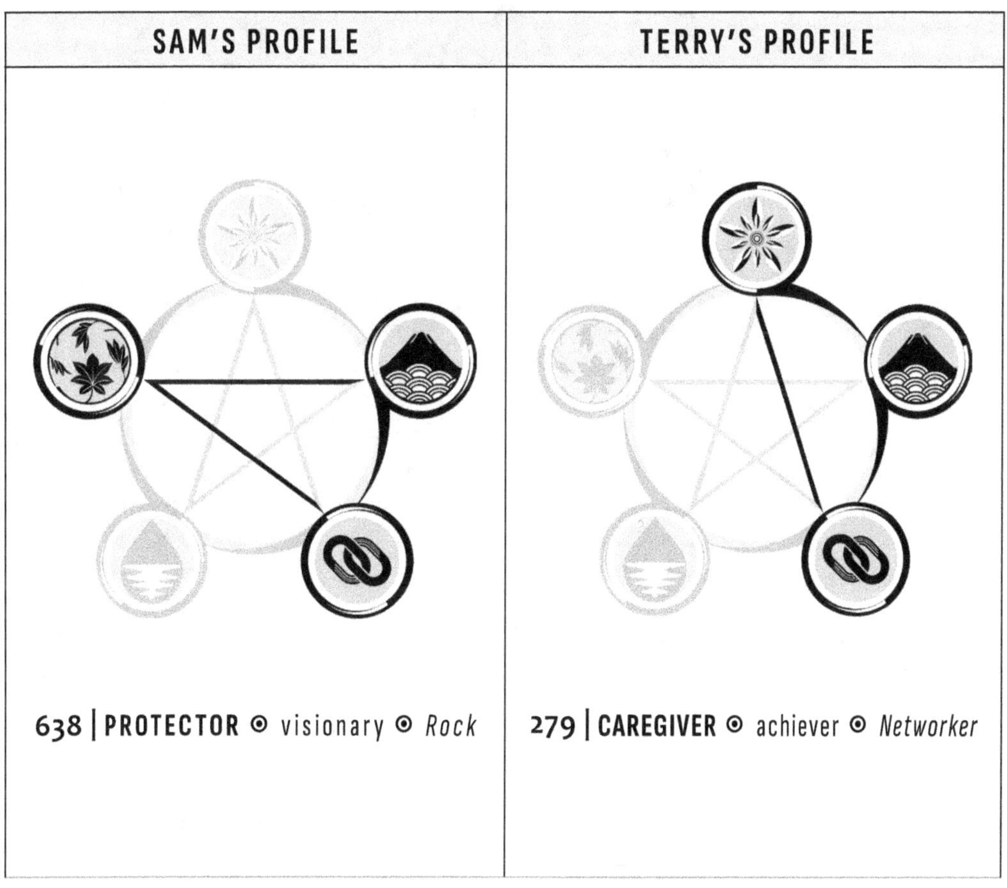

Step 2 | Create a combined chart from the individual charts.

Primary attribute	**BOLD UPPERCASE**
Secondary and Developmental attribute	lowercase letters
Relational attribute	*Italics*

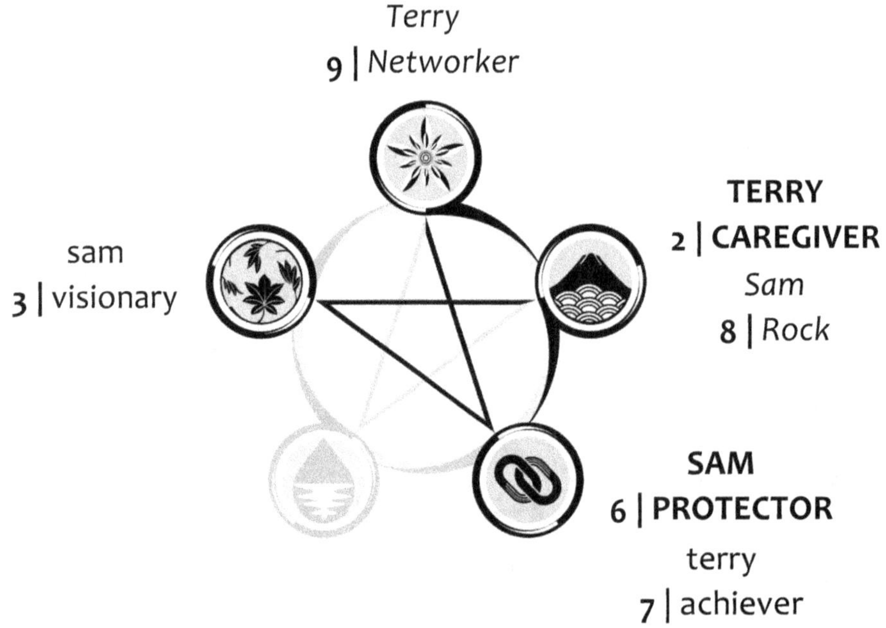

NAME	CODE	ARCHETYPLES
Sam	638	**PROTECTOR** ⊙ visionary ⊙ *Rock*
Terry	279	**CAREGIVER** ⊙ achiever ⊙ *Networker*

Step 3 | Study initial observations on the combined chart.

Upon initial review, Sam's and Terry's chart indicates the following:

- ◉ Of the Five Elements, four (Metal, Wood, Fire and Earth) are present in both of their profiles.

- ◉ There is no Water in their profiles and Wood shows up only in the Secondary attribute

Step 4 | Chart the four scenarios that can occur between Sam and Terry.

Scenario A:

Both are operating from their Primary attributes.

OBSERVATIONS

- ◉ Terry is an Earth|Caregiver and Sam is a Metal|Protector. Earth supports Metal, thus Terry naturally supports Sam. The Caregiver is the Mother archetype and the Protector is the Father archetype in the ancient framework. This is an auspicious and prosperous partnership!

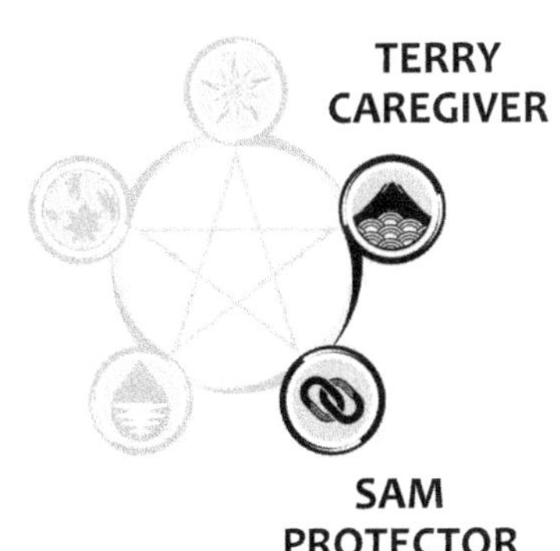

⊙ Their Relational attributes are well positioned, with Terry's Networker and Sam's Rock both respectively supporting their Primary attributes.

Scenario B:

Both are operating from their Secondary attributes.

OBSERVATIONS

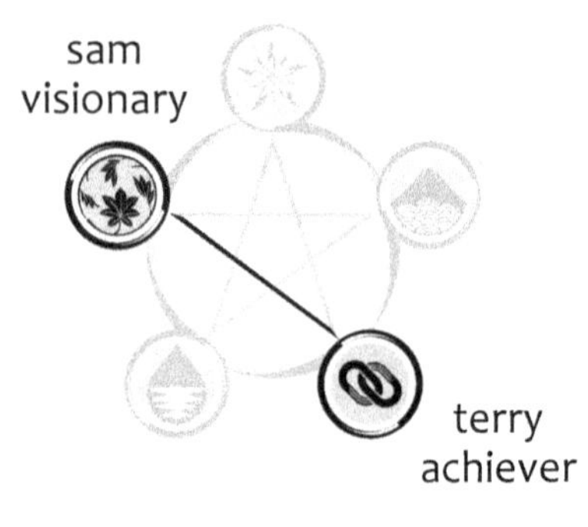

⊙ Terry is a Metal|Achiever and Sam is a Wood|Visionary in this mode. They move from a Supporting to a Restraining relationship with Terry's Metal nature cutting into Sam's Wood nature. This is unfortunate news!

⊙ Both Relational attributes are in Restraining relationships with their respective Secondary attributes. This creates situations where people may be disappointed in their expectations of Sam and Terry.

Scenario C:

Sam is Primary and Terry is Secondary.

OBSERVATIONS

⊙ Terry is a Metal|Achiever and Sam is a Metal|Protector in this mode. Since they are both in Metal, Sam's Primary mode is able to counter Terry's secondary characteristics and actions.

⊙ The Relational attributes are well positioned and generally supportive of this scenario.

Scenario D:

Terry is Primary and Sam is Secondary.

OBSERVATIONS

⊙Terry is an Earth|Caregiver and Sam is a Wood|Visionary in this mode. Because Wood restrains Earth, Sam's secondary mode has the upper hand in this scenario, leaving Terry depleted.

⊙The Relational attributes are well positioned and generally supportive of this scenario. Terry's Fire|Networker attribute helps to facilitate the tension between Wood and Earth.

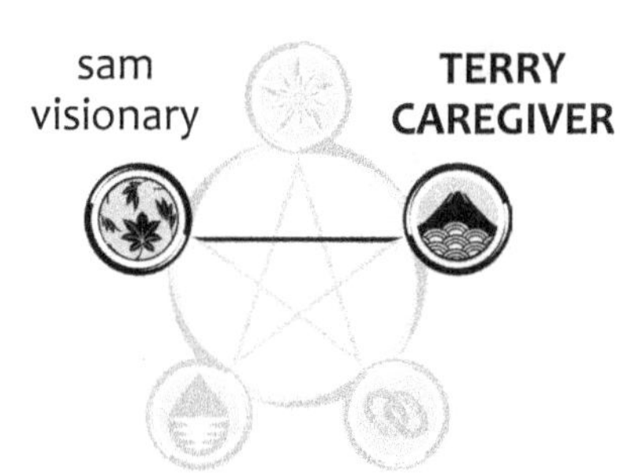

Step 5 | Study the overall observations.

- ⊙ There is no Water in any scenario.

- ⊙ Wood only shows up in the Secondary mode.

- ⊙ The situation is especially precarious when Sam goes into Secondary|Visionary mode. It would be best to try to keep Sam in his Primary|Protector mode.

- ⊙ Scenario A is the most desirable. Scenarios B and D are the least desirable (when Sam is in Secondary|Visionary mode).

Step 6 | Recommendations

The recommendation would be to "water the seeds." Considering the observations in step 5, Sam's and Terry's primary recommendation is to invoke practices to bring more Water and Wood into their relationship.

By "watering the seeds", they can avoid the potential of Sam going into Secondary|Visionary mode. Here are some practices that they could employ to bring in more Water and Wood:

WATER THE SEEDS

⊙ Anchor themselves in an issue or activity that they both feel passionate about.

⊙ Learn and experience by listening. The body part representing Water is the ears. Podcasts, lectures and concerts are good activities to do together.

⊙ Develop a meditation practice, preferably one that involves the sense of hearing (like chanting or toning) that they can engage in together.

⊙ Infuse fun into their daily lives, even if it's a few minutes of dancing to their favorite song. Terry's Caregiver and Sam's Protector make them pretty serious people.

⊙ Go for walks in nature, especially in forests or near water.

⊙ In everything they do, seek to understand and be understood.

⊙ Place a fountain or aquarium along with plants in their living area.

The following steps will assist you in coding and charting an interpersonal profile of your own.

Step 1 | Code and chart the individual profiles and lay them out side by side.

Complete the table for the persons you will be analyzing
Note: If you have not created an individual Five Elements profile for each person, go to Chapter 13 and follow those steps.

Prepare a chart for each person.

NAME	CODE	ARCHETYPLES

Step 2 | Create a combined chart from the individual charts.

Primary attribute	**BOLD UPPERCASE**
Secondary and Developmental attribute	lowercase letters
Relational attribute	*Italics*

NAME	CODE	ARCHETYPLES

Step 3 | List initial observations on the combined chart.

- ⊙ Which elements are present and which are not?

- ⊙ What are the dynamics at play regarding the Supporting and Restraining cycles?

- ⊙ Do *not* make any conclusions or recommendations yet. Simply note the patterns.

Step 4 | Chart the four scenarios that can occur between the individuals.

Scenario A:
Both are operating from their Primary attributes.

OBSERVATIONS

Scenario B:

Both are operating from their Secondary attributes.

OBSERVATIONS

Scenario C:
One person is Primary and the other is Secondary.

OBSERVATIONS

Scenario D:

Switch Primary|Secondary modes from Scenario C.

OBSERVATIONS

Step 5 | Record your overall observations.

⊙ Circle the element(s) that were not represented in any of the charts.

⊙ Which elements would support you in staying in your Primary attributes?

⊙ Which elements would prevent you from moving into your Secondary attributes (your stress modes)?

⊙ Which of these elements would alleviate the tension points in your chart?

⊙ What is the best element you can invoke to keep you healthy, balanced and productive?

Step 6 | Develop your recommendations.

⊙ What are some practices you can employ that are aligned with these recommendations?

 Refer to Appendix III for a list of recommendations.

CHAPTER FOURTEEN RECAP

Analyzing interpersonal dynamics between two people requires the following steps.

Step 1 | Code and chart the individual Five Elements profiles and lay the charts
side by side.

Step 2 | Code and chart a Five Elements pairs profile by combining the information from the two
individual profiles.

Step 3 | Look for overall elemental patterns and dynamics. Which elements are present and which
are not? What are the dynamics at play regarding the Supporting and Restraining cycles?
Do not make any conclusions or recommendations yet; simply note the patterns.

Step 4 | Code and chart the for possible scenarios that can occur between these two people. The
scenarios are:

⦿ Both are operating from their Primary attributes.

⦿ Both are operating from their Secondary attributes.

⦿ Person "A" is operating from their Primary attribute while Person "B" is operating from their Secondary attribute.

⦿ Person "B" is operating from their Primary attribute while Person "A" is operating from their Secondary attribute.

Step 5 | Overlay the Relational attributes on each scenario.

Step 6 | Look for overall elemental patterns and dynamics. Which elements are present and which are not? What are the dynamics at play regarding the Supporting and Restraining cycles?

⦿ What dynamics are occurring between the elements and attributes?

⦿ What is the relationship between your Primary and Relational attributes (when you both are seen at your very best)?

⦿ What is the relationship between your Secondary and Relational attributes (how you are seen when you both are stressed or at your worst)?

⦿ What is the relationship if Person "A" is operating from their Primary attribute and Person "B" is operating from their Secondary attribute?

⦿ What is the relationship if Person "A" is operating from their Secondary attribute and Person "B" is operating from their Primary attribute?

Step 7 | What happens when the Relational attributes are overlayed on all four scenarios?

Step 8 | What observations can you make as these dynamics relate to your individual and collective personality, leadership and communication styles?

Step 9 | If there is an overall pattern or trend becomes evident in Step 6, congratulations! You can now determine what element(s) would contribute to supporting your relationship and develop practices and solutions aligned with that element(s). If there is not an overall pattern or trend, you may need to develop several solutions to respond to the situations as they present themselves.

ADVICE FOR TWO PEOPLE: DEVELOP A CODE

It is important is to check in with each other often to see if you are operating from your Primary or Secondary attributes. Some people have developed a code to communicate with each other: one finger for Primary; two fingers for Secondary. Others have made signs to post on their doors. Some couples are more straightforward and simply ask, "Primary or Secondary today?" Make the ritual yours and have fun with it.

NOTE REGARDING CHILDREN AND TEENS:

If you are coding and charting a profile for a person under
the age of 12, please use their Developmental attribute as your main
reference point. They will not grow into their Primary attribute
until their teens.

If you are coding and charting a profile for a person between
the ages of 12 and 20, use both Developmental and Primary
attributes as main reference points as they are transitioning
from one to the other.

TEENAGERS! *a* FIVE ELEMENTS PERSPECTIVE

"I don't know what happened!" Ava said of her children.

"It's as if extraterrestrials came down and traded our kids for theirs!" her husband Carlos added. "They didn't touch Santiago. He was steady as a rock. Still is."

"But they definitely switched out Grace and Mateo," Carlos continued. "Grace has completely checked out, wearing black and reading Marx. She's even learning Russian so she can read the original Marxist texts. We used to do everything together. Now she doesn't want to have anything to do with me."

When asked about Mateo, Ava answered, "He used to be the popular kid. He excelled at school, sports, music. He always dressed to impress. Now he wears the same thing, day after day. And his grades? Hmph. He has new friends and is never around. I don't know my son."

"I thought whatever we did with Santiago would work for Grace and Mateo, but I was obviously mistaken," Carlos lamented. "I just want to know what to do with these kids until we get our originals back."

Such is the dilemma of millions of families who are living with teenagers and young adults. Why is the developmental path to adulthood easier for some than others?

Behavioral scientists have their explanations as to why this phenomenon called "adolescence" occurs. Yet they struggle to explain why people from the same genetic makeup and living situations have such different experiences. Beyond that, parents, teachers, mentors and family members just want to know how to support their young people in the right way.

The Five Elements may provide some guidance and relief for both teenagers and their loved ones.

The relationship between the Developmental and Primary attributes is crucial in understanding the journey from childhood to adulthood. While the philosophy behind **The Five Elements** states that the Developmental attribute is most prevalent during

Reminder: While the Secondary attribute focuses on the negative characteristics of an archetype, the Developmental attribute includes both the positive and negative characteristics of that archetype.

a person's first two cycles of nine years, or until the age of 18, the transition can last through the late-20s, depending on the situation and elements involved.

As adults, the Developmental attribute takes on a more subtle yet powerful role in influencing our emotional states of being. Like a drop of food coloring that infuses a glass of water, our Developmental attribute is ever present and reflected through our Primary and Relational attributes.

Pathways to Adulthood

Transitions from Developmental to Primary mode, or between childhood and adulthood occur through five pathways. These five pathways are:

These pathways apply to adults who are transitioning from their Secondary attribute (stress mode) to their Primary attribute (strength mode).

I. **I Am Who I Am;**
(When the Developmental and Primary attributes are the same element; for example, Wood and Wood – 344.)

II. **Smooth Sailing;**
(When the Developmental attribute flows towards the Primary attribute in the Supporting Cycle; for example, Earth to Metal – 656.)

III. **Slipping Away;**
(When the Developmental attribute

goes backward to the Primary attribute in the Supporting Cycle; for example, Fire to Wood– 499.)

IV.   **I'm Outta Here;**
(When the Developmental attribute aligns in the direction of the Restraining cycle toward the Primary attribute; for example, Earth to Water – 151.)

V.   **The Hero's Journey.**
(When the Developmental attribute goes against direction of the Restraining cycle toward the Primary attribute; for example, Metal to Fire – 977.)

"I AM WHO I AM"

"I AM WHO I AM"

EXAMPLE: **344**
WOOD AND WOOD

Applies to the following profiles: 115, 225, 252, 288, 335, 344, 436, 445, 528, 555, 582, 665, 674, 766, 775, 822, 858, 885, 995

When the Developmental and Primary attributes are the same archetype (for example, Optimist|Optimist or Rock|Rock) or even within the same element (as in Protector|Achiever or Caregiver|Facilitator), the transition is easy and uneventful. These young people essentially stay in their same element throughout their adolescence; thus, the transition is subtle.

Their physical appearances and personalities typically don't change much. They will just be bigger and more mature versions of their younger selves. People will look at them, even years after adolescence, and say, "You haven't changed a bit."

Because of their subtle transition, they often lack compassion for those who have tougher journeys. They may say of their siblings and peers, "Why are they making life so hard for themselves? Just deal with it."

Depending on their elements, they may assert their independence at a young age. This is more prevalent in the Wood (343, 445) and Metal (665, 766) profiles. Others may find it difficult to leave the comfort of family and explore the world (especially the triple Earths; for instance, 252, 555, and 822).

How to support this young person:

While they are comfortable "in their element", there is a concern that these young people may become too comfortable and complacent with themselves. They may take on an "I Am Who I Am" attitude. The key in supporting them is to look to the following element in the Supporting cycle and develop recommendations based on that element.

Referring to the example in the sidebar, the 344 "triple Wood" person would be most supported by looking to Fire. Focusing the young person's energy and enthusiasm toward something positive would be a step in the right direction. One example is to find a mentor who can provide guidance and a spark of inspiration in the young person's area of interest.

"SMOOTH SAILING"

Applies to the following profiles: 169, 178, 297, 317, 418, 591, 629, 656, 683, 721, 757, 784, 894, 932, 941

This dynamic occurs when the Developmental attribute supports the Primary attribute (for example, Developmental|Earth to Primary|Metal as in 656). The transition occurs in the flow of the Supporting cycle so it is smooth, as if growing up was the most natural thing in the world.

These young people typically carry a perception that life comes relatively easy for them. People are attracted to this energy; thus this young person would be popular among peers.

Like their counterparts above, these young people often lack understanding for others who might struggle with this stage of their lives.

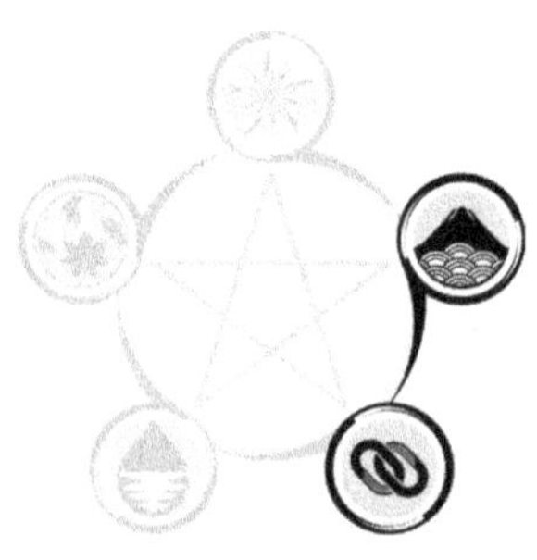

"SMOOTH SAILING"

EXAMPLE: 656
EARTH SUPPORTS METAL

How to support this young person:

Since this young person is already in a positive forward motion in the Supporting cycle, look to the following element and develop recommendations based on that element. This will give the young person the momentum to stay on a generative path.

"Slipping Away"

Applies to the following profiles: 133, 142, 261, 279, 398, 499, 564, 573, 611, 712, 867, 876, 923, 959, 986

When the Developmental attribute follows the Primary attribute (for example, Developmental|Fire to Primary|Wood as in 499), the dynamic is going against the Supporting cycle.

Like a salmon swimming upstream, life is a constant struggle for this young person. Things that come easily for their counterparts above ("I Am Who I Am" and "Smooth Sailing") are elusive. They may retreat and let opportunities slip away, claiming that it's just too hard and they won't succeed anyway.

Depending on the Primary element they are moving toward, this young person may develop a tough skin and strong work ethic (for example, those

EXAMPLE: **499**
FIRE RETREATS TO WOOD

transitioning to Primary Metal, Earth or Fire attributes like 611, 867, or 923). Others may take on a defeatist attitude and blend in with the crowd or become an eccentric (for instance, those transitioning to Primary Wood or Water attributes like 398, 142).

These young people will typically believe that life is an uphill battle. Because of this, they generally don't settle into their Primary element until their mid- to late-20s.

How to support this young person:

Clarity and perspective are the most important ways to support this young person. They are so focused on getting to the next moment—be it the next class, test, social event or end of the school year—that they can't see the forest through the trees.

The tricky part is *how* to provide clarity and perspective. These young people are so fragile (even and especially the ones with tough skins) that one small misjudgment in intent or delivery may result in them rejecting anything you have to offer.

Choosing the right element to bring forth, and understanding the timing and nuances of your approach, will take thought and skill. The key is to look at the elements at play and go to the element that forms a triangle (for example, Fire).

The response has to be well timed and appropriate for the situation. It would be helpful to have several options to play, as you may need to resort to a Plan B, C, or D.

Supporting a young person in this phase is sensitive business. You will make mistakes and need to ask forgiveness from yourself and your adolescent. Be patient because you will be in this for the long haul.

"I'm Outta Here"

Applies to the following profiles: 124, 151, 187, 234, 243, 362, 371, 463, 472, 537, 546, 694, 793, 831, 849, 914

When the Developmental attribute falls in the flow of the Restraining cycle (for example, Developmental|Earth to Primary|Water as in 151), there is such a momentum to move forward that it feels like the young person can't wait to grow up. They will likely exercise their independence in their early teen years and leave all parts of their childhood behind.

Nothing of their past is useful to them anymore. It is all about embracing a new attitude and identity. This young person may take on a new group of friends and interests which, in the eyes of the adults, may or may not meet with their approval.

EXAMPLE: **151**
EARTH RESTRAINS WATER

Experimentation and exploration are big for this young person, as they are figuring out how this new identity fits. The archetypical teenage rebel manifests in this dynamic. External influences, especially peers, will be a key factor in this young person's path.

How to support this young person:

Because of this young person's tendency to be future-oriented and seek community outside of the home, the family of origin or childhood caregivers may not be the most appropriate support network for them. Seeking positive adult role models and peers who have little or no connection to their childhoods may be a more effective approach.

"The Hero's Journey"

Applies to the following profiles: 196, 216, 326, 353, 389, 427, 454, 481, 519, 638, 647, 739, 748, 813, 968, 977

This young person is making the precarious transition against the Restraining cycle (for example, Developmental|Metal to Primary|FIre as in 977). This is the classic hero's journey, where the young person embarks on a quest to fulfill a mission and find a new way of being.

Unlike their counterparts in "I'm Outta Here", this young person is reluctant to let go of the past and move toward the future. Steps are tentative and there may be many false starts. Success and full integration into their Primary attribute will likely not occur until their mid- to late-20s.

That said, the sense of mission and adventure into an unknown future can be established at an early age. The pressure toward the Primary attribute may be internally or externally driven; but despite the fear, the quest is compelling.

The young person may often feel alone on a tightrope, where no one else can see the dangers ahead. People may be impatient with them and tell them to just grow up. Once they reach their Primary attribute, there is a deep sense of appreciation for the journey. For this young person, the hero's journey will likely become a metaphor for their adulthood.

How to support this young person:

Since this a classic Restraining cycle dynamic, the solution is to turn to the circle and bring in the element that will facilitate movement toward the Supporting cycle, and positive responses.

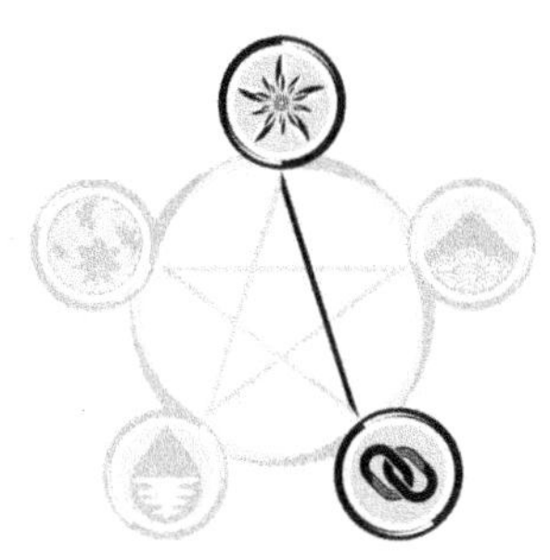

"THE HERO'S JOURNEY"

EXAMPLE: **977**
METAL IS MELTED BY FIRE

Because of this young person's tendency to be future-oriented and seek community outside of the home, the family of origin or childhood caregivers may not be the most appropriate support network for them. Seeking positive adult role models and peers who have little or no connection to their childhood may be a more effective approach.

How did this information help Carlos and Ava manage the young people in their home? Let's take a look at each of their children's profiles and see.

SANTIAGO
885 | *Rock ⊙ Rock ⊙ Facilitator*

SANTIAGO

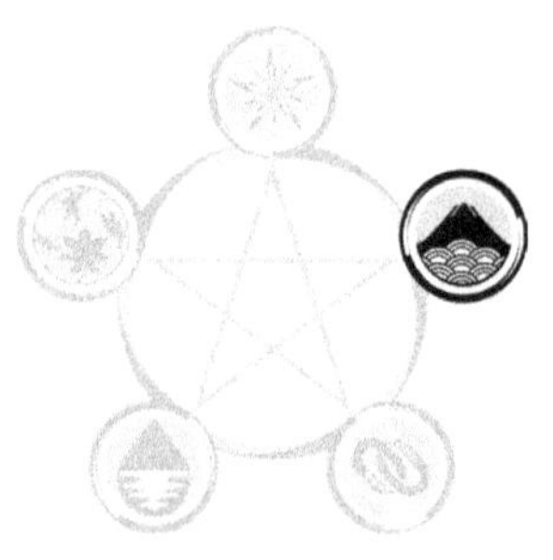

885
ROCK | ROCK
FACILITATOR

Carlos joked that the extraterrestrials didn't touch Santiago. "He was steady as a rock. Still is."

Since both of his Developmental and Primary attributes are Rock, Santiago remained steadfast and predictable throughout his adolescence. He retained his essential nature as he matured, both in personality and physical appearance. His strengths and quirks never wavered, and his parents knew how to deal with them.

As a "triple Earth", Santiago's consistency kept him grounded in any situation. He is thriving in college and is planning to attend medical school.

GRACE
187 | *Philosopher ⊙ Rock ⊙ Achiever*

Like her older brother, Grace was a Rock as a child—solid, steady and dependable. She was also an Achiever (Relational) and engaged in everything with her dad, from volunteering with Habitat for Humanity to bungee jumping.

But as she reached her early teens, Grace left her Rock nature behind, said "I'm Outta Here" and ran toward her Primary|Philosopher identity. (Earth restrains Water, so Grace's journey from Rock|Earth to Philosopher|Water was quick and natural.)

As an emerging Philosopher, Grace was compelled to discover a deeper truth. It was no longer satisfactory for her to trust the process of life. She wanted to know what it was all about. Grace developed a deep interest in Marxism and adopted new friends, leaving her parents concerned that she was immersing herself so deeply in this topic that she wouldn't find her way out.

MATEO
499 | *Optimist* ⊙ *Networker* ⊙ *Networker*

MATEO

499
OPTIMIST | NETWORKER
NETWORKER

When Ava said that she did not know her son anymore, it was the result of Mateo slipping back from Fire to Wood, a move against the current of the Supporting cycle. His Networker's sense of focus, confidence and swagger gave way to a more adaptable "whatever, it's all good" attitude that people found puzzling.

Mateo began to question why things like ironing his clothes and being the most popular boy in school were important. For Mateo, there was a sense of confusion about his identity, as if he was losing his way in a world of which he'd once had a clear command.

When we place their charts side-by-side . . .

SANTIAGO

885
ROCK | ROCK
FACILITATOR

GRACE

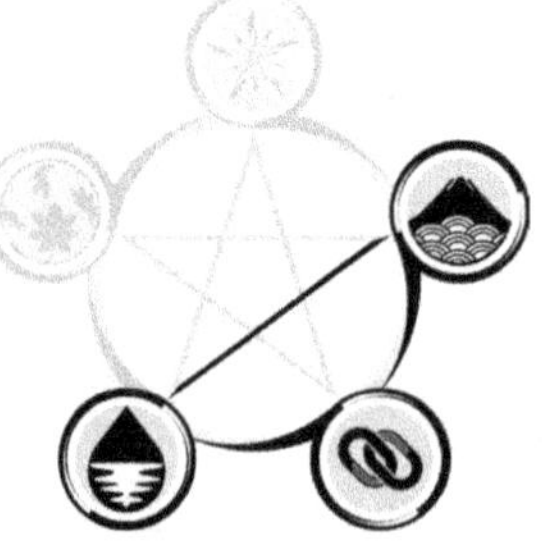

187
PHILOSOPHER | ROCK
ACHIEVER

MATEO

499
OPTIMIST | NETWORKER
NETWORKER

. . . we can see how different the profiles of these three siblings are, and how different their pathways to health and balance needed to be. Santiago's adolescent journey reflected "I Am Who I Am." Grace's journey was "I'm Outta Here" and Mateo's was "Slipping Away."

It's no wonder that their parents were perplexed. While it was clear to Carlos and Ava that the approach for one child would not work for the other, they did not know what approach *would* work.

The Five Elements gave them a simple, elegant framework to understand the journey to adulthood for each of their children, and to find ways to give them exactly what they needed to support them in their life journeys.

As a Rock, Santiago was sure of his course and didn't need much beyond added focus, direction and clarity. If Carlos and Ava continued to shine light on and affirm Santiago's journey (Fire), he would have the confidence to draw upon his internal resources (Earth) to implement his plans (Metal).

Grace needed Metal to provide a framework for her inquiries in philosophy. The recommendation that I gave was to create a structure and routine for Carlos and Ava to engage in activities with Grace that aligned with her interests. Carlos agreed to attend

FORGE YOUR TOOLS	GET IT IN GEAR	JUST ADD WATER
RECOMMENDATIONS TO HELP SANTIAGO	*RECOMMENDATIONS TO HELP GRACE*	*RECOMMENDATIONS TO HELP MATEO*

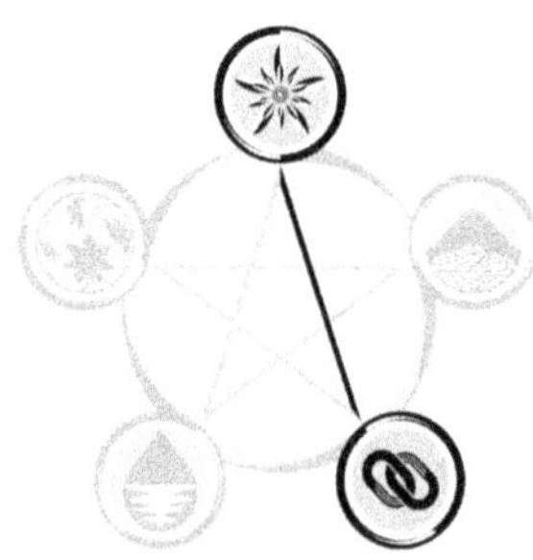 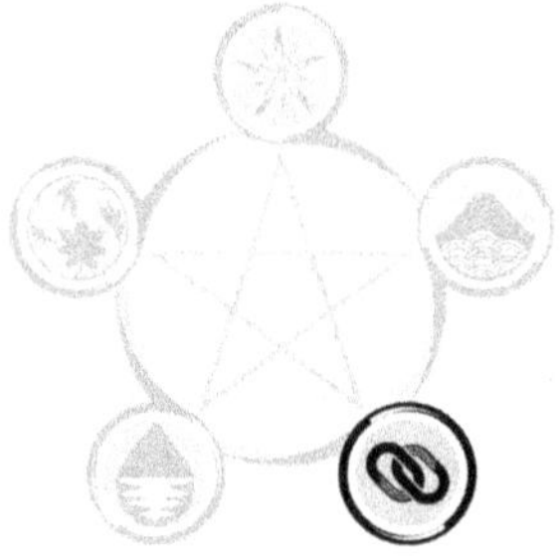 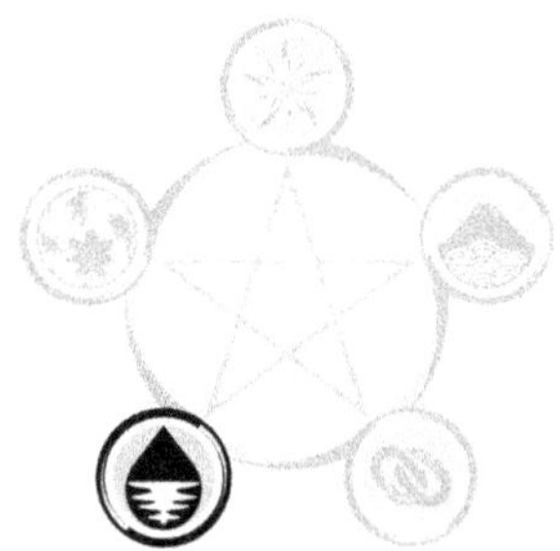

855	187	499
ROCK | ROCK	PHILOSOPHER | ROCK	OPTIMIST | NETWORKER
FACILITATOR	ACHIEVER	NETWORKER

lectures with Grace (as long as they went out to dinner and a walk beforehand, drawing upon Grace's Earth tendencies to nurture relationships), and Ava started learning Russian. In this manner, Grace was able to draw upon her Rock characteristics to be more engaged with others.

Mateo, who was normally so focused and directed by being in his Fire|Networker mode, was overwhelmed by his transition to Wood|Optimist mode. He needed a way to anchor himself in a deeper purpose and meaning, and water the seeds that would reorient him in a clear path.

The recommendation to add Water was a new approach for Carlos and Ava, as they had always provided him with various activities to fuel his enthusiasm for life (Wood supporting Fire). They felt that the depth and seriousness of Water would snuff his light.

As it turned out, Mateo accompanied Grace and Carlos to a lecture on Marxist theory, and a seed was planted. Mateo integrated the creative and innovative characteristics of the Optimist with the clear and intuitive nature of the Networker by joining the debate club at school. He is finding his swagger again.

While these pathways may not provide a magic wand that will take away the challenges of adolescence, they hopefully provide some clarity for young adults, their families and supporters on how to employ communication and behavioral strategies and practices that will yield positive and healthy outcomes.

CHAPTER FIFTEEN RECAP

⊙ The relationship between the Developmental and Primary attributes is crucial in understanding the journey from childhood to adulthood. While the philosophy behind The Five Elements states that the Developmental attribute is most prevalent during a person's first two cycles of nine years, or until the age of 18, the transition can last through the late-20s depending on the situations and elements involved.

⊙ According to **The Five Elements**, there are five ways that the transitions occur from Developmental to Primary mode, or between childhood and adulthood. These pathways are:

I.	I Am Who I Am;
II.	Smooth Sailing;
III.	Slipping Away;
IV.	I'm Outta Here; and
V.	The Hero's Journey.

⊙ The pathway is determined by the relationship between one's Developmental and Primary archetypes. For instance, if both archetypes are contained within the same elements (for example, Primary is Protector|Metal and Developmental is Achiever|Metal), the pathway is "I Am Who I Am." If the Primary archetype restrains the Developmental archetype (for instance, Primary is Philosopher|Water and Developmental is Networker|Fire), the pathway is "The Hero's Journey."

⊙ These pathways also apply to adults who are transitioning from their Secondary attribute (stress mode) to their Primary attribute (strength mode).

NOTE REGARDING CHILDREN AND TEENS:

If you are coding and charting a profile for a person under the age of 12, please use their Developmental attribute as your main reference point. They will not grow into their Primary attribute.

If you are coding and charting a profile for a person between the ages of 12 and 20, use both Developmental and Primary attributes as main reference points as they are transitioning from one to the other.

THE FIVE ELEMENTS *at* WORK *and at* HOME

"My leadership team is very functional and productive," Diane, the CEO of a tech startup, said. "For the most part, we communicate well and get along. But I must admit, at times, a couple of the team members exhaust me. It seems like when the rest of them are focused on doing the work, they are off in some corner, thick as thieves, cooking up some new thing that is totally irrelevant to the work at hand. If I could figure out a constructive way to deal with them, I would sleep much better."

Laura is the principal of an elementary school where she oversees 100 teachers and support staff. While her primary responsibility is to ensure a safe and positive learning environment for 800 students, she also wants to create a school culture that embraces the values of community, respect, acceptance, joy and love.

"Chaos is the norm at any school," Laura commented. "You've got hundreds of kids running about with a range of stories and needs, parents trying to manage their many responsibilities, substitute teachers to orient, and an overflowing toilet in the boy's bathroom."

People look to Laura to set the tone and embody the values of the school.

"I get that," Laura said, "but how can I keep a calm and friendly demeanor with all of this going on?"

People are diverse and complex beings. Because people comprise organizations, the concepts and systems of any company must be designed to respond to the diversity and complexity of the people in it. Both Diane and Laura needed ways to assess and understand these dynamics in order to create and sustain positive and productive work environments.

This chapter will guide you in assessing leadership and communication dynamics through **The Five Elements** perspective. An assessment can be conducted between two or 2,000+ people. The only information required is birth dates to determine each person's Five Elements profile.

This chapter will guide you in assessing leadership and communication dynamics through The Five Elements perspective.

An assessment can be conducted between two or 2,000+ people. The only information required is birth dates to determine each person's profile.

With that information, you can map the profiles on **The Five Elements** chart and analyze the patterns that emerge. As you will see, in both of the above cases, the imbalance between the elements—and the solutions needed to maintain balance—were clear. Through their team assessments, Diane and Laura developed a plan of action to build and sustain a positive, values-aligned work environment.

Any number of people may participate in this process. They are less personal, but larger groups can reveal patterns, especially in leadership and communication styles, that may be impacting group or organizational culture. Taking larger group dynamics into consideration can help teams develop appropriate responses. I recommend conducting smaller team or departmental assessments to address the nuances within those groups.

For example, in addition to providing Laura with an assessment of her 100 staff, I also assessed of each of her teams (for example, the first-grade teaching team, the administrative staff and the leadership team), which provided a comprehensive set of solutions. Case studies for both Diana and Laura are provided so you can see how the assessment works for both small and large groups.

Developing a Five Elements Group Assessment

I.   Gather each person's birthdate (mm/dd/yyyy). Code and record their individual Five Elements profiles on the table provided below.

II.   Record all of the Five Elements profiles onto a master chart. If there are fewer than 10 people, record

Refer to Chapter 13 to learn how to code and chart an individual Five Elements profile.

individual names (see Diane's case study). If there are more than 10 people, record the number of people in each element (see Laura's case study).

III. Code and chart for the possible scenarios that can occur. The scenarios are:

⊙ Everyone is operating from their Primary attributes.

⊙ Everyone operating from their Secondary attributes.

⊙ Some people are operating from their Primary attribute while others are operating from their Secondary attribute.

IV. Overlay the Relational attributes on each scenario.

V. Look for overall patterns and dynamics. Which elements are present and which are not? What are the dynamics at play regarding the Supporting and Restraining cycles?

⊙ What dynamics are occurring between the elements and attributes?

⊙ What is the relationship between the Primary and Relational attributes (when everyone is at their very best)?

⊙ What is the relationship between your Secondary and Relational attributes (when everyone is seen at their worst)?

⊙ What is the relationship between the Primary, Secondary and Developmental attributes?

⊙ What observations can you make about how these dynamics relate to your organizational culture and experience?

VI.   If there is an overall pattern or trend, congratulations! You can determine what element(s) would contribute to supporting your relationship and then develop practices and solutions aligned to that element(s).

If there is not an overall pattern or trend, you may need to develop several solutions to respond to the situations as they present themselves.

Reality Check

In group situations, it is rare when everyone is operating from their Primary or Secondary attributes at any given point in time. More often, some people are operating from their Primary attributes while others are operating from their Secondary attributes. This dynamic can change from day to day or even moment to moment. To accommodate this, it may be helpful to code an additional chart with the following scenario:

⊙ Randomly select half of your team members and code their Primary attributes.

⊙ Then code the remaining team members with their Secondary attributes.

⊙ Does the pattern change? If so, what solutions do you need to employ?

As you become more experienced with this method, you can check in with your team in real time to see if you are operating from your Primary or Secondary attributes.

Case Study | Diane's Leadership Team – Assessing a Smaller Group/Team

Diane wanted to maintain a cohesive vision that was anchored in a clear mission and core values. Because of the iterative nature and volatility of the industry, Diane used **The Five Elements** throughout her organization as a guide to build a coordinated and integrated work environment. Her leadership team was especially adept at using the system to understand and manage change.

The leadership team is comprised of Diane and the vice presidents of product development (Ash), finance and administration (Huilan), strategy (DJ), manufacturing (Tom) and sales (Zoe).

 Refer to Chapter 13 to learn how to code and chart an individual Five Elements profile. Reminder: The labels for the charts are: **PRIMARY: BOLD UPPERCASE**; secondary: lowercase; *Relational: Italics*

Step 1 | Code each individual profile and complete the table below.

NAME	PROFILE	PRIMARY ATTRIBUTE	SECONDARY ATTRIBUTE	RELATIONAL ATTRIBUTE
	Your intrinsic nature and optimal potential.	Characteristics that arise when you are stressed.	How you are viewed by others.
Diane	766	**ACHIEVER**	protector	*Protector*
DJ	941	**NETWORKER**	optimist	*Philosopher*
Zoe	941	**NETWORKER**	optimist	*Philosopher*
Ash	169	**PHILOSOPHER**	protector	*Networker*
Tom	638	**PROTECTOR**	visionary	*Rock*
Huilan	528	**FACILITATOR**	caregiver	*Rock*

Step 2 | Map out everyone's attributes on a chart.

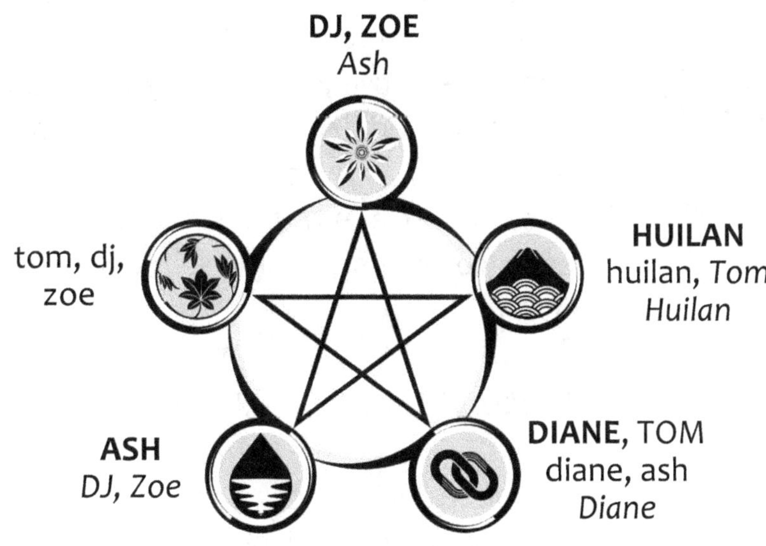

Step 3 | Develop an analysis of each of the attribute charts.

- ⊙ What elements/archetypes are represented?

- ⊙ What characteristics are represented in those elements/archetypes?

- ⊙ What elements/archetypes are missing?

- ⊙ What characteristics are needed in those elements/archetypes?

ANALYSIS OF RELATIONAL ATTRIBUTES

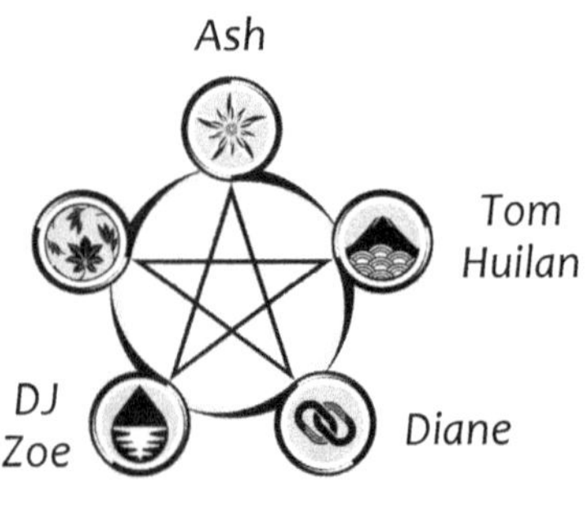

Notice that there's a pretty even distribution of the Relational attributes. This lends the perception that the staff is well rounded. They have a reputation of being values-driven and strategic (Water), focused (Fire), caring and compassionate (Earth) and task-oriented (Metal). There is no representation of Wood archetypes. This may lead to the perception that the leadership team is not particularly visionary, innovative or fun.

ANALYSIS OF PRIMARY ATTRIBUTES

Like the Relational chart, there is a pretty even distribution of the Primary attributes. When members are all working from their strengths, they are a well-rounded team that is values-driven and strategic (Water), focused (Fire), caring and compassionate (Earth) and task-oriented (Metal). Again, there is no representation of Wood, meaning that the team lacks vision, innovation and a sense of joy. The alignment between the Relational and Primary attributes suggests that when the team is working from their strengths, what you see is what you get.

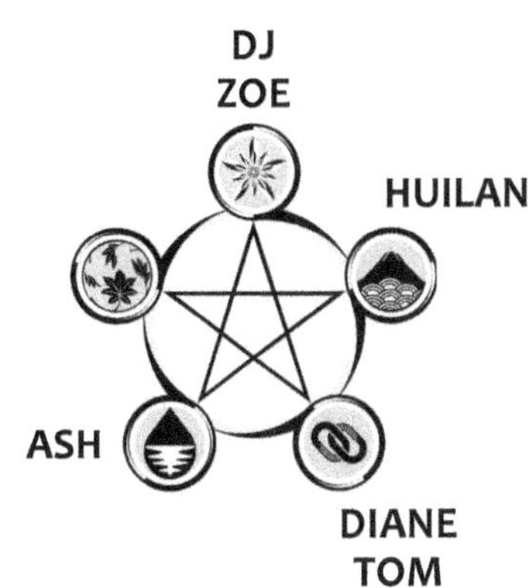

ANALYSIS OF SECONDARY ATTRIBUTES

When the staff collectively goes into stress mode (Secondary attribute), things change. The resulting dynamics are a sense of forgetfulness (Wood), passive-aggressive behavior (Earth) and stubbornness (Metal). The lack of focus and purpose (Fire and Water) tends to keep the team feeling adrift, without a sense of direction and a compass to guide them through this phase.

Step 4 | Determine recommendations to attain and sustain balance.

- ◉ Focus on the missing element(s)/archetype(s).

- ◉ What characteristics/tools are needed to manifest those element(s)/archetype(s).

Recommendation for Diane's Leadership Team: Tend the Garden

In all three attribute charts (Relational, Primary, Secondary), Wood was either missing or, in the case of the Secondary chart, a contributing factor to the imbalance of the team (half of them manifest Wood as their Secondary attribute).

The clear recommendation for this team is to manifest more Wood. Short of hiring a Wood person, what might this look like?

HERE ARE SOME RECOMMENDATIONS TO TEND THE GARDEN.

In all that you do, hold a sense of curiosity and wonder toward a new way of imagining the world.

"Consider posing these questions at every meeting:

- ⊙ "What are three out-of-the-box ways to get this job done?"

- ⊙ "How does this topic or activity allow us to stay on the cutting edge?"

- ⊙ "How does this topic or activity differentiate us from our competition?"

- ⊙ "Are we having fun yet?"

TEND THE GARDEN

⊙ Be very visual with your processes. Chart, write and draw things out so you can focus. Rub your hands together for energy.

⊙ During meetings, have a standing brainstorming session. Bring blocks and crafts supplies to encourage creativity.

Step 5 | Conduct a reality check.

While the analyses of the Relational, Primary and Secondary attributes in Step 2 reveal inherent patterns, they often do not reflect the dynamics that are occurring in real time. In group situations, it is rare when everyone is operating from their Primary or Secondary attributes at any given time. More often, some people are operating from their Primary attributes while others are operating from their Secondary attributes. This dynamic can change from day to day or even moment to moment.

In Diane's case, she opened her weekly team meetings with the following questions:

⊙ Are you showing up at work in your Primary or Secondary attribute?

⊙ What can I do to support you in showing up in your Primary attribute?

⊙ What can you do to assure that you are operating in your Primary attribute?

⊙ What can we do as a leadership team to create conditions for everyone to show up in their Primary attributes?

In this manner, everyone could see who was feeling strong or "in their element" (Primary attribute), and who was feeling stressed (Secondary attribute). As a team, they could discuss how to support each other—either by staying in their Primary attributes, or moving from their Secondary to their Primary attributes.

At a recent leadership team meeting, the group responded to question 1, on the previous page, in this manner:

Primary attribute	**BOLD UPPERCASE**
Secondary and Developmental attribute	lowercase
Relational attribute	*Italics*

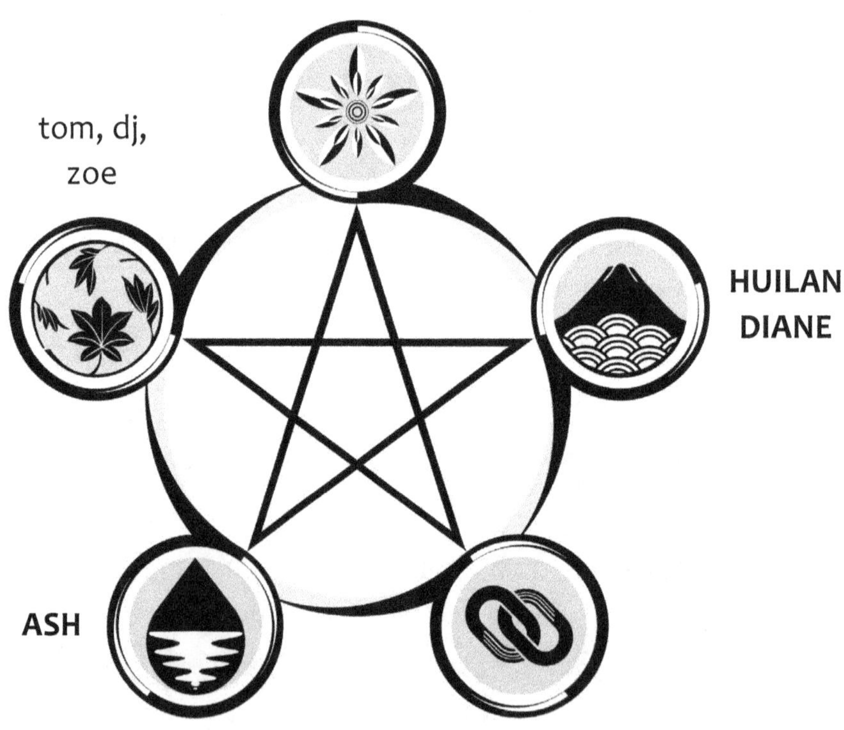

Reality Check - Analysis of Combined Attributes

In this scenario, Diane, Huilan and Ash indicated that they were operating from their Primary attributes. They felt balanced and strong about their work and their lives in general. Tom, DJ and Zoe indicated that they were operating from their Secondary attributes. Tom had an impending deadline that concerned him. DJ's child had chicken pox, and Zoe was preparing for an important client visit.

The key question is how can Ash, Diane and Huilan support their colleagues through this phase and move them back into their Primary attributes?

Recommendation: Tend the Garden and Let the Sun Shine In

The standing recommendation for Diane's team—Tend the Garden—is still relevant in this and any situation. Even though there is representation in Wood from Tom, DJ and Zoe, they are manifesting Wood from their Secondary attributes, which is not healthy or productive; therefore, it is still important to focus on Wood.

In addition, I recommended manifesting Fire and to Let the Sun Shine In. This will help move DJ and Zoe

TEND THE GARDEN

LET THE SUN
SHINE IN

299

into their Primary attributes/elements, and bring the necessary warmth, direction and focus needed to instill support and unity.

Be an advocate for Fire through language that inspires people to expand and connect. Consider these questions:

- ⊙ How can we shed some light on this topic and look at the big picture?

- ⊙ Are we seeing things eye to eye?

- ⊙ Are we clear on our intention, messages and priorities?

- ⊙ How does this topic or activity lead to new or expanded opportunities?

Be very visual with your processes. Chart, write and draw things out so you can focus. Rub your hands together to generate heat and energy.

If you need to ponder or talk about something serious, take a walk in the sun.

Between meetings, some members of Diane's team developed a code to inform each other on a daily basis: One finger for Primary; two fingers for Secondary. Others made signs to post on their doors. Others were more straightforward and simply asked, "Primary or Secondary today?" In the end, they created their own rituals and had fun with it.

What about the two team members who were causing Diane to lose sleep?

Referring back to the general chart of the leadership team's leadership profile, we see that Diane is a triple Metal (all three of her attributes are Metal).

NAME | PROFILE	PRIMARY ATTRIBUTE	SECONDARY ATTRIBUTE	RELATIONAL ATTRIBUTE
	Your intrinsic nature and optimal potential.	Characteristics that arise when you are stressed.	How you are viewed by others.
Diane | 766	**ACHIEVER**	protector	*Protector*

The elements that impact Metal in the Restraining cycle are Fire and Wood. Upon closer look at the chart, we see that DJ and Zoe both have Fire and Wood in their charts. In addition, their leadership profiles are identical (941 or Networker|Fire – Optimist|Wood – Philosopher|Water).

NAME | PROFILE	PRIMARY ATTRIBUTE	SECONDARY ATTRIBUTE	RELATIONAL ATTRIBUTE
	Your intrinsic nature and optimal potential.	Characteristics that arise when you are stressed.	How you are viewed by others.
Diane | 766	**ACHIEVER**	protector	*Protector*
Zoe | 941	**NETWORKER**	optimist	*Philosopher*
DJ | 941	**NETWORKER**	optimist	*Philosopher*

When Diane said . . .

"A couple of the team members exhaust me. It seems like when the rest of them are focused on doing the work, they are off in some corner, thick as thieves, cooking up some new thing that is totally irrelevant to the work at hand."

. . . she was referring to DJ and Zoe. If we remove the other team members from the chart, the dynamic is more evident.

Primary attribute	**BOLD UPPERCASE**
Secondary and Developmental attribute	lowercase letters
Relational attribute	*Italics*

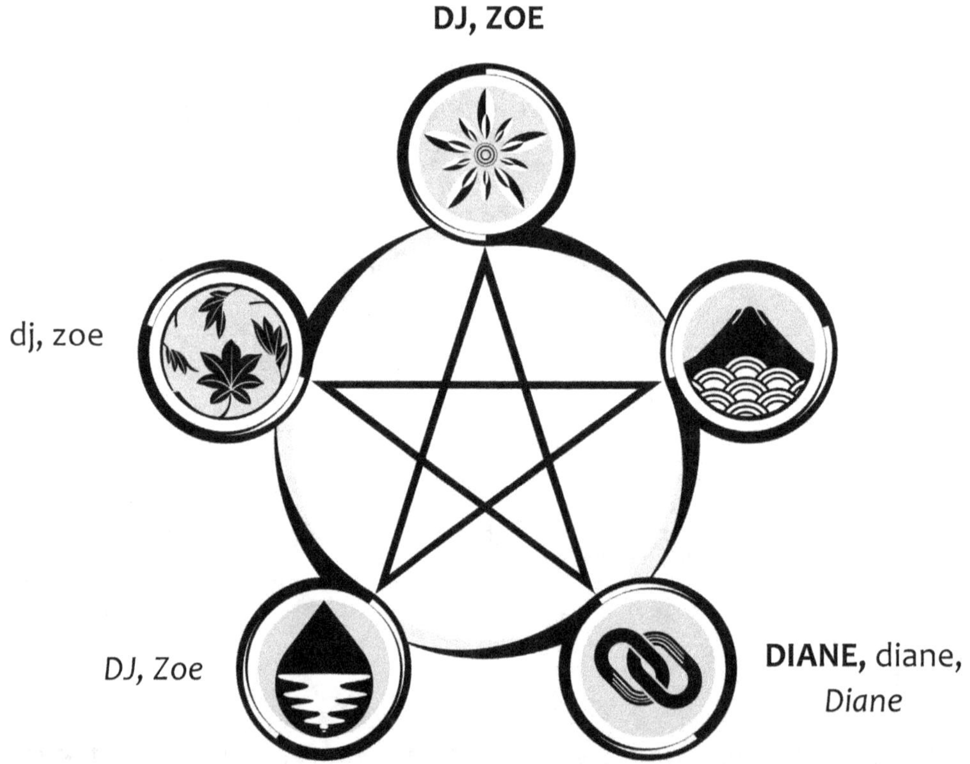

As a triple-Metal, Diane is a no nonsense, task-oriented person. With the combination of Fire, Wood and Water, DJ and Zoe have no grounding and task orientation in their charts. They get things done, but in a free-flowing way that annoys Diane. And since DJ and Zoe have identical profiles, they are like peas in a pod—or in Diane's words, "thick as thieves."

Recommendation

The element that is missing in this chart is Earth, representing the lack of common ground, trust, empathy and communication that exists between Diane and her colleagues.

As a triple-Earth, Huilan can be called upon as a resource to facilitate the relationship. In addition, I recommended the following processes for Diane, DJ and Zoe to "Stay Grounded."

Be an advocate for Earth through language that nurtures and supports. Consider the following language:

STAY GROUNDED

- ⊙ "Before we get started, let's review our ground rules."

- ⊙ "What are the needs and implications from a human perspective? What are the operational needs?"

◉"What do we need to do work together in a
spirit of support?"

Develop a practical nature to all aspects of your life. Intentionally give and seek support every day. Do something that builds your community every day; for example, have daily contact with a friend or loved one, make a daily to-do list or cook more often.

Case Study: Laura's Elementary School – Assessing a Larger Group/Team

What if you are assessing a larger group, as in Laura's case? The process is identical, regardless of whether you are working with five or 500 people. With any group larger than 30, it is more difficult to provide individualized recommendations. Instead, look for general trends and patterns to develop the best solutions.

As appropriate, you may also choose to conduct assessments of smaller teams or departments (for example, Diane's leadership team or Laura's second-grade team) to allow for more individualized attention.

Let's walk through the steps to assess a larger organization.

Step 1 | Code each person's profile and complete the table below.

 Refer to Chapter 13 to learn how to code and chart an individual Five Elements profile.

NAME | PROFILE	POSITION	PRIMARY ATTRIBUTE	SECONDARY ATTRIBUTE	RELATIONAL ATTRIBUTE
Laura | 656	Principal	**PROTECTOR**	facilitator	Protector
Stevie | 611	Dean of Students	**PROTECTOR**	philosopher	Philosopher
Milla | 968	Dean of Students	**NETWORKER**	protector	Rock
Aubrey | 187	Secretary	**PHILOSOPHER**	rock	Achiever
Aidan | 481	PreK Teacher	**OPTIMIST**	rock	Philosopher
Alex | 398	Kindergarten	**VISIONARY**	networker	Rock
Sofia | 822	Kindergarten	**ROCK**	caregiver	Caregiver
Shep | 977	Kindergarten	**NETWORKER**	achiever	Achiever
Whitney | 591	K-Para Pro	**FACILITATOR**	networker	Philosopher
Chas | 822	1st Grade Teacher	**ROCK**	caregiver	Caregiver
Sarah | 481	1st Grade Teacher	**OPTIMIST**	rock	Philosopher
Ryan | 519	1st Grade Teacher	**FACILITATOR**	philosopher	Networker
Eric | 418	1st Grade Teacher	**OPTIMIST**	philosopher	Rock

The chart continues to list the 100+ staff, with 2nd - 5th grade faculty and support/operations staff.

Step 2 | Map out everyone's attributes on a chart.

Primary attribute	**BOLD UPPERCASE**
Secondary and Developmental attribute	lowercase letters
Relational attribute	*Italics*

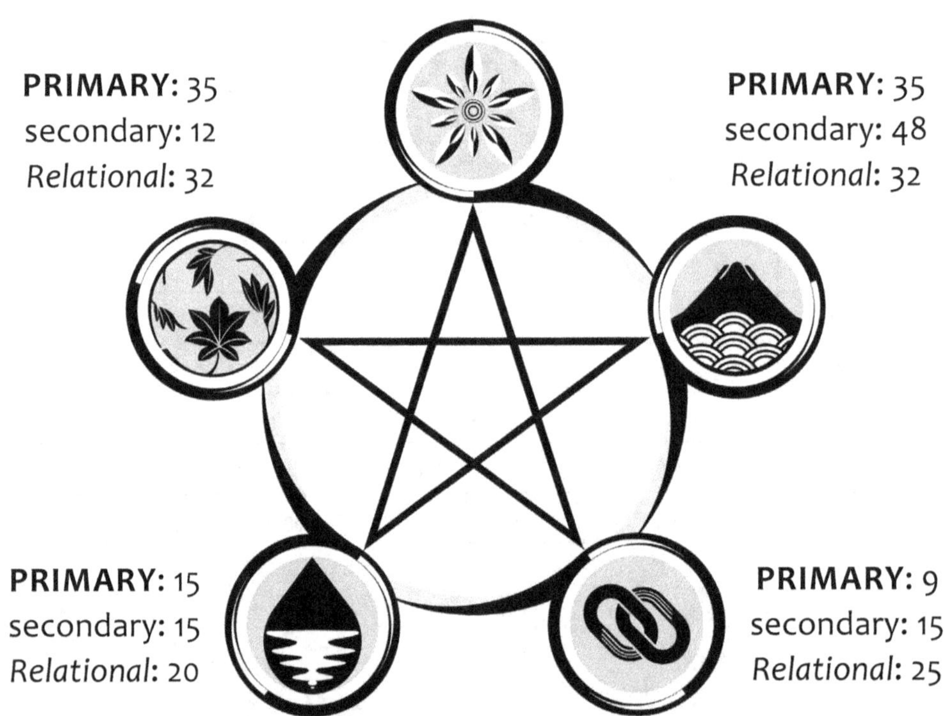

Step 3 | Develop an analysis of each of the attribute charts.

- ⊙ What elements/archetypes are represented?

- ⊙ What characteristics are represented in those elements/archetypes?

- ⊙ What elements/archetypes are missing?

- ⊙ What characteristics are needed in those elements/archetypes?

ANALYSIS OF RELATIONAL ATTRIBUTES

We can see that there's a pretty even distribution of the Relational attributes. This lends the perception that the staff is well rounded. They are values-driven and strategic (Water), creative and optimistic (Wood), caring and compassionate (Earth) and task-oriented (Metal). There is a larger representation in Earth and Wood, which is typical in schools and youth-serving organizations. There is little representation of the Fire archetype (Networker), which leads to a reputation that the school lacks focus, direction and the ability to communicate.

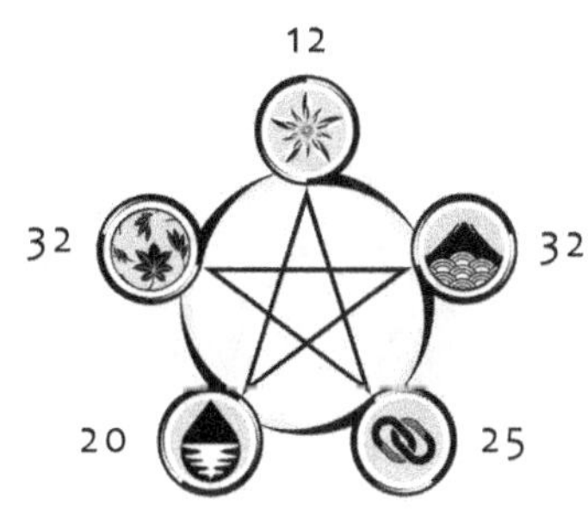

ANALYSIS OF PRIMARY ATTRIBUTES

The highlight here is the lack of Fire. The lack of Metal also indicates that the staff might not live up to their achievement-oriented reputation.

ANALYSIS OF SECONDARY ATTRIBUTES

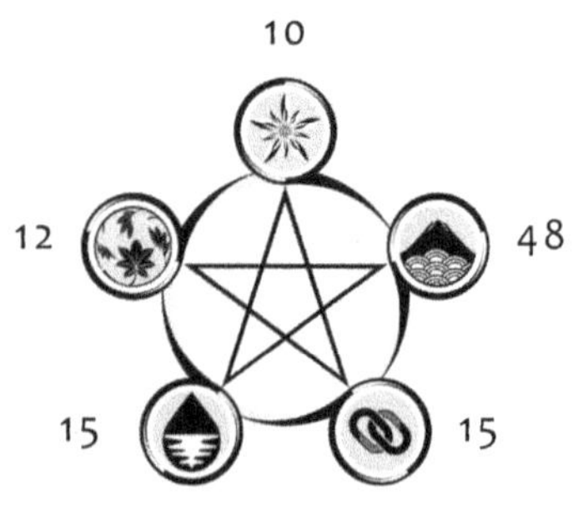

When the staff collectively goes into stress mode (Secondary attribute), nearly half manifest Earth. The resulting dynamics are stubbornness, passive-aggressive behavior, and a sense of too many cooks and not enough chefs. There's a quality of "stuckness" in this dynamic, as if the staff can't move forward without great effort.

Step 4 | Determine recommendations to attain and sustain balance.

- ⦿ Focus on the missing element(s)/archetype(s).

- ⦿ What characteristics/tools are needed to manifest those element(s)/archetype(s)?

RECOMMENDATION FOR LAURA'S ELEMENTARY SCHOOL: FORGE YOUR TOOLS

All three of the attribute charts reflect a need for more Fire to balance the elements. This involves bringing more focus, direction and discernment to prevent the staff from feeling depleted (Wood to Earth). With the abundance of Wood in the Primary chart, the staff is not lacking for new and creative ideas. The question at hand is if those ideas will help the school be more effective in realizing its mission.

In addition to adding more Fire, I recommended adding Metal to assure that the structure and accountability mechanisms are in place for success.

In all that you do, seek clarity and focus to assist you in accomplishing your goals.

The transitions between these two elements are Focus and Meltdown. Be especially aware of the timing and tone of communication. Everything can fall apart with one ill-timed word.

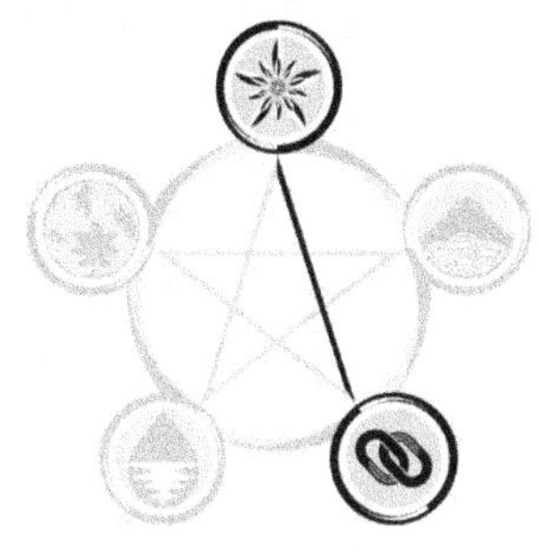

FORGE YOUR TOOLS

Be an advocate for Fire and Metal through language that affirms and encourages the power of the team and values cooperation and compassion.

- ◉ "Keep up the good work! I believe in you!"

- ◉ "Let's keep communicating! What do you need and how can we support each other?"

- ◉ "Let's take a quick look at the workplan and see where we stand. What adjustments, if any, do we need to make?"

- ◉ "What can we do to make sure we stay organized and coordinated?"

Focus on small tasks and maintain a checklist. When you accomplish those tasks, make sure you celebrate.

Organize short "standing meetings" that focus on troubleshooting and mutual support. Serving coffee and snacks will help build a sense of teamwork and camaraderie.

Step 5 | Conduct a reality check.

While the analyses of the Relational, Primary and Secondary attributes in step 2 reveal inherent patterns, they often do not reflect the dynamics that are occurring in real time.

In group situations, it is rare when everyone is operating from their Primary or Secondary attributes at any given time. More often, some people are operating from their Primary attributes while others are operating from their Secondary attributes. This dynamic can change from day to day or even moment to moment.

Since the full staff met infrequently, Laura instituted a "Where do you stand?" activity at all staff meetings by asking the following question:

> ⊙ Are you showing up at work in your Primary or
> Secondary attribute?

Her assistant principals followed up with the following questions during the weekly team meetings:

> ⊙ What can I do to support you in showing up in your
> Primary attribute?

> ⊙ What can you do to assure that you are operating in your
> Primary attribute?

⊙ What can we do as a team to create conditions for everyone to show up in their Primary attributes?

In this manner, everyone could see who was feeling strong or "in their element" (Primary attribute), and who was feeling stressed (Secondary attribute). As a team, they could discuss how to support each other—either by staying in their Primary attributes, or moving from their Secondary to their Primary attributes.

Like Diane's group, Laura's teams also developed a code to inform each other on a daily basis: One finger for Primary; two fingers for Secondary. Others made signs to post on their doors. Others were more straightforward and simply asked, "Primary or Secondary today?" In the end, they created their own rituals and had fun with it.

Laura set the example of "Forging the Tools" by embodying the school's values of community, respect, acceptance, joy and love. Each morning, she stood at the entrance of the school and greeted every student as they arrived. She posted the school's mission and values in every classroom and instilled a "value of the week" program to ensure that the values were known and practiced by students, parents and faculty alike.

CHAPTER SIXTEEN RECAP

Analyzing interpersonal dynamics among a group of people requires the following steps.

⊙ Determine each person's individual Five Elements profiles and list them out on the chart provided on page 314.

⊙ Map out everyone's Five Elements profiles on the chart provided on page 315. If the group is smaller than 10, list their names. If the group is larger, simply list the number of people per element.

⊙ Develop an analysis on each of the attribute charts provided on page 316. Look for overall patterns and dynamics. Which elements are present and which are not? What characteristics are represented in those elements/archetypes? What characteristics are needed to bring forth the elements/archetypes that are missing? What are the dynamics at play regarding the Supporting and Restraining cycles? What is the relationship between your Primary and Relational attributes (when you are seen at your very best)? What is the relationship between your Secondary and Relational attributes (when you are stressed or at your worst)?

⊙ Determine recommendations to attain and sustain balance. Focus on the missing element(s)/archetype(s). What characteristics/tools are needed to manifest those element(s)/archetype(s)? Determine what element(s) would contribute to supporting your relationship and develop practices and solutions aligned to that element(s). Refer to Appendix III for a list of recommendations.

⊙ Conduct a reality check. The most important thing to do in this and any group situation is to check in with each other often to see if you are operating from your Primary or Secondary attributes. This will allow for the most appropriate solutions at any given point in time. Remember that the patterns will still apply but as people change, you may need to adjust your strategies and recommendations accordingly.

⊙ Update your chart on a regular basis. This will account for staff transitions (people leaving, new hires and promotions).

FIGURE 12
GROUP FIVE ELEMENTS PROFILE CHART

NAME | PROFILE	POSITION	PRIMARY ATTRIBUTE	SECONDARY ATTRIBUTE	RELATIONAL ATTRIBUTE

FIGURE 13
GROUP FIVE ELEMENTS CHART

FIGURE 14
ANALYSIS OF RELATIONAL ATTRIBUTES

FIGURE 15
ANALYSIS OF PRIMARY ATTRIBUTES

FIGURE 16
ANALYSIS OF SECONDARY ATTRIBUTES

CHAPTER SEVENTEEN
TRANSFORMING CONFLICT

When it comes to conflict, the Law of Nature is stark and unquestionable, and **The Five Elements** clearly affirms it:

- Water extinguishes Fire.

- Fire tempers or melts Metal.

- Metal chops Wood.

- Wood depletes the nutrients from the Earth.

- Earth contains Water.

We can learn a lot from the tension that exists between the elements, especially in the Restraining cycle. When they are in full force, they can be dangerous and destructive. The conflict is unforgiving and can only be resolved when one element prevails over the other.

But is that always the case?

If we observe the subtleties between the elements in the Restraining cycle, we find that conflict can be not only resolved, but transformed into something good. For instance:

- ◉ When we apply Fire to Water in just the right degree, the result is the perfect bath temperature, or a low simmer that produces a delicious pot of soup.

- ◉ The proper flame can temper Metal to a sharp and useful blade.

- ◉ That blade, correctly applied, can prune a tree to maximize its growth.

- ◉ Plants have the capacity to transform barren land into fertile soil.

- ◉ Earth and Water, appropriately combined, produces clay that can be shaped into useful and beautiful objects.

Human behavior operates in a similar fashion. Conflict resolution often means two sides invoking their full power upon each other until one side prevails. Our military, legal, athletic and political systems confirm this winner-take-all dynamic.

But nature shows us that conflict transformation is possible under the right conditions. It takes a keen degree of awareness and skill to hold a healthy tension and prevent disaster.

If a flame is adjusted by just one degree, a perfectly formed blade could melt away into a formless puddle of liquid metal. Likewise, one ill-timed look, gesture or "hmph" can result in a complete meltdown of emotions.

This chapter explores the fine line of conflict transformation from The Five Elements perspective. The following case studies featuring interactions between two people demonstrate the tension between the elements in the Restraining cycle. An analysis and recommended solutions for each are presented, as well.

Smolder

Vinh and Conner have been best friends since they met in their seventh-grade metalwork class. They went to art school together and, for the past six years, have devoted much of their time and passion to creating stunning works of art for Burning Man, the annual festival in Black Rock Desert, Nevada. From concept to execution, each installation takes 10 months.

Their current project—a phoenix rising from the ashes—is their most complex and ambitious to date. They intend to mount a mechanized frame on a van and embellish it with feathers constructed of stained glass and mirrors. Special effects included strobe lights, dry ice, pyrotechnics, and sound effects. They named their installation "Walter" in honor of their metalwork teacher.

Vinh and Conner spent hundreds of hours designing and building prototypes before deciding on their final model. Then one day, this conversation occurred.

> **Vinh:** "This thing is a piece of junk. It's never going to work."

> **Conner:** "What are you saying?"

> **Vinh:** "I'm saying that we've lost the vision. Walter has no passion. No inspiration. He's not feeding my soul. We need trash him and start over."

> **Conner:** "I don't know what you're talking about. If you just open your eyes, you will see that there is soul written all over him."

Vinh: "You mean to tell me if the real Walter Whitney was standing here, he would be proud of this project? He'd approve of how we constructed the hoist mechanism which only works half the time? Besides, we still haven't figured out how the feathers can withstand the pyrotechnics."

Conner: "Dude, that's not fair bringing Mr. Whitney into this. This project is good and we can't throw out all of our time, energy and money with the bathwater just because you think that Walter has no soul."

Conner: "You gotta give me something, Vinh."

Vinh: "Let me think about it and I'll let you know."

The next day, Vinh told his friend, "I know Walter is good, Conner. I just want him to be great."

ANALYSIS

This conflict is an example of the tension between Water and Fire. Vinh's fears got the best of him and those fears threatened to sink their project, resulting in a misunderstanding between lifelong friends.

"I kind of lost it," Vinh said in retrospect.

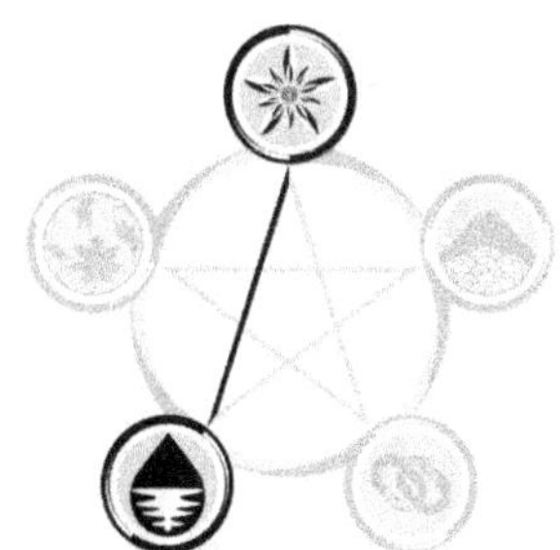

To him, it felt like Conner was running away with the vision and leaving him behind. If Vinh had expressed his concerns earlier instead of waiting to release the floodwaters of doubt all at once, the situation would not have reached a boiling point.

Fortunately, Conner and Vinh had a solid enough friendship to withstand the deluge of doubt. For Vinh, talking about the installation was one thing, but committing to it for all the world to see was quite another. It was important that they review some of the philosophical and technical issues, but not dwell on them too long at the risk of losing momentum.

Conner had enough faith to hold the vision, and he refused to give up on both Vinh and Walter. In his request to his friend, "You gotta give me something," Conner was looking for a sign of hope from Vinh.

Vinh delivered on that request the following day, offering the perspective that he wanted Walter to not just be good, but great. This deepened both Vinh's and Conner's commitment to the project and to each other.

SOLUTION | TEND THE GARDEN

In order for Vinh and Conner to move forward in a healthy way, they needed to Tend the Garden by revisiting Wood. The sense of hope and possibility would assuage Vinh's doubts and reignite his excitement and inspiration for the project.

Vinh and Conner took a short break from the logistics of the project and engaged in a session of "what if?" Their point was to think as far out of the box as possible. Here are some thoughts that they developed:

- ◉ "What if we could record the real Walter Whitney's voice reading an instruction manual and broadcast it out of the phoenix's mouth?"
- ◉ "What if we made Walter a purple boa?"
- ◉ "What if Walter tossed chocolate kisses to his adoring masses?"

This activity reminded the two friends of the reason why they were doing this in the first place: to have fun. Having rediscovered those seeds of joy, they had a good laugh and got back to work.

Transforming Conflict between Water and Fire

The relationship of Water and Fire is one of the most rewarding and sustaining between two elements. Recall a time when you eased yourself into a bath and the water temperature was just right; or prepared a simmering pot of soup on the stove, with the flame

The relationship of fire and water is one of the most rewarding and sustaining between two elements.

Find the right temperature between parties and work to maintain that temperature.

not too high or too low. When we attain the right balance between Water and Fire, the results can be magical.

In human interactions, the balance between Water and Fire is knowing how much Wood, or fuel, to add. Not enough innovation, brainstorming, joy and adventure results in a tepid experience with a lack of enthusiasm. In Vinh's eyes, this was the "good" version of Walter.

Too many ideas and an overemphasis on innovation can result in a bunch of hot air, where style trumps substance and the energy quickly dissipates. If Vinh and Conner focused all of their energies on the "what if" scenarios, they would have run out of fuel and called it day before making any tangible progress on Walter.

The key in transforming these potential conflicts is to find the right temperature between parties and work to maintain that temperature. (I call it the Goldilocks zone.) It starts with identifying what seeds or qualities will support the common vision, and watering the seeds you wish to cultivate that will provide the right fuel for that vision.

In the case of Vinh and Conner, those seeds were friendship, fun, creativity, adventure, joy, challenge, and wow! Anchoring those values into their purpose and vision helped them to focus on seeing their project through.

Meltdown

Anthony, a high school sophomore, was preparing his poster board for a presentation at a regional science fair. He had won both the school-wide and citywide science fairs to qualify, and had spent six weeks gathering additional research for the regionals.

Michelle, a doctor, was especially proud of her son for doing so well on this project. While she had hoped for and nurtured his passion for science, Michelle was glad to see that Anthony had taken an interest in the subject on his own.

Michelle was used to helping her son with his school projects, and for his part, Anthony welcomed her feedback. In fact, it was a source of pride for him that he and his mother could connect on this level.

As usual, Michelle gave Anthony a few helpful suggestions about his poster board, like changing some language to sharpen up his presentation, placing the charts higher to bring focus on the data, etc. As Michelle brought Anthony a sandwich, she looked at the poster board and said, "You know, if you just . . ."

Then it happened.

Anthony: "I'm done with this!" He tossed the poster board on the floor.

Michelle: "What the?"

Anthony: "Just quit butting in and leave me alone."

Michelle: "But I was only trying to help."

Anthony: "You think you're helping but it feels like you're criticizing everything. I can't do anything right with you standing over me all the time."

Michelle: "Look, let's just pick this up and see what we can do to put it back together."

Anthony: "Mom. Didn't you hear me? I'm done! No more science fairs. No more AP classes. No more going to lectures with you. From now on, you'll have to find someone else to pick on."

ANALYSIS

With the best of intentions, Michelle was trying to be an extra set of eyes for Anthony and provide some helpful suggestions. From Anthony's perspective, the first three suggestions were fine; the fourth and fifth were annoying. By the time Michelle offered her sixth comment, Anthony had reached his melting point and was finished with anything that had to do with science and his mother. The sad thing was, he actually loved both.

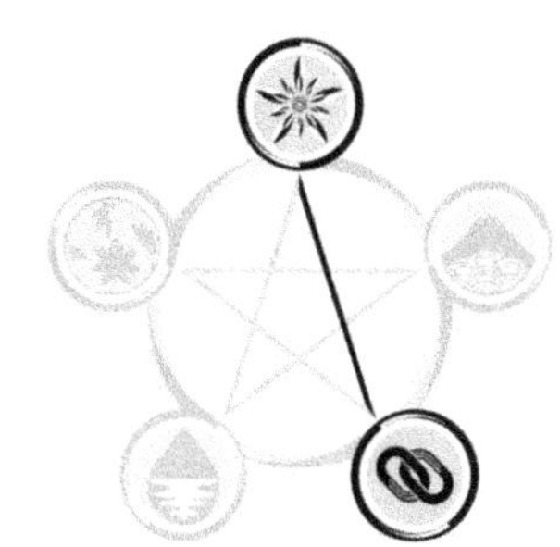

The dynamic between Fire and Metal is the most difficult to repair because the result is a complete meltdown. When, and if, the metal reconstitutes, the structure may never be the same.

The meltdown scenario is commonly referred to as "burnout." People become so fed up with a situation or relationship that they will walk away without turning back. The damage is often permanent.

When placed in this situation, people claim that it feels like being in a pressure cooker, stuck in a steel container and placed under extreme heat. While the experience can be transformational in positive ways, it also runs the risk of blowing its top and causing a great deal of destruction.

Anthony was in that pressure cooker, and neither he nor Michelle realized it until it was too late. With Anthony in meltdown/burnout mode, it was up to Michelle to rectify the situation.

SOLUTION | GET GROUNDED

When a meltdown/burnout situation occurs, stability and connection are the most important factors to consider. These characteristics are indicative of Earth.

As the source of the fire, Michelle needed to get grounded in order to turn down the heat and establish the right conditions for rebuilding the relationship. While it was important for her to give Anthony some space to cool down, she also needed to provide some structure and context.

Being mindful of the Earth attributes of compassion, care and connection, Michelle:

- Apologized to Anthony;

- Agreed that he did not have to participate in the science fair, but for his own sake, suggested that he complete the project;

- Promised not to bother him; and

- Offered to pick up any supplies that he needed.

Michelle also contacted Anthony's science teacher and mentor (whom she knew he would contact) to give him a heads up. Anthony finished the project with his science teacher's guidance and participated in the fair. Although Michelle did not attend the event, she met Anthony afterwards at his favorite restaurant to celebrate.

Once they reconnected, Michelle and Anthony made amends. He knew that his mother meant well and that she played a positive role in sharpening his skills and developing his passion for science. Michelle became more aware of the fine line between offering constructive feedback and meddling. When they re-established common ground, they were able to find a way to relate to each other with care and compassion.

Transforming Conflict between Fire and Metal

From a perspective of human relations, Fire is one of the easiest elements to regulate, but we often fail at doing so. Many people can't resist offering unsolicited advice or too much information.

Fire is represented by the eyes; therefore, it is important for people who are in the Fire stage to access all of their levels of seeing. Besides what they may be actually viewing with their physical eyes, what is their mind's eye telling them? What are the underlying patterns and dynamics at play, and how might they inform one's response?

Since the nature of Fire is to shed light on a topic, people in this stage may know more than what might be appropriate to share. Think about the Earth characteristics of compassion, care and connection, and ask yourself, "What is best for everyone concerned?"

The smallest adjustment in the flame can make a difference between tempered and liquid metal. Human emotions are much more fragile than metal, thus exercising discernment is key in transforming conflict.

Chopped

Jessie and Chris have been married for seven years. They co-own a small catering business, which provides the opportunity for them to pursue their common passion for cooking and have the flexibility to spend time with their kids.

Since Jessie is in charge of sales and administration, they decided that she would attend a business development conference while Chris stayed home to take care of the children and the business. The conference was very successful, and Jessie returned home excited to share what she had learned and the meetings she'd had with several potential clients.

Although they typically get along, Chris had been avoiding Jessie since her return, claiming that he was too busy to talk. Whenever she approached Chris, he would put his hands up and say, "Can't you see we've got work to do? Just cut it out."

After several days, Jessie asked a neighbor to watch the kids and invited Chris for a walk around a small lake and a cup of tea. As they sipped their tea, they talked.

> **Jessie:** "It's been a while since I returned and we still haven't talked about the conference. So, I thought I'd arrange this time for me to ..."

> **Chris:** "Hold up right there, Jess. With you gone, I was so overwhelmed with work and the kids. I had all pistons running and was just barely keeping things functioning. You wanted to talk, but I literally didn't have the time. Plus, I was feeling angry that you went away and left me with all the work."

> **Jessie:** "I was so excited to share everything I learned at the conference that I thought you'd be excited too. And I ..."

> **Chris:** "That's exactly my point. You're coming home with all these new ideas, which

means more work for me. Even if they're good ideas, I don't see how we can implement them."

Jessie: "And I was going to say that I was excited to see you and the kids too. I understand that you're stressed, but your attitude just takes the wind out of my sails. Now I can't even remember why I went."

Chris: "I'll tell you why you went. You went to find out how to fulfill our dream and grow our business. And I should have trusted that you've already weeded out the bad ideas and would only come to me with the good ideas."

Jessie: "You're right, and I did weed out the bad ideas on the trip home. Why don't we talk about how to redistribute the workload first and then I can share a couple of the good ideas?"

Chris: "Sounds like a plan."

ANALYSIS

Like an axe chopping down a tree, Chris' attitude and constant interruptions were obstructing Jessie's sense of hope and enthusiasm. In this interaction, Jessie's seeds of confidence and joy were being replaced with doubt and guilt. The way she interpreted Chris' perspective was that there was too much work and they needed to cut back, not grow.

This scenario underscores the tension between Metal and Wood. It can be subtle, like a gardener pruning a tree; or drastic, like chopping the tree down. The intensity of the interaction depends on the attitude and actions of the person in Metal.

The most positive outcome would result in a controlled pruning of ideas, thereby providing a realistic framework on the creative process. Taking steps back and reflecting on the bigger picture could offer a deeper perspective and prevent ideas from getting too out of hand.

Chris was in such a panic mode that the mere thought of Jessie's ideas was a threat. Jessie was astute enough to see this, and she offered to talk about redistributing the workload, bringing in Earth to support Metal, before bringing up new ideas. This put Chris at ease, and re-established the conditions for him to engage in a conversation.

SOLUTION | JUST ADD WATER

When Metal restrains Wood, it is important to go back to the beginning and ask, "Why are we doing this?" When people are in Metal mode, they can sometimes

get so caught up in the tasks that they lose sight of the purpose. The same dynamic can happen when people are generating ideas in the Wood stage.

When Chris talked about fulfilling their dream and growing their business, he added some Water. He and Jessie found a comfort in seeking the qualities of Water: purpose, values, and deep listening. Jessie had the foresight to bring in Water by planning a trip to the lake and having tea. By surrounding themselves with the actual element they'd hoped to invoke, the pathway toward engaging in healthy communication was easier.

Adding Water provided a way for Chris and Jessie to affirm and anchor their common vision. Upon doing so, they were able to seek ways to understand and be understood.

Transforming Conflict between Metal and Wood

In Traditional Chinese Medicine, an excess of Metal leads to rash speech and actions, rigidity, arrogance, and isolation. People with too much Metal often feel as if they are suffocating under the weight of their responsibilities. In many ways, they are their own worst enemies.

The body part related to Metal is the lungs. Breathing is something we do automatically. It's a function that runs 24/7, like a machine. When the lungs stop working, so do we. It is this pressure that drives people in the Metal stage to keep going at all costs.

The simplest way to manage this tension is to focus on the lungs and take deep breaths. Fresh air acts as a lubricant for our thoughts and actions, bringing perspective and connection to the present moment. Taking three slow, conscious breaths allows one to focus on what is essential and ask, "Why am I doing this?"

Reflecting back on Chris and Jessie's conversation, if Chris was more conscious of his breathing, perhaps he wouldn't have been so inclined to cut Jessie off. The pathways toward listening and understanding would have been open so that he could see the benefit of Jessie's ideas.

The organization Tools for Peace has a saying:

Stop. Breathe. Think.

These three simple acts may be the solution to preventing potential destruction from happening.

Depleted

Nani and Layla are co-workers at a clothing store that caters to young women. Layla, the store manager, has been recognized as a top producer and innovator in the company. Her store has been number one in sales for the past year.

Nani was excited to be hired as the assistant manager and was looking forward to learning all she could about the business from Layla. They hit it off immediately and Layla agreed to be Nani's mentor.

Layla had a habit of coming to work every day with a list of ideas on how to improve the customer experience. Here's an example of a typical walk-through with Nani.

> **Layla:** "Let's move these displays over here and change the signage out front."

> **Nani:** "Yes, ma'am."

> **Layla:** "I'm thinking of bringing in more music from this artist I heard last night. I can't remember his name but you can look it up. He just played at The Blue Note."

> **Nani:** "Got it."

Layla: "Since spring is coming, I want to feature all of our pink clothes up front."

Nani: "Okay."

Layla talked through a few more ideas on her list as Nani took meticulous notes. Even though she did not completely understand the vision, Nani didn't question Layla and agreed with everything she said.

"Consider it done," Nani said, as Layla left for a meeting. Several hours later, Layla returned to the store.

Layla: "What's this music?"

Nani: "It's the artist you told me about. I had one of our employees look him up and make a playlist."

Layla: "I was just thinking out loud, Nani. I didn't mean that you should actually do it. Please put the old music back on."

Nani: "Yes, ma'am."

Layla: "And why is all the pink merchandise up front?"

Nani: "You said that you wanted it moved, so I had four employees do it. We also moved the displays and changed the signage."

Layla: "Look, Nani. You're a terrific worker and you have a lot of potential. But you need to understand that there's a difference between what I want, what I'm thinking and what needs to be done. Am I making myself clear?"

ANALYSIS

Nani wanted to say, "No Layla, you are not making yourself clear. I spend 60 hours a week at this store trying to implement your ideas. The staff and I work our fingers to the bone, only to have you come in and tell us you were just 'thinking out loud.' You have to know how exasperating that is. I want to succeed in this business. I want to please you. I want to learn from you. And I want you to be clear."

Nani wanted to say this in spite of her desire to keep the peace. Out of respect for lines of authority, she refrained from doing so.

The earth provides the nutrients for plants to draw upon. The same principle applies to people. There are those who are innovate and those who maintain.

Society tends to reward the pioneers and visionaries, rather than those who organize and facilitate the work. It is the dynamic of Wood restraining Earth.

The Wood stage can infuse new ideas and breakthroughs in an environment. Many of Layla's ideas were good and provided the company with fresh approaches in sales and customer service. Through Layla's skills at innovation, Nani saw the world in ways she would not have imagined.

This stage can also deplete resources while pursuing plans that are not seriously considered or vetted. Layla's lack of filtering her ideas and considering the impact on Nani, as well as the rest of the staff, drained everyone's energy and morale. Even the best ideas need a reality check.

It is important to understand the difference between depletion and burnout. In Anthony's case, he had thrown up his hands and was ready to walk away from science and his mother. When people experience burnout, they are saying, "Peace out. I'm done."

Nani was not burnt out, but depleted. Instead of checking out, she was saying, "Even if it kills me, I will stick with it and get it right." It is that sense of unfettered loyalty that is the mark of Earth.

There is a difference between burnout ("Peace out. I'm done."), and depletion (I will stick with this even if it kills me).

The key to this dynamic is scale. While one suggestion can create a feeling of breakthrough, 17 suggestions will likely be overwhelming and result in feelings of depletion. Leaders and managers should be mindful of the timing, the messenger, and the cost-benefit of presenting the idea.

SOLUTION | TEND THE FIRE

Turning to Fire would have assisted Layla and Nani in transforming their conflict. Confidence, clarity and consideration are key factors when facilitating the tension between Wood and Fire.

If Layla took a moment to shed some light on the big picture and provide a story that related to the customer experience, it would have provided Nani and the staff a point of reference for them to gain a deeper understanding of the reason behind the change. In addition, if Nani took the time to review her understanding of Layla's comments, and perhaps even developed a chart ("random thoughts", "consider but don't take action", "green light - take action"), it would have prevented wasted time and energy on items that were not a priority.

By stepping into the light, Layla and Nani could see eye to eye on the path ahead, and assure that their steps are coordinated toward successful and sustainable outcomes.

Transforming Conflict between Wood and Earth

Transforming conflict in this dynamic is especially relevant in our age of social media. Every day, we are bombarded with data from multiple sources. Every few seconds, our personal devices buzz, click, ring or vibrate, notifying us of some new and perhaps life-changing bit of information.

People are both seduced and repelled by this dynamic. Many profess to check their social media for "just a minute" only to find that an hour has passed. How do we control this?

Fire is regulated primarily by fuel and air. Consider ideas, information and data as our fuel, and the time that we spending reading, viewing, thinking, talking and communicating about it as our air. If we can regulate our fuel (input) and air (time) by setting time limits on social media (for example, three, 15-minute sessions/day), we will be able to shine light on the issue and better prioritize our time and energy.

Stuck

Jeremy, Nicole and Brett had been neighbors for more than 10 years. They were friendly but not close, greeting each other as they came and went, or talking over the fence as they tended to their respective backyards. Nicole and Brett's son, Kaleo, liked to go next door and play with Jeremy's dog. One day, Jeremy, Nicole and Kaleo were talking over the fence, complaining about the small size of their inner-city yards.

> **Kaleo:** "Why don't we just tear down the fence and have one big yard?"

> **Jeremy:** "You know, that's not a bad idea."

> **Nicole:** "We could combine our gardens and have extra space for your dog to play."

> **Kaleo:** "Plus, I won't have to go out on the street to come visit. I can just come around the back."

> **Nicole:** "It'll be a win-win. Who knows? Maybe all of our neighbors will tear down their fences and we'll have a big community space."

> **Jeremy:** "Let me look into it and I'll get back to you."

Jeremy researched and discussed the following options:

◉ Were there any tax or property implications?

- ◉ Would we need a permit from the city?

- ◉ Do we need some sort of legal agreement?

- ◉ What if my dog tears up your yard?

- ◉ What if one of us moves?

- ◉ What if one of us doesn't like the situation after a while?

- ◉ What if one of us does 90% of the gardening and starts to resent the other?

- ◉ If I have a barbeque in my backyard, am I obligated to invite you because it's your backyard too?

A year passed and a fence still divided the two yards when they engaged in another conversation. This time, they were joined by Brett.

Kaleo: "Whatever happened to my idea of tearing down the fence?"

Nicole: "I think it was a good idea in spirit, but we kind of got mired down in the details."

Jeremy: "Yeah, I'm sorry I took us down that road. I didn't mean to go that deep but as I talked to more people about it, one question led to another, then another . . ."

Kaleo: "That's too bad. I thought it was a good idea."

Jeremy: "It still is a good idea. We just couldn't make it happen."

Nicole: "Why not? We've been neighbors for all these years. Who cares what other people think?"

Jeremy: "You've got a point. Maybe we should just do it."

Brett: "How about this? Instead of bringing down the whole fence, we could cut down a section and build a gate. That way, we can try it out and if we like it, then we can remove the rest of the fence. If not, we'll leave the gate as a safe way for Kaleo and the dog to go back and forth."

Everyone agreed and within minutes, Brett had brought out his power saw and began cutting a hole in the fence. They spent the rest of the day building a gate and celebrating their new arrangement. Three months later, they agreed to tear down the rest of the fence.

ANALYSIS

This is a classic example of progress being entrapped by process. The neighbors were clear on their common philosophy of combining their resources, expanding their sense of family, and affirming their value of community (Water). As Nicole said, "It's a win-win."

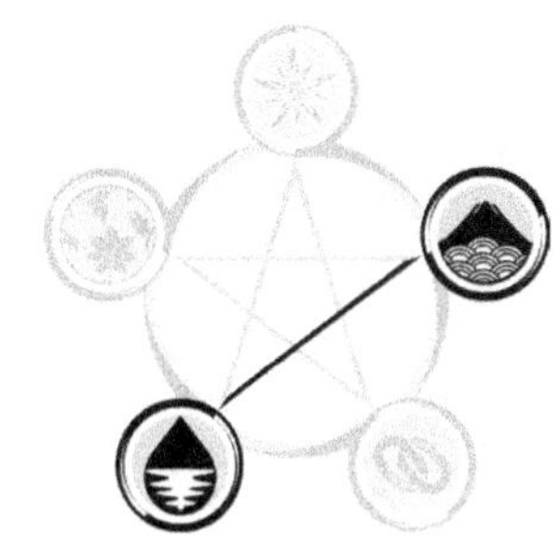

But in Jeremy's attempt to assure harmony for the long run (Earth), his questions and contingencies overrode any progress. The combination of Earth and Water resulted in them being stuck in the mud. Every time he tried to dig himself out, the situation became more complex. They all felt paralyzed by the process and it wasn't important enough for any of them to push through and make it happen. Kaleo's continued advocacy and unwillingness to let the idea go was the key factor in seeing it through.

SOLUTION | PUT THE PEDAL TO THE MEDAL

When someone is stuck in the mud, they need a cable to pull themselves out. In the framework of **The Five Elements**, it demonstrates the restraining nature of Earth and Water. Nicole and Jeremy, having been deeply involved in the process for a year, were trapped by the situation.

Brett stepped in with a fresh perspective and offered a compromise that aligned with their original purpose. The compromise of the gate was particularly important. When people are stuck in the mud, they can, for better or worse, get comfortable enough to the point that they would prefer to stay stuck than choose a way out. Brett's compromise was an example of providing a step-by-step plan of action that would be palatable for the more process-oriented qualities found in Earth and Water.

In the end, this plan gave them the needed lifeline to get them unstuck and move toward action (Metal) so they could eventually achieve their mission.

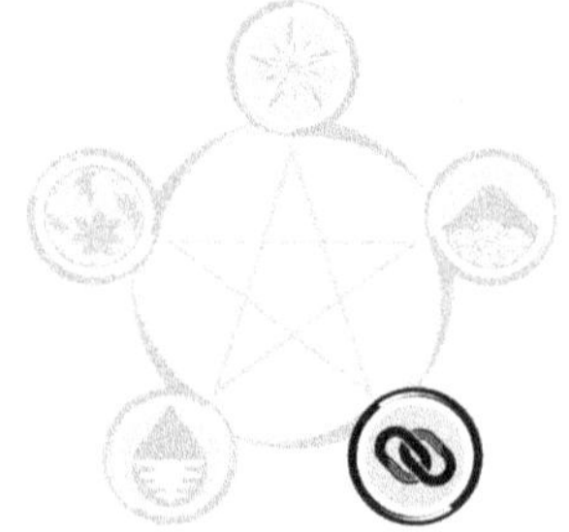

Transforming Conflict between Earth and Water

The Earth stage thrives in busy work, which may or may not be productive. The goal of this stage is to establish the conditions for health, harmony and productivity. When one introduces philosophical concepts (Water), such as . . .

- ⊙ How can we be sure that our policies and procedures are aligned with our values?

- ⊙ What does true success look and feel like?

. . . it muddies the process with issues that should have been discussed and established in the Wood and Fire stages. The Earth stage loves process and errs on the side of caution, so the temptation to stay in the mud bath and not move on to Metal is strong.

The dilemma with this conflict is that it is so sneaky. Many have found that they are unknowingly trapped in a process of their own making. Sometimes it takes a third party (like Brett) to point it out and perhaps provide a way out.

Developing a step-by-step action plan is the best way to get unstuck.

The key is to follow the gut instead of the head. In Traditional Chinese Medicine, the body part representing Earth is the abdomen, especially the area just below and behind the navel. It has been said that this area is the source of intuition and will guide us more effectively than our heads. If you find yourself entrapped in a muddy situation, try not to think yourself toward a solution, but take a moment to breathe, and see what answers arise.

This dynamic also tends toward isolation. To seek community and ask for support is a big step in transforming this conflict. Celebrate each step toward action and integration, however small, because it is not easy to walk in quicksand.

CHAPTER SEVENTEEN RECAP

⊙ Just as important in understanding the elements themselves are the transitions between the elements.

⊙ The ability to understand and navigate these parts of the system will lead to more harmonious and prosperous outcomes.

⊙ The transitions within the Restraining cycle are:

⊙ The responses generally tend toward the negative within the Restraining cycle (for example, confusion, meltdown, obstruction, depletion, and entrapment). Transitions are typically more intense at the beginning and decrease as the change process progresses.

⊙ There may be times when it is advantageous to utilize the positive response within the Restraining cycle; however, it takes a skilled practitioner of **The Five Elements** to utilize the Restraining cycle in this manner.

⊙ Responses within the Restraining cycle also tend to be much more subtle. A word or glance will likely be enough to make a shift from positive to negative, or vice versa. Again, the more skill and experience one has with The Five Elements, the more one can recognize the areas that are unaligned and then develop strategies to maintain balance.

"The language of the elements is also the language of the heart, spoken with the crystal clarity of a quiet mind, linked to all that has come before, and all that will come after. There is a simple natural, harmonious magic to it, which we are all in tune with if we can learn to listen."

KATHERINE METZ
The Art of Placement

CHAPTER EIGHTEEN

INTEGRATING *the* FIVE ELEMENTS *as a* DAILY PRACTICE

When I was beginning my study of **The Five Elements**, I would spend several days each season with my teacher Katherine Metz. She lived in Redstone, Colorado at the time, a one-street town nestled high in the Rocky Mountains along the banks of the Crystal River. With limited Wi-Fi access, we were literally disconnected from the rest of the world.

Our sessions were intense, as Katherine filled our heads with wisdom from traditions that date back thousands of years. In addition to sharing her own vast repository of knowledge, Katherine brought in master teachers of Tibetan Buddhism, *Yin Yang* Theory, the I Ching, and the Ba Gua, providing a comprehensive education on the principles and practice of *qi*.

After each session, Katherine instructed her students to go out in silence, to listen and notice. Sometimes, I went for long walks by the river, and sometimes I just sat on the bench in front of the general store.

It didn't take long for nature to respond, perhaps in the form of a falling autumn leaf, or the bite of the winter air as I took in a deep breath. Sometimes I closed my eyes in order to "see" better, noting the sound of the babbling brook, a conversation between a mother and child, or a logging truck in the distance. In the springtime, I felt the familiar itch in my nose and eyes responding to the pollen in the air. With the coming of summer, I experienced the joy of wiggling my toes in the firm red clay and easing myself in the healing waters of the hot spring.

It was during those moments that **The Five Elements** came alive for me. I felt them in every cell of my body and in every interaction I encountered. I experienced color, taste, weather, formations, beauty, music, language, joy and wonder through new eyes. The language of **The Five Elements**— in its simplicity and elegance—became a new way of being. To honor Katherine's teachings, I pass her advice onto you.

Now that you have completed an immersion in this methodology, I invite you to put the book down and go out in silence to _experience_ The Five Elements.

Release the formulas, archetypes and attributes for the moment and simply allow the elements to manifest in your world. It doesn't matter whether you're in the city or the country; the elements will always show up. Be sure to tap into _all_ of your senses.

I invite you to -

- Notice the sparkle of sunshine on a puddle (Water and Fire).

- Feel the slight breeze against your face (Wood).

- Hear an airplane passing overhead (Metal).

- Taste the richness of braised carrots (Earth and Wood).

- Inhale the fresh scent of the air after a spring rain (Water and Wood).

Observe what is present, as well as what is absent. If movement and noise predominate, stillness and silence will be the contrasting features. Noticing these contradictions will hone your skills in assessing which elements are predominant, and which are needed.

Bring **The Five Elements** into your home and workspace to create an environment that promotes health, balance and prosperity. Make sure your bedding reflects colors that support your Primary attribute. Adjust your meditation and self-care practices to align with the recommendations for your profile. Make sure your meetings coincide with formations that work best for your team. Organize your clothes by elemental colors. Think about who and what you will be facing each day and choose what you will wear accordingly.

As you integrate **The Five Elements** into your daily routine, share your Five Elements profile with others and determine their profiles by referring to Chapter 3 or using our app at my5elements.life. In this manner you can identify the interpersonal dynamics and patterns that exist and determine what solutions will bring about positive outcomes.

And if you need more assistance, please don't hesitate to contact us at my5elements.life for individual or group consultations.

In this increasingly complex and diverse world, **The Five Elements** transcends issues and identity factors such as gender, age, position and title, race, sexual orientation, language, topic, culture and more.

The Five Elements present themselves without bias or judgment. It simply says, "This is what needs to be done to bring you back to balance in a good way." Because the system is based on the laws of nature, the process is sensible and simple to learn and apply.

My grandmother relied on **The Five Elements** every day to keep her and her family well. On behalf of my grandmother and all of my teachers and ancestors, I hold you in deep regard and fond aloha in your journey toward health, balance and prosperity with **The Five Elements**.

THE FIVE ELEMENTS

APPENDIX I

CHARTS *to* DETERMINE *a* FIVE ELEMENTS PROFILE

PRIMARY ATTRIBUTE CHART
FIGURE 17
1910 -2035

9	8	7	6	5	4	3	2	1
Networker	Rock	Achiever	Protector	Facilitator	Optimist	Visionary	Caregiver	Philosopher
1910	1911	1912	1913	1914	1915	1916	1917	1918
1919	1920	1921	1922	1923	1924	1925	1926	1927
1928	1929	1930	1931	1932	1933	1934	1935	1936
1937	1938	1939	1940	1941	1942	1943	1944	1945
1946	1947	1948	1949	1950	1951	1952	1953	1954
1955	1956	1957	1958	1959	1960	1961	1962	1963
1964	1965	1966	1967	1968	1969	1970	1971	1972
1973	1974	1975	1976	1977	1978	1979	1980	1981
1982	1983	1984	1985	1986	1987	1988	1989	1990
1991	1992	1993	1994	1995	1996	1997	1998	1999
2000	2001	2002	2003	2004	2005	2006	2007	2008
2009	2010	2011	2012	2013	2014	2015	2016	2017
2018	2019	2020	2021	2022	2023	2024	2025	2026
2027	2028	2029	2030	2031	2032	2033	2034	2035

SECONDARY AND DEVELOPMENTAL ATTRIBUTE CHART

FIGURE 18

Primary Attribute	9	8	7	6	5	4	3	2	1
	Net	Rock	Ach	Pro	Fac	Opt	Vis	Care	Phil
Birthdate (MM|DD)									
4 Feb – 5 Mar	5	2	8	5	2	8	5	2	8
6 Mar – 4 Apr	4	1	7	4	1	7	4	1	7
5 Apr – 5 May	3	9	6	3	9	6	3	9	6
6 May – 5 Jun	2	8	5	2	8	5	2	8	5
6 Jun – 7 Jul	1	7	4	1	7	4	1	7	4
8 Jul – 7 Aug	9	6	3	9	6	3	9	6	3
8 Aug – 7 Sept	8	5	2	8	5	2	8	5	2
8 Sept – 8 Oct	7	4	1	7	4	1	7	4	1
9 Oct – 7 Nov	6	3	9	6	3	9	6	3	9
8 Nov – 7 Dec	5	2	8	5	2	8	5	2	8
8 Dec – 5 Jan	4	1	7	4	1	7	4	1	7
6 Jan – 3 Feb	3	9	6	3	9	6	3	9	6

RELATIONAL ATTRIBUTE CHART
FIGURE 19
WITH REFERENCE PAGES TO INDIVIDUAL ASSESSMENTS

914 (pg. 403)	813 (pg. 398)	712 (pg. 393)	611 (pg. 389)	519 (pg. 384)	418 (pg. 379)	317 (pg. 374)	216 (pg. 370)	115 (pg. 365)
923 (pg. 403)	822 (pg. 399)	721 (pg. 394)	629 (pg. 389)	528 (pg. 384)	427 (pg. 379)	326 (pg. 375)	225 (pg. 370)	124 (pg. 365)
932 (pg. 403)	831 (pg. 399)	739 (pg. 394)	638 (pg. 390)	537 (pg. 385)	436 (pg. 380)	335 (pg. 375)	234 (pg. 371)	133 (pg. 366)
941 (pg. 404)	849 (pg. 400)	748 (pg. 395)	647 (pg. 390)	546 (pg. 385)	445 (pg. 380)	344 (pg. 376)	243 (pg. 371)	142 (pg. 367)
959 (pg. 404)	858 (pg. 400)	757 (pg. 395)	656 (pg. 391)	555 (pg. 386)	454 (pg. 381)	353 (pg. 377)	252 (pg. 372)	151 (pg. 367)
968 (pg. 405)	867 (pg. 401)	766 (pg. 396)	665 (pg. 391)	564 (pg. 386)	463 (pg. 381)	362 (pg. 377)	261 (pg. 372)	169 (pg. 368)
977 (pg. 405)	876 (pg. 401)	775 (pg. 397)	674 (pg. 392)	573 (pg. 387)	472 (pg. 382)	371 (pg. 377)	279 (pg. 373)	178 (pg. 368)
986 (pg. 406)	885 (pg. 402)	784 (pg. 397)	683 (pg. 392)	582 (pg. 387)	481 (pg. 383)	389 (pg. 378)	288 (pg. 373)	187 (pg. 369)
995 (pg. 407)	894 (pg. 402)	793 (pg. 398)	692 (pg. 393)	591 (pg. 388)	499 (pg. 383)	398 (pg. 378)	297 (pg. 374)	196 (pg. 369)

LUNAR NEW YEAR DATES

FIGURE 20

1910 - 2035

1910 Feb. 10	**1911** Jan. 30	**1912** Feb. 18	**1913** Feb. 6	**1914** Jan. 26	**1915** Feb. 14	**1916** Feb. 3	**1917** Jan. 23	**1918** Feb. 11
1919 Feb. 1	**1920** Feb. 20	**1921** Feb. 8	**1922** Jan. 28	**1923** Feb. 16	**1924** Feb. 5	**1925** Jan. 24	**1926** Feb. 13	**1927** Feb. 2
1928 Jan. 23	**1929** Feb. 10	**1930** Jan. 30	**1931** Feb. 17	**1932** Feb. 6	**1933** Jan. 26	**1934** Feb. 14	**1935** Feb. 4	**1936** Jan. 24
1937 Feb. 11	**1938** Jan. 31	**1939** Feb. 19	**1940** Feb. 8	**1941** Jan. 27	**1942** Feb. 15	**1943** Feb. 4	**1944** Jan. 25	**1945** Feb. 13
1946 Feb. 1	**1947** Jan. 22	**1948** Feb. 10	**1949** Jan. 29	**1950** Feb. 17	**1951** Feb. 6	**1952** Jan. 27	**1953** Feb. 14	**1954** Feb. 3
1955 Jan. 24	**1956** Feb. 12	**1957** Jan. 31	**1958** Feb. 18	**1959** Feb. 8	**1960** Jan. 28	**1961** Feb. 15	**1962** Feb. 5	**1963** Jan. 25
1964 Feb. 13	**1965** Feb. 2	**1966** Jan. 21	**1967** Feb. 9	**1968** Jan. 30	**1969** Feb. 17	**1970** Feb. 6	**1971** Jan. 27	**1972** Feb. 15
1973 Feb. 3	**1974** Jan. 23	**1975** Feb. 11	**1976** Jan. 31	**1977** Feb. 18	**1978** Feb. 7	**1979** Jan. 29	**1980** Feb. 16	**1981** Feb. 5
1982 Jan. 25	**1983** Feb. 13	**1984** Feb. 2	**1985** Feb. 20	**1986** Feb. 9	**1987** Jan. 29	**1988** Feb. 17	**1989** Feb. 6	**1990** Jan. 27
1991 Feb. 15	**1992** Feb. 4	**1993** Jan. 23	**1994** Feb. 10	**1995** Jan. 31	**1996** Feb. 19	**1997** Feb. 7	**1998** Jan. 28	**1999** Feb. 16
2000 Feb. 5	**2001** Jan. 24	**2002** Feb. 12	**2003** Feb. 1	**2004** Jan. 22	**2005** Feb. 9	**2006** Jan. 29	**2007** Feb. 18	**2008** Feb. 7
2009 Jan. 26	**2010** Feb. 14	**2011** Feb. 3	**2012** Jan. 23	**2013** Feb. 10	**2014** Jan. 31	**2015** Feb. 19	**2016** Feb. 8	**2017** Jan. 28
2018 Feb. 16	**2019** Feb. 5	**2020** Jan. 25	**2021** Feb. 12	**2022** Feb. 1	**2023** Jan. 22	**2024** Feb. 10	**2025** Jan. 29	**2026** Feb. 17
2027 Feb. 6	**2028** Jan. 26	**2029** Feb. 13	**2030** Feb. 3	**2031** Jan. 23	**2032** Feb. 11	**2033** Jan. 31	**2034** Feb. 19	**2035** Feb. 8

APPENDIX II

SUMMARY *of* FIVE ELEMENTS PROFILES

115 | *Philosopher ⊙ Philosopher ⊙ Facilitator*
Of the Five Elements, your chart manifests two: Water and Earth, bringing a depth of reflection, synthesis and organization into your work. Your transition from positive to stressed mode (Primary to Secondary) is very subtle, which makes you difficult to read. If you can be transparent in communicating whether you are leading from your Primary or Secondary attribute, it will help ease your relationships with others.

124 | *Philosopher ⊙ Caregiver ⊙ Optimist*
Your chart manifests three elements: Water, Wood and Earth. When you are operating from your Primary attribute, your inward tendency to integrate

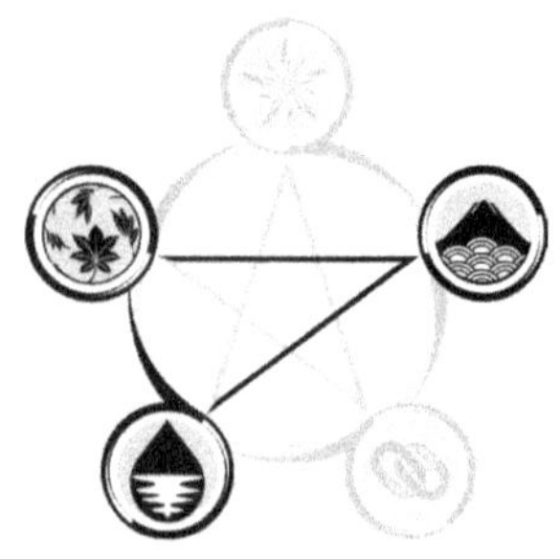

values and philosophy complements your public persona of looking on the bright side of situations. When you are operating from your Secondary mode, your outward tendency to be open, flexible and creative digs into your inward tendencies to control and manipulate. People may get confused by your attitudes and actions, as they don't match up with who you are when you're operating under stress. In all that you do, seek clarity and focus to assist you in accomplishing your goals.

133 | *Philosopher* ⊙ *Visionary* ⊙ *Visionary*

Your chart manifests two elements: Water and Wood. When you are operating from your Primary attribute, your inward tendency to integrate values and philosophy anchors your public persona of being creative and pioneering. Since your Secondary and Relational attributes are identical (Visionary), your attitudes and behaviors align well with peoples' perceptions of you; however, others may carry the impression that you are unreliable and flighty. The period of your late-teens and early-20s was likely difficult, as you became more serious and reflective, and less fun-loving and spontaneous. You likely lost your childhood friends and found people who could understand your deeper side. In all that you do, seek clarity and focus to assist you in accomplishing your goals.

142 | *Philosopher* ◉ *Optimist* ◉ *Caregiver*

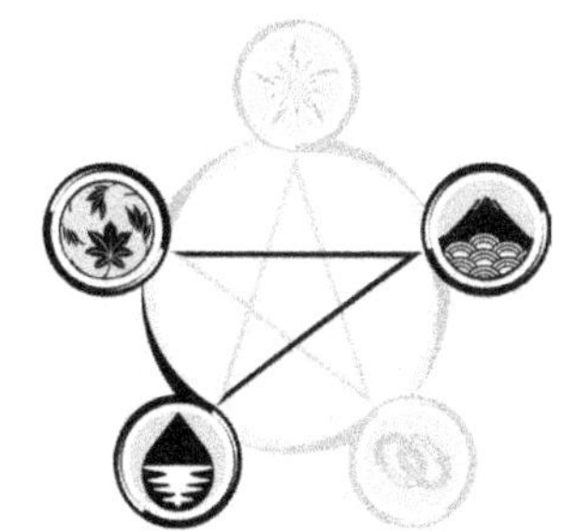

Your chart manifests three elements: Water, Wood and Earth. In relation to your Primary|Philosopher and Relational|Caregiver elements, people may be confused by the reclusive and perhaps cynical nature of the Philosopher with the nurturing side of the Caregiver. This may cause you to feel trapped or stuck between your outward desire to be in community and your inner desire to be alone. Because Water nurtures Wood, it is pretty easy for you to slip into your Secondary mode. You may experience difficulty breaking out of that mode and back into your Primary attribute, as you are going against the current of the Supporting cycle. In all that you do, seek clarity and focus to assist you in accomplishing your goals.

151 | *Philosopher* ◉ *Facilitator* ◉ *Philosopher*

Your chart manifests two elements: Water and Earth. Since your Primary and Relational elements are identical (Philosopher), your attitudes and behaviors align well with peoples' perceptions of you. In other words, what they see is what they get, and people can rely upon the consistency of your actions with your public persona. Your transition from Developmental|Facilitator to Primary|Philosopher (the period of your late-teens and early-20s) was likely smooth, as you were seeking a deeper truth and meaning through service. Focusing on tasks and seeking solutions that involve action will keep you in balance.

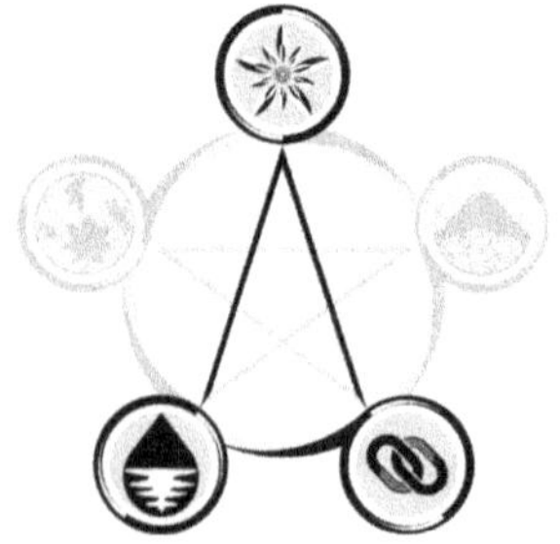

169 | *Philosopher* ⊙ *Protector* ⊙ *Networker*

Your chart manifests three elements: Water, Fire and Metal. Upon first meeting you, people get the impression that you are a Networker. Yet as they get to know you, they discover that you are really a Philosopher at heart, as your thoughtful, reflective inward nature runs counter to your extroverted and vivacious public persona. There is an inherent tension between your Relational attribute and your Secondary attribute. Your outward persona to be in the moment and enjoy life competes with your desire to be in control. This may cause some internal stress, as the Networker in you says, "Relax, we have plenty of time"; while your inner Dictator just wants to put the pedal to the floor and get the job done. To maintain balance, find creative ways to maintain connection and stability.

178 | *Philosopher* ⊙ *Achiever* ⊙ *Rock*

Your chart manifests three elements: Water, Earth and Metal. In relation to your Primary and Relational attributes, people may be confused by the reclusive and perhaps cynical nature of the Philosopher with the steady, dependable side of the Rock. This may cause you to feel trapped or stuck between your outward desire to be of service and your inner desire to be alone. In relation to your Secondary and Relational attributes, people may look to you for action, but find that you are mired in process and details. This causes confusion and distress, both for yourself and others, as expectations are not clear and grounded. In all that you do, be mindful of the balance between curiosity and clarity, focus and ambiguity.

187 | *Philosopher* ⊙ *Rock* ⊙ *Achiever*

Your chart manifests three elements: Water, Earth and Metal. Your task-oriented Achiever persona supports your Philosopher's desire to seek the truth and deepen impact. In relation to your Secondary and Relational attributes, people may look to you to get things done, but find that you are mired in process and details. This causes confusion and distress, both for yourself and others. Your transition from Developmental to Primary stages (the period of your late-teens and early-20s) was likely smooth, as you were seeking deeper truth and meaning through service. In all that you do, be mindful of the balance between curiosity and clarity, focus and ambiguity.

196 | *Philosopher* ⊙ *Networker* ⊙ *Protector*

Your chart manifests three elements: Water, Fire and Metal. Your strategic, take-the-lead Protector persona supports your Philosopher's desire to seek and understand the truth. There is an inherent tension between your Relational attribute and your Secondary attribute. While your Protector just wants to put the pedal to the floor and get the job done, your inner diva says, "Relax, we have plenty of time." Your transition from Developmental to Primary (the period of your late-teens and early-20s) was likely difficult, as you became less fun-loving and spontaneous, and more serious and contemplative.

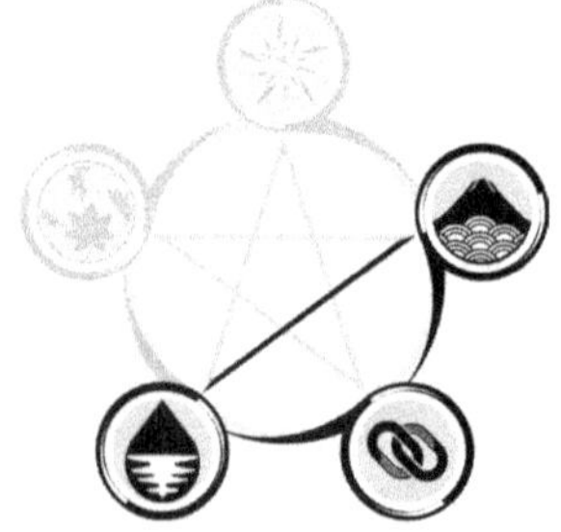

216 | *Caregiver* ⊙ *Philosopher* ⊙ *Protector*

Your chart manifests three elements: Earth, Metal and Water. When you are operating from your Primary attribute, you project the characteristics of a caring parent, embodying the right balance between the archetypical mother (Caregiver) and father (Protector). When you are operating from your Secondary mode, your tendency towards procrastination and cynicism goes against the current of your relational tendencies to be action-oriented. Your teenage years were likely not easy, as may have felt stuck, even paralyzed. This flares up as an adult when you are confronted with tough decisions. The dynamic creates a cycle that at times can feel like you are mired in mud, but you have the internal capacity and means to pull yourself out by engaging in small, achievable tasks.

225 | *Caregiver* ⊙ *Caregiver* ⊙ *Facilitator*

All of your attributes are based in Earth, which means that your attitudes and behaviors align well with peoples' perceptions of you. In other words, what they see is what they get. The key is whether your impressions are positive or negative. When you are operating from your Primary mode, you express a desire to connect and be of service which, when paired with your Relational mode, imparts caring, attentive and organizing qualities. When you are operating from your Secondary mode, people may experience the passive-aggressive side of you, which is prone toward guilt-tripping and holding grudges. Overall, your Earth attributes result in you being grounded and self-assured in your place and purpose in the world.

234 | *Caregiver* ⊙ *Visionary* ⊙ *Optimist*

Your chart manifests two elements: Earth and Wood. Your Primary and Relational attributes are well matched, as your outward tendency to be affectionate and courteous complements your natural strengths of being nurturing and supportive. Given these combined attributes, you will tend to say yes to everything and not want to disappoint others. This can lead to a sense of depletion and lack of self-care. Your transition from Developmental to Primary was likely smooth, as you were seeking to channel your innovative ideas through service and connection. The opportunity lies in finding ways to shed some light on this dynamic and bring more realistic perspectives that will help you prioritize your commitments and draw out your creative nature.

243 | *Caregiver* ⊙ *Optimist* ⊙ *Visionary*

Your chart manifests two elements: Wood and

Earth. Your Primary and Relational attributes are well matched, as your outward tendency to be creative and interested in others complements your natural strengths at being nurturing and supportive. Given these combined attributes, you will have a tendency to say yes to everything and not want to disappoint others. This can lead to a sense of depletion and lack of self-care. The opportunity lies in finding ways to shed some light on this dynamic and bring more realistic perspectives that will help you prioritize your commitments and draw out your creative nature.

252 | *Caregiver* ⊙ *Facilitator* ⊙ *Caregiver*

All of your attributes are based in Earth, which means that your attitudes and behaviors align well with peoples' perceptions of you. In other words, what they see is what they get. The key is whether your impressions are positive or negative. When you are operating from your Primary mode, you express a desire to connect and be of service which, when paired with your Relational mode, is a perfect alignment of perception and reality. When you are operating from your Secondary mode, people may experience the manipulative and controlling side of you. Your Earth attributes result in you being grounded and self-assured in your place and purpose in the world.

261 | *Caregiver* ⊙ *Protector* ⊙ *Philosopher*

Your chart manifests three elements: Earth, Metal and Water. In relation to your Primary and Relational attributes, your preference to stay on the sidelines is aligned. However, people may be confused by the distant, intellectual nature of the Philosopher with the nurturing side of the Caregiver. This may cause you to feel trapped or stuck in a paradigm between being head- and heart-centered. Because Earth supports Metal, it is pretty easy for you to slip into your Secondary mode. The dynamics create a cycle that at times can feel like you are mired in mud, but you have the internal capacity and means to pull yourself out by engaging in small, achievable tasks.

279 | *Caregiver* ⊙ *Achiever* ⊙ *Networker*

Your profile manifests three elements: Earth, Metal and Fire. In reference to your Relational and Primary attributes, people will find your warmth and charm well matched with your caring and nurturing side. There is an inherent tension between your Relational and Secondary attributes, as your public persona to be in the moment and enjoy life competes with your drive to win. People may get confused by your intentions and actions when you are in this mode. Your transition from Developmental to Primary stages (ages 14 to 24) was likely difficult and stressful, as you were going against the grain of the Supporting cycle. To maintain balance, seek clarity and alignment to understand and be understood.

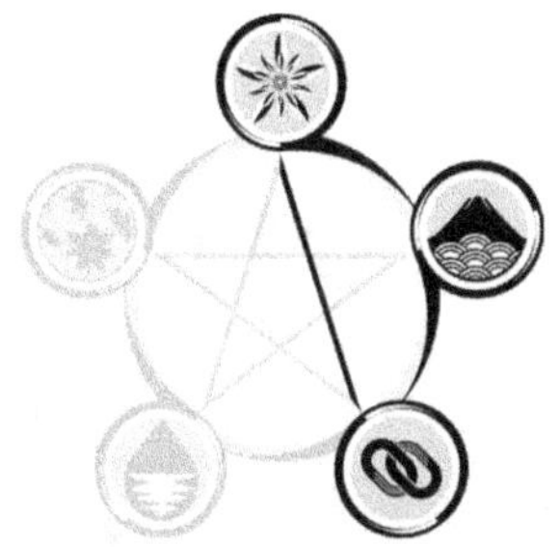

288 | *Caregiver* ⊙ *Rock* ⊙ *Rock*

All of your attributes are based in Earth, which means

that your attitudes and behaviors align well with peoples' perceptions of you. In other words, what they see is what they get, and the key is whether your impressions are positive or negative. When you are operating from your Primary mode, you express a desire to connect and be of service which, when paired with your Relational mode, imparts caring and reliable qualities. When you are operating from your Secondary mode, people may experience the stubborn, brooding side of you, which is prone to outbursts. Your Earth attributes result in you being grounded and self-assured in your place and purpose in the world.

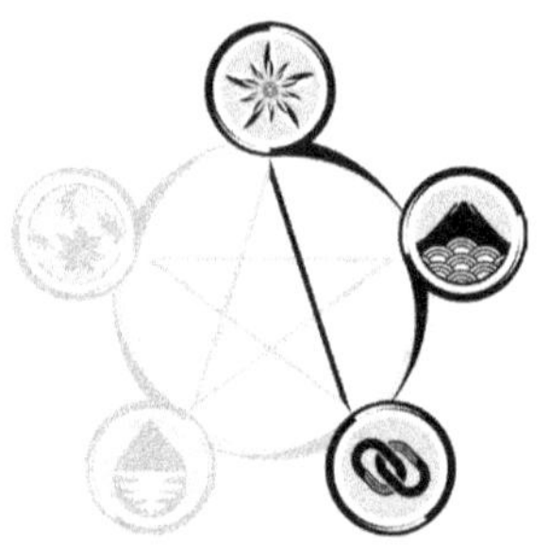

297 | *Caregiver* ⊙ *Networker* ⊙ *Achiever*

Your chart manifests three elements: Fire, Earth and Metal. In reference to your Primary and Relational attributes, people will find that your caring, nurturing side balances well with your determination and drive. The Achiever in you will keep things moving and be your self-advocate, while the Caregiver in you will foster compassion and temperance. There is an inherent tension between your Relational and Secondary attributes. Your internal drive to be in the moment and enjoy life competes with your outward desire for accomplishment. Maintain balance by striving to seek connection, consensus and stability.

317 | *Visionary* ⊙ *Philosopher* ⊙ *Achiever*

Your chart manifests three elements: Wood, Water

and Metal. The dynamics between the public persona of your Relational and Primary attributes create a sense of mystery about you. Your outward desire toward accomplishing tasks cuts into your internal drive to be open, flexible and creative. When you are operating from your Secondary mode, your tendency towards procrastination and cynicism goes against the current of your Relational tendencies to be action-oriented. You can maintain balance by seeking clarity and alignment to understand and be understood.

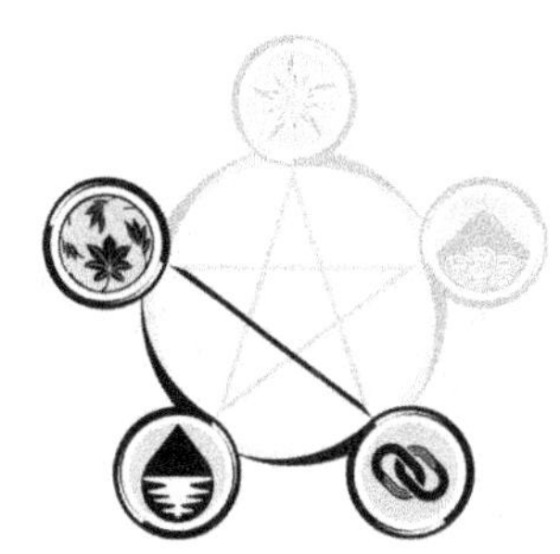

326 | *Visionary* ⊙ *Caregiver* ⊙ *Protector*

Three elements manifest in your chart: Wood, Earth and Metal. The dynamics between the public persona of your Relational with your Primary attributes create a sense of mystery about you. Your outward desire to accomplish tasks and adhere to tradition cuts into your internal drive to be open, flexible and creative. In relation to your Secondary and Relational attributes, people may look to you for guidance and strategy, but find that you are mired in process and details. This causes confusion and distress, both for yourself and others. In all that you do, be mindful of the alignment between your purpose and values with your vision and priorities.

335 | *Visionary* ⊙ *Visionary* ⊙ *Facilitator*

Your chart manifests two elements: Wood and Earth. Upon first meeting you, people get the impression that you are a Facilitator; yet as they get to know you,

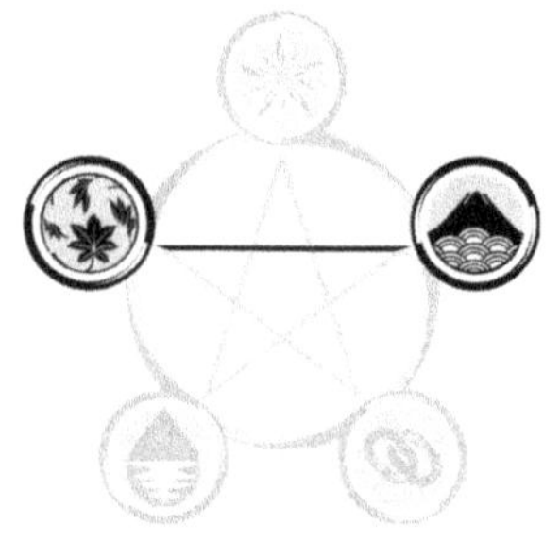

they discover that you are really a Visionary at heart. Because your Primary and Secondary attributes are identical (Visionary), your transition from childhood to adulthood was relatively smooth. People who knew you when you were a child may likely say that you haven't changed a bit. Likewise, your transition from positive to stressed mode (Primary to Secondary) is very subtle, which makes you difficult to read. If you can be transparent in communicating whether you are leading from your Primary or Secondary attribute, it will help ease your relationships with others.

344 | *Visionary* ◉ *Optimist* ◉ *Optimist*

All of your attributes are based in Wood, which means that your attitudes and behaviors align well with peoples' perceptions of you. The key is whether your impressions are positive or negative. When you are operating from your Primary mode, you are outgoing, innovative and inspirational which, when paired with your Relational mode, imparts a fun-loving and energetic person. When you are operating from your Secondary mode, people may experience the gullible and unreliable side of you. Because your Secondary and Relational attributes are the same, this can leave a lasting impression that will be hard to change. Be mindful of the alignment between your mission and values with your priorities and goals to maintain balance.

353 | *Visionary* ◉ *Caregiver* ◉ *Visionary*

Your chart manifests two elements: Wood and Earth. Since your Primary and Relational attributes are identical (Visionary), your attitudes and behaviors align well with peoples' perceptions of you. When you are in your Secondary mode, your outward tendency to be open, flexible and creative digs into your inward tendencies to control and manipulate. The opportunity lies in finding ways to shed some light on this dynamic to bring more common sense and realistic perspectives that will help you prioritize your commitments and draw out your creative nature.

362 | *Visionary* ◉ *Protector* ◉ *Caregiver*

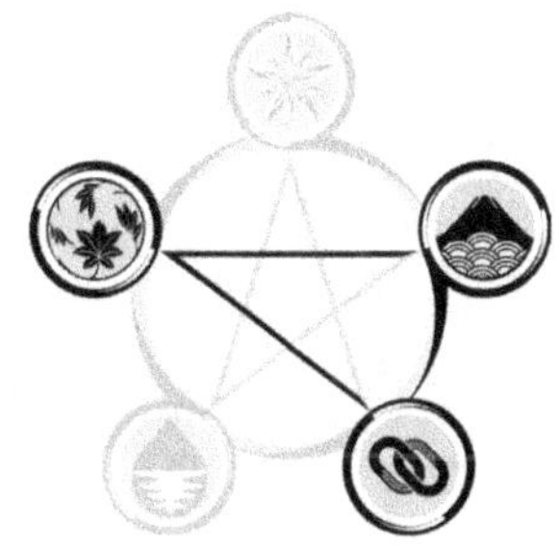

Your chart manifests three elements: Earth, Metal and Wood. The dynamics between the public persona of your Relational with your Primary elements are well aligned. Your outward desire for harmony and connection complements your inherent gift of being fun-loving and spontaneous. However, your desire to please others and tendency to be everything to everyone may deplete you. In order to remain balanced, be mindful of the alignment between your purpose and values with your priorities and goals.

371 | *Visionary* ◉ *Achiever* ◉ *Philosopher*

Your chart manifests three elements: Wood, Water and Metal. The dynamics between your Relational

and Primary attributes create a sense of mystery about you. Your outward desire toward deep, systematic thinking cuts into your internal drive to be open, flexible and creative. People may get confused by your intentions and actions, as they don't match up with who you are when you're operating at your best. To maintain balance, make sure you are confident in your vision and direction before taking action.

389 | *Visionary* ⊙ *Rock* ⊙ *Networker*

Your chart manifests three elements: Wood, Fire and Earth. The dynamics between your Relational and Primary attributes create a sense of warmth and energy that attracts people to you. Your outward desire for connection is fueled by your inner drive for knowledge and innovation. In relation to your Secondary and Relational attributes, people may look to you for clarity and inspiration, but find that you are mired in process and details. In all that you do, be mindful of the alignment between your purpose and values with your priorities and goals.

398 | *Visionary* ⊙ *Networker* ⊙ *Rock*

Your chart manifests three elements: Wood, Fire and Earth. The dynamics between your Relational and Primary attributes create a sense of mystery about you. Your inherent tendency to be fun-loving and spontaneous runs counter to your outward persona of being steady and dependable. Thus, you may not be who people expect you to be. Because

Wood fuels Fire, it is pretty easy for you to slip into your Secondary mode. You may experience difficulty breaking out of that mode and back into your Primary attribute, as you are going against the current of the Supporting cycle. In all that you do, seek solutions that involve action toward deeper understanding and impact.

418 | *Optimist* ⊙ *Philosopher* ⊙ *Rock*

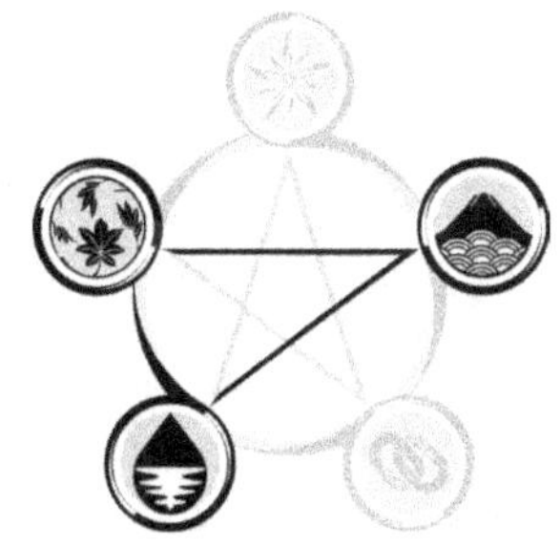

Your chart manifests three elements: Wood, Earth and Water. The dynamics between your Relational and Primary attributes create a sense of mystery about you. Your inherent tendency to be fun-loving and spontaneous runs counter to your outward persona of being steady and dependable. In relation to your Secondary and Relational attributes, your preference to stay on the sidelines is aligned. However, people may be confused by the reclusive and perhaps cynical nature of the Philosopher with the nurturing side of the Rock. In order to maintain balance, be mindful of the balance between curiosity and clarity, focus and ambiguity.

427 | *Optimist* ⊙ *Caregiver* ⊙ *Achiever*

Your chart manifests three elements: Wood, Earth and Metal. The dynamics between the public persona of your Relational and Primary attributes create a sense of mystery about you. Your outward desire toward competition and accomplishing tasks cuts into your inner drive to be open, flexible and creative.

When you are operating from your Secondary mode, your tendency towards procrastination goes against the current of your relational tendencies to be action-oriented. The dynamic between your Primary and Secondary attributes creates an internal tension that could be depleting. The opportunity lies in finding ways to shed some light on this dynamic to bring more common sense and realistic perspectives that will help you prioritize your commitments and draw out your creative nature.

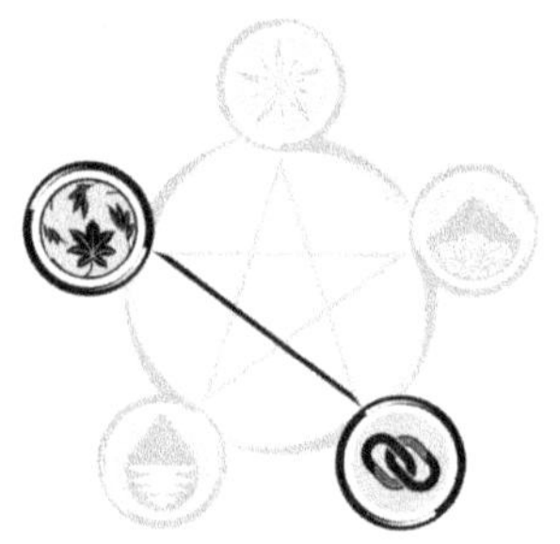

436 | *Optimist* ◉ *Visionary* ◉ *Protector*

Your chart manifests two elements: Wood and Metal. The dynamics between your Relational and Primary and Secondary attributes create a sense of mystery about you. Your outward desire to accomplish tasks and adhere to tradition cuts into your inner drive to be open, flexible and creative. Because your Primary and Secondary attributes are both in Wood, people who knew you when you were a child may likely say you haven't changed a bit. Likewise, your transition from positive to stressed mode (Primary to Secondary) is very subtle, which makes you difficult to read. If you can be transparent in communicating whether you are leading from your Primary or Secondary attribute, it will help ease your relationship with others.

445 | *Optimist* ◉ *Optimist* ◉ *Facilitator*

Your chart manifests two elements: Wood and Earth. Upon first meeting you, people get the impression that you are a Facilitator. Yet as they get to know you, they discover that your pragmatic "let's get organized" Facilitator runs counter to your spontaneous Optimist. This pattern arises especially when you are under stress. Because your Primary and Secondary attributes are identical (Optimist), people who knew you when you were a child may likely say you haven't changed a bit. Likewise, your transition from positive to stressed mode (Primary to Secondary) is very subtle, which makes you difficult to read. If you can be transparent in communicating whether you are leading from your Primary or Secondary attribute, it will help ease your relationship with others.

454 | *Optimist* ⊙ *Facilitator* ⊙ *Optimist*
Your chart manifests two elements: Earth and Wood. Since your Primary and Relational elements are identical (Optimist), what people see is what they get, and they can rely upon the consistency of your actions. When you are manifesting your Secondary attribute, the dynamic between your Primary and Relational modes creates a tension that will leave you feeling overwhelmed and depleted. The opportunity lies in finding ways to shed some light on this dynamic to bring more common sense and realistic perspectives that will help you prioritize your commitments and draw out your creative nature.

463 | *Optimist* ⊙ *Protector* ⊙ *Visionary*
Your chart manifests two elements: Metal and Wood.

When you are operating from your Primary mode, your attitudes and behaviors align well with peoples' perceptions of you, and people can rely upon the consistency of your actions. When you are operating from your Secondary mode, your drive to accomplish your tasks and adhere to tradition (Protector) cuts into your relational tendencies to be open and creative (Optimist). This creates an internal tension that could be confusing and at times paralyzing. The opportunity lies in finding ways to turn these obstructions into guideposts to bring more common sense and realistic perspectives that will frame your creative nature.

472 | *Optimist* ⊙ *Achiever* ⊙ *Caregiver*

Your chart manifests three elements: Wood, Earth and Metal. The dynamics between your Relational and Primary are well aligned. Your outward desire for harmony and connection complements your inherent gift of spreading joy and inspiration. Yet in your desire to please others, people may take advantage of your giving nature and you may end up feeling depleted. This creates an internal tension that could be confusing and at times paralyzing. There is some degree of self-sabotage caused by obstructions that you create for yourself (Metal cuts into Wood). The opportunity lies in finding ways to turn those obstructions into guideposts to bring more common sense and realistic perspectives that will frame your creative nature.

481 | *Optimist ◉ Rock ◉ Philosopher*

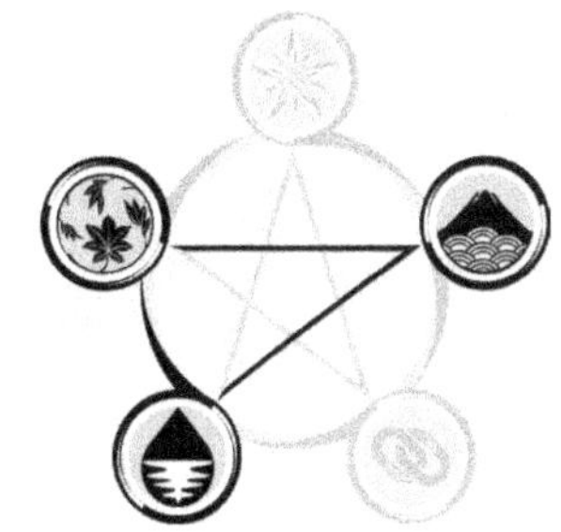

Your chart manifests three elements: Wood, Earth and Water. In general, the alignment between your public persona and leadership skills is good. There is harmony between your more thoughtful, values-anchored Philosopher and your fun-loving, inspirational Optimist. In reference to your Relational and Secondary attributes, people may be confused by the volcanic side of the Rock and the reclusive nature of the Philosopher. This may cause you to feel trapped or stuck between your outward desire to express yourself and your inner desire to want to be alone. Focusing on simple, attainable tasks will alleviate this dynamic.

499 | *Optimist ◉ Networker ◉ Networker*

Your chart manifests two elements: Wood and Fire. The dynamics between your Relational and Primary attributes create a sense of warmth and energy that attracts people to you. Your outward desire for warmth and connection is fueled by your inner drive for curiosity and joy. When you are operating from your Secondary mode, people may experience an arrogant, self-centered side of you. Because your Secondary and Relational attributes are the same, this can leave a lasting impression that will be hard to change. Make sure that you find time for reflection and relaxation to keep yourself in a positive place .

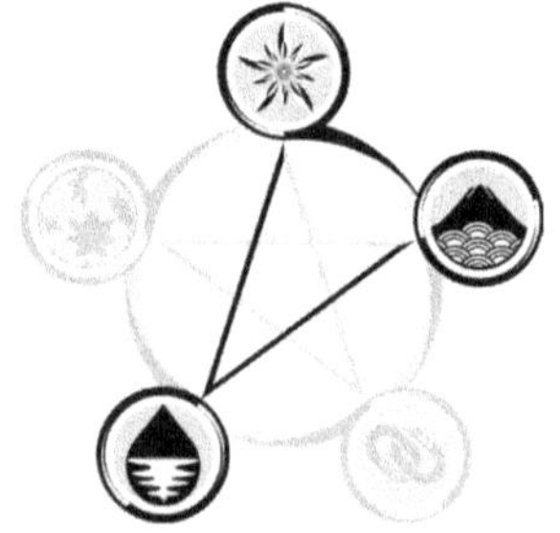

519 | *Facilitator* ◉ *Philosopher* ◉ *Networker*

Of the Five Elements, your chart manifests three: Water, Fire and Earth. In reference to your Networker and Facilitator archetypes, people will find you warmth and charm well matched with your nurturing side. When you are operating from your Philosopher mode, there is conflict with your Networker archetype. Your cynical nature runs counter to the outgoing spokesperson that people expect. The dynamics of Water in relation to Earth and Metal create a cycle that at times can feel like you are mired in mud, but you have the internal capacity and means to gain perspective on the situation by drawing on your Networker archetype.

528 | *Facilitator* ◉ *Caregiver* ◉ *Rock*

All of your attributes are based in Earth, which means that your attitudes and behaviors align well with peoples' perceptions of you. In other words, what they see is what they get, and people can rely upon the consistency of your actions and motivations with your public persona. The key is whether your impressions are positive or negative. When you are operating from your Facilitator attribute, you express a desire to connect and be of service, which when paired with your Rock archetype imparts organized and reliable qualities. When you are operating from your Secondary attribute, people may experience the passive-aggressive side of you, which is prone toward guilt-tripping and holding grudges. Your Earth attributes result in your being grounded and self-assured in your place and purpose in the world.

537 | *Facilitator* ⊙ *Visionary* ⊙ *Achiever*

Your chart manifests three elements: Earth, Metal and Wood. When you are operating from your Primary attribute, your inward tendency to organize and build consensus complements your action-oriented public persona. The dynamic between your Secondary and Primary attributes creates an internal tension that could be depleting. There is some degree of self-sabotage by overextending yourself. The key is to be mindful of the alignment between your purpose and values with your priorities and goals.

546 | *Facilitator* ⊙ *Optimist* ⊙ *Protector*

Your chart manifests three elements: Earth, Metal and Wood. When you are operating from your Primary attribute, your inward tendency to organize and build consensus complements your strategic, take-charge Relational mode. The dynamic between your Secondary and Primary attributes creates an internal tension that could be depleting. There is some degree of self-sabotage by overextending yourself. The key is to be mindful of the alignment between your purpose and values with your priorities and goals.

555 | *Facilitator ⊙ Facilitator ⊙ Facilitator*

All of your attributes are based in Earth, which means that your attitudes and behaviors align well with peoples' perceptions of you. In other words, what they see is what they get, and people can rely upon the consistency of your actions and motivations with your public persona. The key is whether your impressions are positive or negative. When you are operating from your Primary attribute, you express a desire to connect and organize which, when paired with your Relational attribute, imparts caring and reliable qualities. When you are operating from your Secondary attribute, people may experience the controlling, manipulative side of you. Because all of your attributes are the same element, this can leave a lasting impression that will be hard to change. Your Earth attributes result in you being grounded and self-assured in your place and purpose in the world.

564 | *Facilitator ⊙ Protector ⊙ Optimist*

Your chart manifests three elements: Earth, Metal and Wood. Your Primary and Relational attributes are well matched, as your outward tendency to be upbeat and courteous complements your natural strengths to seek cooperation and consensus. Given these combined attributes, you will have a tendency to say yes to everything and not want to disappoint others. This can lead to a sense of depletion and lack of self-care. When you are operating from your Secondary mode, there is conflict with your Relational attribute. Your drive to accomplish tasks and adhere to tradition cuts into your Relational tendencies to be open and creative. In all that you do, be mindful of the alignment between your purpose and values with your priorities and goals.

573 | *Facilitator* ⊙ *Achiever* ⊙ *Visionary*

Your chart manifests three elements: Earth, Metal and Wood. Your Primary and Relational attributes are well matched, as your outward tendency to be creative and interested in others complements your natural strengths at being nurturing and supportive. Given these combined attributes, you will tend to say yes to everything and not want to disappoint others. This can lead to a sense of depletion and lack of self-care. When you are operating from your Secondary mode, your drive to accomplish tasks cuts into your Relational tendencies to be open, flexible and creative. People may get confused by your attitudes and actions, as they don't match up with who you are when you're operating at your best. In all that you do, be mindful of the alignment between your purpose and values with your priorities and goals.

582 | *Facilitator* ⊙ *Rock* ⊙ *Caregiver*

All of your attributes are based in Earth, which means

that your attitudes and behaviors align well with peoples' perceptions of you. In other words, what they see is what they get, and people can rely upon the consistency of your actions and motivations with your public persona. The key is whether your impressions are positive or negative. When you are operating from your Facilitator mode, you express a desire to connect and organize which, when paired with your Caregiver archetype, imparts a caring, reliable quality. When you are operating from your Rock archetype people may experience the stubborn and volatile side of you. Your Earth attributes result in you being grounded and self-assured in your place and purpose in the world.

591 | *Facilitator* ⊙ *Networker* ⊙ *Philosopher*

Your chart manifests three elements: Water, Fire and Earth. In relation to your Primary and Relational attributes, your preference to stay on the sidelines is aligned. However, others may be confused by the distant nature of the Philosopher with the nurturing side of the Facilitator. This may cause you to feel trapped or stuck in a paradigm between being head- and heart-centered. When you are operating from your Secondary mode, your tendency to be quiet and reflective runs counter to your inner tendencies to create a scene. To maintain balance, seek creative solutions to accomplish your tasks.

611 | *Protector ⊙ Philosopher ⊙ Philosopher*

Your chart manifests two elements: Metal and Water. When you are operating from your Primary attribute, your attitudes and behaviors align well with peoples' perceptions of your Relational attribute. Your drive for integrity and order will support your outward tendency to look for deeper meaning, impact and alignment of values. Because your Secondary and Relational attributes are both in Water, people may know you as a cynic and someone who might protect through fear and doubt. The dynamics of competition and integration are also at play. In this manner, you may be your own worst enemy, establishing a standard of excellence that is too high to surmount. In all that you do, consider how to infuse fun and creativity in staying organized and connected.

629 | *Protector ⊙ Caregiver ⊙ Networker*

Your chart manifests three elements: Fire, Metal and Earth. Upon first meeting you, people get the impression that you are a Networker. Yet as they get to know you, they discover that you are really a Protector at heart. Your inspirational "let's get this party started" Networker runs counter to your practical "I've got your back" Protector. This may cause some confusion for people, as they may not be clear about how your actions match your words. In all that you do, seek clarity and alignment to understand and be understood.

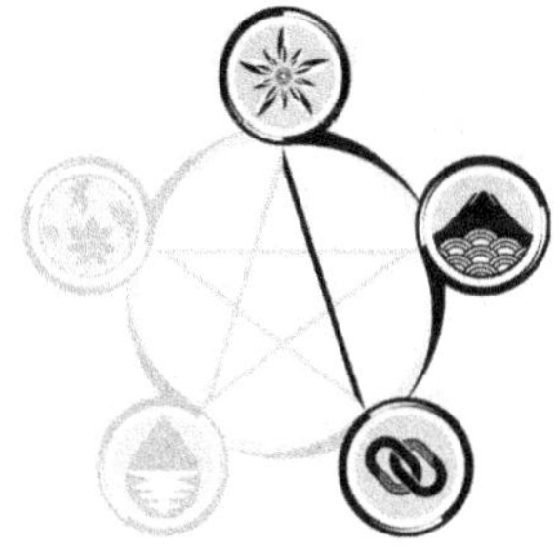

638 | *Protector ⊙ Visionary ⊙ Rock*

Your chart manifests three elements: Metal, Wood and Earth. When you are operating from your Primary mode, you are perceived as a dependable leader who will keep things safe and orderly. When you are operating from your Secondary mode, there is conflict with your Relational attribute, as your forgetful nature runs counter to the reliable Rock that people expect. At times, the dynamic between all of the elements creates an internal tension that could be confusing and paralyzing. There is some degree of self-sabotage present, as you create obstacles in your life that result in your feeling depleted. Relief comes when you are able to really be "in your element" as a Protector.

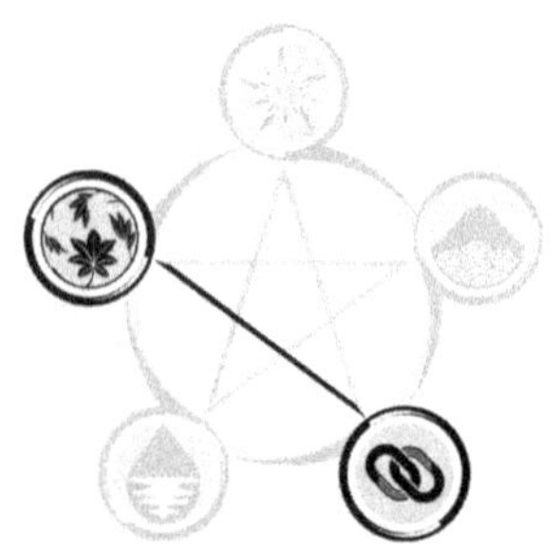

647 | *Protector ⊙ Optimist ⊙ Achiever*

Your chart manifests two elements: Metal and Wood. Since your Primary and Relational attributes are both based in Metal, your attitudes and behaviors align well with peoples' perceptions of you. The dynamics between your Relational and Secondary attributes create a sense of mystery about you. Your outward desire to accomplish tasks cuts into your inner drive to be open, flexible and creative. When stressed, you may shed your need to take responsibility for everything, sit back and say, "It's all good," and let deadlines slip by. Anchoring yourself in your mission and values will help you stay on track.

656 | *Protector ⊙ Facilitator ⊙ Protector*

Your chart manifests two elements: Metal and Earth. Since your Primary and Relational elements are identical (Protector), your attitudes and behaviors align well with peoples' perceptions of you, and they can rely upon the consistency of your actions. Since Earth supports Metal, your transition from Developmental to Primary (the period of your late-teens and early-20s) was relatively smooth. In fact, you may have developed your Primary traits in your early teens and felt a sense of relief in getting to your Primary mode. It's important for you to stay grounded, focusing on systems, processes and relationships to keep you balanced .

665 | *Protector ⊙ Protector ⊙ Facilitator*

Your chart manifests two elements: Earth and Metal. Upon first meeting you, people get the impression that you are a Facilitator. Yet as they get to know you, they discover that you are really a Protector at heart. At times, your pragmatic "let's get organized" Facilitator complements your "I've got your back" Protector. But when you're under stress, there may be a conflict between your consensus-building Facilitator and your "it's my way or the highway" Protector. Because your Primary and Secondary attributes are identical (Protector), you tend to isolate yourself from others. If you can be transparent in communicating whether you are leading from your

Primary or Secondary attribute, it will help ease your relationship with others.

674 | *Protector* ◉ *Achiever* ◉ *Optimist*

Your chart manifests two elements: Metal and Wood. Upon first meeting you, people get the impression that you are an Optimist. Yet as they get to know you, they discover that you are really a Protector at heart. Your practical, take-charge approach runs counter to your "it's all good" Optimist. People will conclude that you are not who they thought you were and their first impression was incorrect. This dynamic is more pronounced when you are in your Secondary mode. Because your Primary and Secondary attributes are both Metal, your transition from positive to stressed mode is very subtle, which makes you difficult to read. If you can be transparent in communicating whether you are leading from your Primary or Secondary attribute, it will help ease your relationship with others.

683 | *Protector* ◉ *Rock* ◉ *Visionary*

Your chart manifests three elements: Metal, Wood and Earth. Upon first meeting you, people get the impression that you are a Visionary. Yet as they get to know you, they discover that you are really a Protector at heart. Your practical, take-charge approach runs counter to your "anything's possible" Visionary. People will conclude that you are not who they thought you were and their first impression was incorrect. The dynamic between all of the attributes creates an internal tension that could be confusing in the least and at times paralyzing. There is some degree of self- sabotage present, as you create obstacles in your life that result in your feeling depleted. Relief comes when you are able to really be "in your element" as a Protector.

692 | *Protector* ⊙ *Visionary* ⊙ *Caregiver*

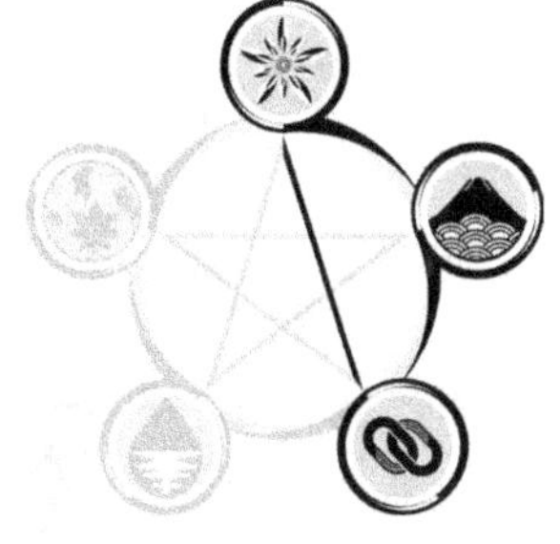

Your chart manifests three elements: Fire, Earth and Metal. When you are operating from your Primary attribute, your attitudes and behaviors align with characteristics of a caring parent, embodying the right balance between the archetypical mother (Caregiver) and father (Protector). When you go into stress, it is a step backward from Protector to Networker mode, indicating a big resistance to go there. People will rarely see you in the Diva mode. Instead, you likely act out the negative characteristics through your Protector attribute (the Dictator). Your internal drive to build walls and isolate yourself competes with your outward desire for harmony. People won't know how to support you in these times. In all that you do, seek clarity and alignment to understand and be understood.

712 | *Achiever* ⊙ *Philosopher* ⊙ *Caregiver*

Your chart manifests three elements: Metal, Water and Earth. Your inner drive for accomplishment competes with your outward desire for harmony and

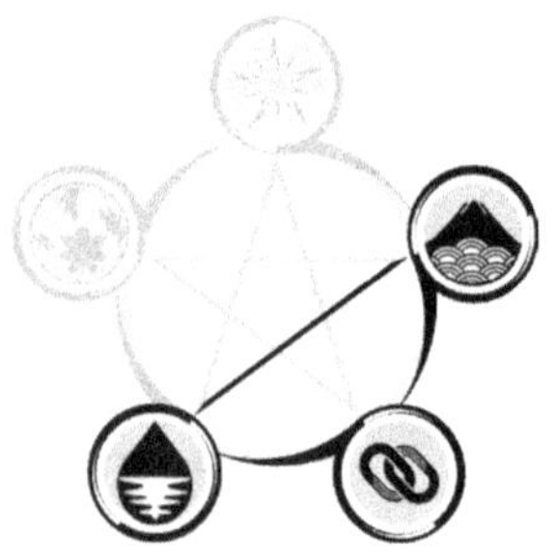

connection. This may cause some internal stress, as you try to please everyone but also feel compelled to just get the job done. Because Metal flows into Water, it is easy for you to slip into your Secondary mode. Once you get into your reclusive, cynical mode, it is hard to draw you out. The dynamics of these three elements create a cycle that at times can feel like you are mired in mud, but you have the internal capacity and means to pull yourself out by engaging in small, achievable tasks.

721 | *Achiever* ⊙ *Caregiver* ⊙ *Philosopher*

Your chart manifests three elements: Water, Earth and Metal. When you are operating from your Primary attribute, your drive to accomplish tasks will support your outward tendency to look for deeper meaning and impact. In reference to your Relational and Secondary attributes, the reclusive nature of both may cause you to feel trapped or stuck. People will tend to leave you alone, thinking that you will find your way out. Engaging in small, achievable tasks will help you stay on the generative side of your attributes.

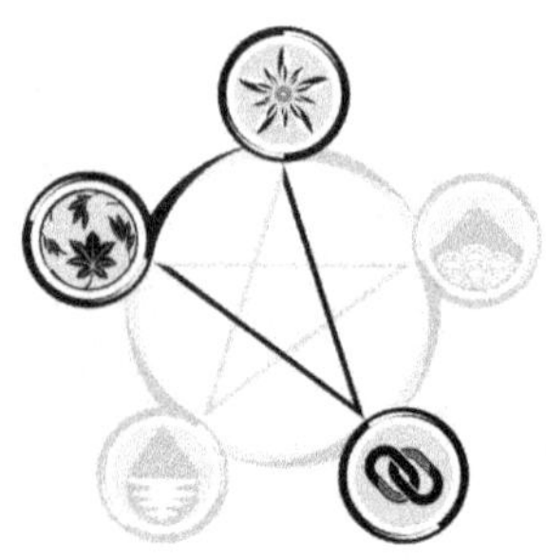

739 | *Achiever* ⊙ *Visionary* ⊙ *Networker*

Your chart manifests three elements: Metal, Wood and Fire. Upon first meeting you, people get the impression that you are a Networker. Yet as they get to know you, they discover that your inspirational "let's get this party started" Networker runs counter to your practical "let's do it" Achiever. This may cause some confusion for people, as they may not be clear about what you are doing. The dynamic between all of the elements creates an internal tension that could be confusing in the least and at times paralyzing. There is some degree of self-sabotage present as you create obstacles in your life that result in your feeling depleted. Relief comes when you are able to really be "in your element" as an Achiever.

748 | *Achiever* ◉ *Optimist* ◉ *Rock*

Your chart manifests three elements: Metal, Earth and Wood. When you are operating from your Achiever mode, you are perceived as a person who can be accountable for getting things done. When you are operating from your Optimist mode, your forgetful nature runs counter to the reliable Rock that others expect. People may get confused by your attitudes and actions, as they don't match up with who you are when you're operating at your best. The dynamic between all of the elements creates an internal tension that could be confusing in the least and at times paralyzing. There is some degree of self-sabotage present, as you create obstacles in your life that result in your feeling depleted. Relief comes when you are able to really be "in your element" as an Achiever.

757 | *Achiever* ◉ *Facilitator* ◉ *Achiever*

Your chart manifests two elements: Metal and

Earth. Since your Primary and Relational elements are identical (Achiever), your attitudes and behaviors align well with peoples' perceptions of you. Since Earth supports Metal, your transition from Facilitator to Achiever (the period of your late-teens and early-20s) was relatively smooth. In fact, you may have developed your Primary traits in your early teens and felt a sense of relief in getting to your Primary mode. It's important for you to stay grounded and focus on systems, processes, and relationships to keep you balanced.

766 | *Achiever* ⊙ *Protector* ⊙ *Protector*

All of your attributes are based in Metal, which means that your attitudes and behaviors align well with peoples' perceptions of you, and they can rely upon the consistency of your actions and motivations with your public persona. The key is whether your impressions are positive or negative. When you are operating from your Primary mode, you are driven and goal-oriented which, when paired with your Relational mode, reveals a leader who gets things done. When you are operating from your Secondary mode, people may experience the arrogant, domineering and judgmental side of you. Because your Secondary and Relational attributes are the same, this can leave a lasting impression that will be hard to change. In all that you do, lean on the strength of your relationships to understand and be understood.

775 | *Achiever* ⊙ *Achiever* ⊙ *Facilitator*

Your chart manifests two elements: Metal and Earth. Your pragmatic "let's get organized" Facilitator complements your "let's do it" Achiever. But when you're under stress, there may be a conflict between your consensus-building Facilitator and your "win at all costs" Achiever. This may cause some confusion for people, as they may not be clear on your motivations. If you can be transparent in communicating whether you are leading from your Primary or Secondary attribute, it will help ease your relationships with others.

784 | *Achiever* ⊙ *Rock* ⊙ *Optimist*

Your chart manifests three elements: Metal, Earth and Wood. Upon first meeting you, people get the impression that you are an Optimist. But as they get to know you, your practical "let's do it" Achiever runs counter to your "anything is possible" Optimist. People will conclude that you are not who they thought you were and their first impression was incorrect. Your steady, responsible and sometimes stubborn Rock runs counter to the free-thinking Optimist that people thought you were. The dynamic between all of the arrows creates an internal tension that could be confusing in the least and at times paralyzing. There is some degree of self-sabotage between who you really are and who you project to be (Metal cutting into Wood). Staying anchored in your mission and values will keep you focused.

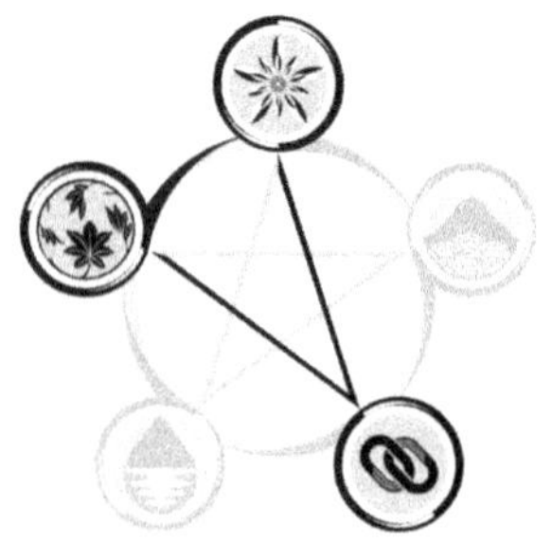

793 | *Achiever ⊙ Networker ⊙ Visionary*

Your chart manifests three elements: Metal, Fire and Wood. Upon first meeting you, people get the impression that you are a Visionary. Yet as they get to know you, they discover that your practical "let's do it" approach runs counter to your "anything is possible" Visionary. People will conclude that you are not who they thought you were and their first impression was inaccurate. When you are operating from your Secondary mode, there is conflict with your Visionary. Your tendency to act out and be self-centered goes against your Relational tendencies to be upbeat and curious of others. The dynamic between all of the arrows creates an internal tension that could be confusing in the least and at times paralyzing. Seek connections and support to understand and be understood.

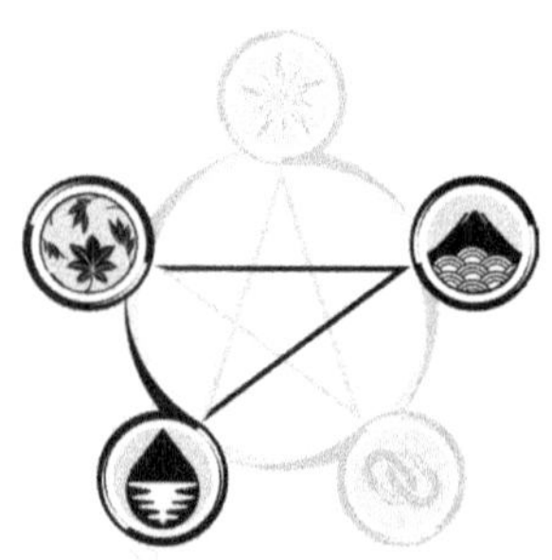

813 | *Rock ⊙ Philosopher ⊙ Visionary*

Your chart manifests three elements: Earth, Water and Wood. Your Primary and Relational attributes are well matched, as your outward tendency to be creative and interested in others complements your natural strengths at being nurturing and supportive. Given these combined attributes, you will tend to say yes to everything and not want to disappoint others. This can lead to a sense of depletion and lack of self-care. Keeping your eye on the goal and staying focused on the vision will keep you balanced.

822 | *Rock ◉ Caregiver ◉ Caregiver*

All of your attributes are based in Earth, which means that your attitudes and behaviors align well with peoples' perceptions of you, and they can rely upon the consistency of your actions and motivations with your public persona. The key is whether your impressions are positive or negative. When you are operating from your Rock mode, you are steady and resourceful which, when paired with your Caregiver mode, imparts caring, attentive and dependable qualities. When you are operating from your Secondary mode, people may experience the needy side of you (the Martyr). Your Earth attributes result in your being grounded and self-assured in your place and purpose in the world. Because you focus so much on others, self-care is a low priority. Keeping your eye on the goal and staying focused on the vision will keep you balanced.

831 | *Rock ◉ Visionary ◉ Philosopher*

Your chart manifests three elements: Earth, Water and Wood. In relation to your Primary and Relational attributes, your preference to stay on the sidelines are aligned, but people may be confused by the distant, intellectual nature of the Philosopher with the nurturing side of the Rock. This may cause you to feel trapped or stuck in a paradigm between being head- and heart-centered. The opportunity lies in finding ways to shed some light on this dynamic to bring more common sense and realistic perspectives that will help you prioritize your commitments and draw out your creative nature.

849 | *Rock* ⊙ *Optimist* ⊙ *Networker*

Your chart manifests three elements: Wood, Fire and Earth. Your Rock and Fire elements are well matched, as your outward tendency to be affectionate and courteous complements your natural strengths at being nurturing and supportive. Given these combined attributes, you will have a tendency to say yes to everything and not want to disappoint others. This can lead to a sense of depletion and lack of self-care. Keeping your eye on the goal and staying focused on the vision will keep you balanced.

858 | *Rock* ⊙ *Facilitator* ⊙ *Rock*

All of your attributes are based in Earth, which means that your attitudes and behaviors align well with peoples' perceptions of you. In other words, what they see is what they get, and people can rely upon the consistency of your actions. The key is whether your impressions are positive or negative. When you are operating from your Primary mode, you are steady and resourceful, which is perfectly aligned with your Relational attribute. When you are operating from your Secondary mode, people may experience the manipulative, controlling side of you. Your Earth attributes result in you being grounded and self-assured in your place and purpose in the world. Keeping your eye on the goal and staying focused on the vision will keep you balanced.

867 | *Rock* ⊙ *Protector* ⊙ *Achiever*

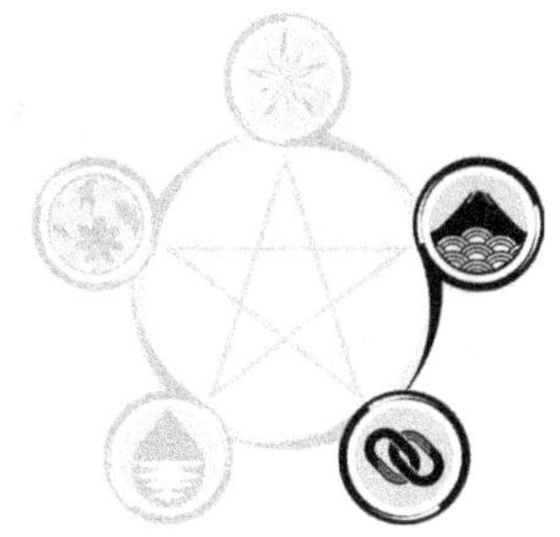

Your chart manifests two elements: Earth and Metal. In reference to your Rock and Achiever archetypes, people will find that your steadfast nature balances well with your determination and drive. The Achiever in you will keep things moving, while the Rock in you will foster patience and perspective. When you are operating from your Secondary mode, you may be prone to arrogance and even bullying, and people will keep their distance from you. The combination of these elements indicates a sense of self-containment that may be unhealthy. Seeking community support will ensure that you stay in your Primary attribute.

876 | *Rock* ⊙ *Achiever* ⊙ *Protector*

Your chart manifests two elements: Earth and Metal. In reference to your Rock and Protector archetypes, people will find that your steadfast nature balances well with your desire to lead others. The Protector in you will provide order, while the Rock in you will foster patience and stability. When you are operating from your Secondary mode, you may be prone to meanness, and people will keep their distance from you. The combination of these elements indicates a sense of self-containment that may be unhealthy.

Seeking community support will ensure that you stay in your Primary attribute.

885 | *Rock* ⊙ *Rock* ⊙ *Facilitator*

All of your attributes are based in Earth, which means that your attitudes and behaviors align well with peoples' perceptions of you. In other words, what they see is what they get, and people can rely upon the consistency of your actions. The key is whether your impressions are positive or negative. When you are operating from your Secondary mode, people may experience the stubborn and volatile side of you. Because your Secondary and Relational attributes are the same element, this can leave a lasting impression that will be hard to change. Your Earth attributes result in you being grounded and self-assured in your place and purpose in the world. Keeping your eye on the goal and staying focused on the vision will keep you balanced.

894 | *Rock* ⊙ *Networker* ⊙ *Optimist*

Your chart manifests three elements: Wood, Fire and Earth. Your Primary and Relational attributes are well matched as your outward tendency to be affectionate and courteous complements your natural strengths at being nurturing and supportive. Given these combined attributes, you will tend to say yes to everything and not want to disappoint others. This can lead to a sense of depletion and lack of self-care. Focusing on practical, achievable tasks will help you stay in balance.

914 | *Networker ⊙ Philosopher ⊙ Optimist*

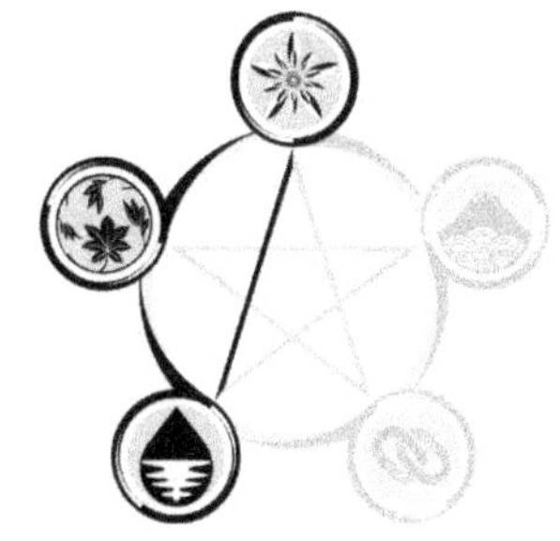

Your chart manifests three elements: Fire, Wood and Water. There is harmony between your more innovative, inspiring Optimist and the intuitive communication skills of your Networker archetypes. When you move to your Secondary mode, your tendency towards procrastination and cynicism goes against the current of your Relational tendencies to be positive and innovative. Seeking support from community to accomplish your tasks will keep you in your Primary mode.

923 | *Networker ⊙ Caregiver ⊙ Visionary*

Your chart manifests three elements: Fire, Wood and Earth. There is a harmony between your more innovative, inspiring Visionary and the intuitive communication skills of your Networker archetypes. When you are operating from your Secondary mode, there is conflict with your Relational attribute. Your outward tendency to be open, flexible and creative digs into your inner tendencies to please everyone. You may be overwhelmed and depleted by this dynamic. Anchor yourself in your purpose and values, so you can stay focused on your priorities.

932 | *Networker* ⊙ *Visionary* ⊙ *Caregiver*
Your chart manifests three elements: Fire, Wood and Earth. Your complementary qualities of connecting (Networker) and nurturing (Caregiver) make you a warm, dependable advocate and friend. When you are operating from your Secondary mode, your tendency to be self-absorbed runs counter to the nurturing Caregiver that people expect. People may get confused by your attitudes and actions, as they don't match up with their expectations. Focus on seeking solutions that involve action toward deeper understanding and impact.

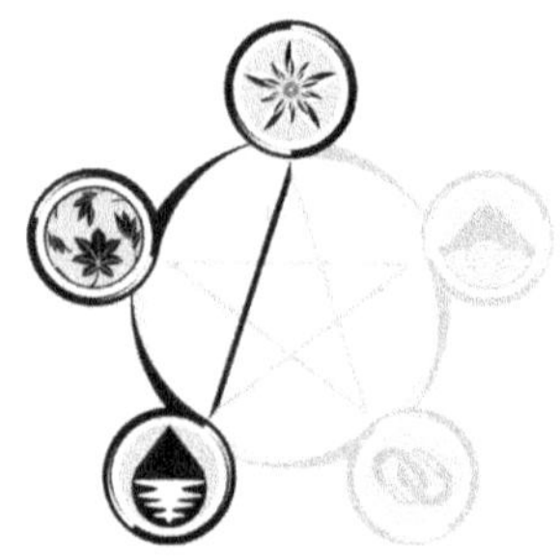

941 | *Networker* ⊙ *Optimist* ⊙ *Philosopher*
Your chart manifests three elements: Fire, Wood and Water. The dynamics between the public persona of your Philosopher with your Networker archetypes create a sense of mystery about you. Your calling to be quiet and reflective conflicts with your internal drive to be social and in the center of things. People may get confused by your intentions and actions, as they don't match up with who you are when you're operating at your best. In relation to your Secondary attribute, people may look to you for wisdom, but find that you are lost in the clouds. This causes confusion and distress, both for yourself and others, as the directions are not clear and anchored. You can counter this effect by seeking confidence and unity toward a plan of action.

959 | *Networker* ◉ *Facilitator* ◉ *Networker*

Your chart manifests two elements: Fire and Earth. Since your Primary and Relational attributes are identical (Networker), your attitudes and behaviors align well with peoples' perceptions of you. When you are operating from your Facilitator mode, your outward tendency to be open and flexible digs into your inner tendencies to control and manipulate. People may get confused by your attitudes and actions, as they don't match up with who you are when you're operating under stress. You may find yourself up nights worrying, especially about unfounded perceptions. The opportunity lies in finding ways to shed some light on this dynamic to bring more common sense and realistic perspectives that will help you prioritize your commitments and draw out your intuitive nature.

968 | *Networker* ◉ *Protector* ◉ *Rock*

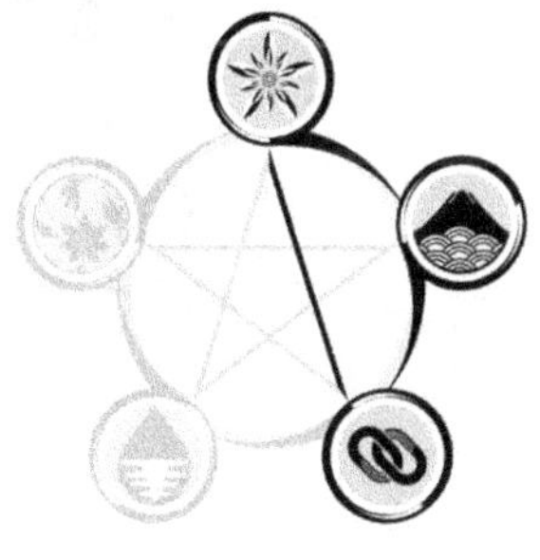

Your chart manifests three elements: Fire, Earth and Metal. Your complementary qualities of connecting (Networker) and nurturing (Rock) make you a dependable advocate and friend. Your transition from Protector to Networker (the period of your late-teens and early-20s) was likely not an easy one, feeling under fire. You likely experienced a series of meltdowns during this period, which flares up as an adult when you are not in charge. Seeking clarity and alignment to understand and be understood will support your ability to stay balanced.

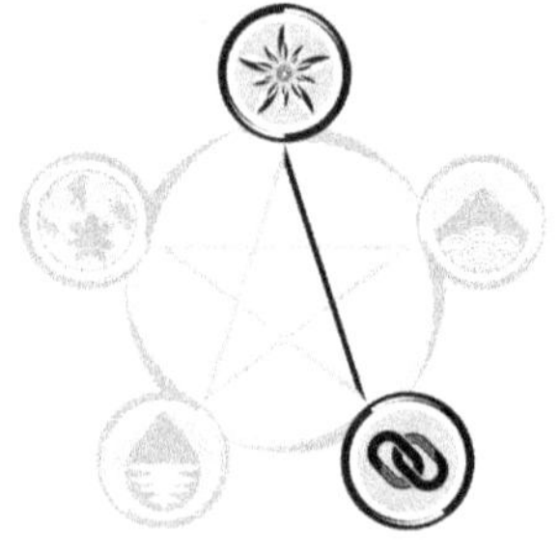

977 | *Networker* ⊙ *Achiever* ⊙ *Achiever*

Your chart manifests two elements: Fire and Metal. Your inspirational "spread the love" Networker runs counter to your practical "let's do it" Achiever. This creates an internal tension that could either really sharpen your focus and intensity, or lead to a total meltdown. Your transition from Protector to Networker (the period of your late-teens and early-20s) was likely not an easy one, feeling under fire. You likely experienced a series of meltdowns during this period, which flares up as an adult when you are not in charge. Seeking clarity and alignment in your purpose and priorities will support your ability to stay balanced.

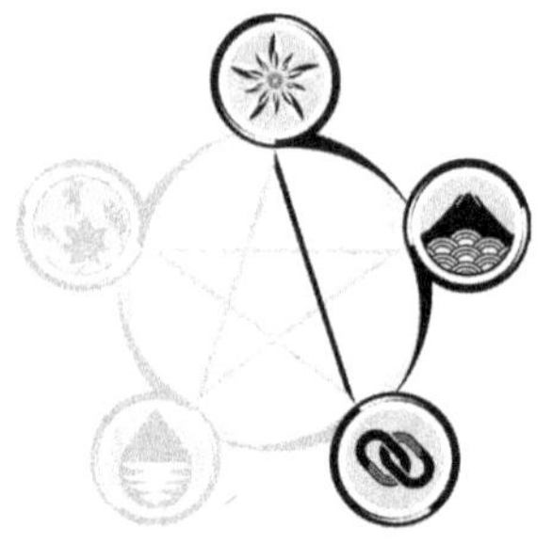

986 | *Networker* ⊙ *Rock* ⊙ *Protector*

Your chart manifests three elements: Fire, Earth and Metal. Your inspirational "spread the love" Networker runs counter to your practical, serious "I've got your back" Protector nature. This may cause some confusion for people, as they may not be clear on your intentions. Your transition from Rock to Networker (the period of your late-teens and early-20s) was likely not an easy one, feeling under fire. You likely experienced a sense of apprehension, as there was pressure (internal or external) for you to step out on the stage, when all you wanted to do was quietly retreat. Seeking clarity and alignment in your purpose and priorities will support your ability to stay balanced.

995 | *Networker ☉ Networker ☉ Facilitator*

Your chart manifests two elements: Fire and Earth. Your complementary qualities of connecting (Networker) and coordinating (Facilitator) make you a warm, organized advocate and friend. If people meet you under stress, they may find that you are leading with a self-serving agenda that does not engender trust or confidence. Because your Primary and Secondary attributes are identical (Networker), your transition from childhood to adulthood was relatively smooth. People who knew you when you were a child may likely say you haven't changed a bit. If you can be transparent in communicating whether you are leading from your Primary or Secondary attribute, it will help ease your relationships with others.

APPENDIX III

SUMMARY *of* RECOMMENDATIONS *for* EACH PROFILE

Just Add Water

Featured Element: Water

Recommendations for Profiles 436, 463, 647, 674

In everything that you do, seek to understand and be understood.

The body parts that correlate with Water are the ears. Therefore, start and end your day listening to your favorite music or an inspiring message that connects you to your deeper purpose.

Be an advocate for Water through language that inspires strategic thinking and values integration. Consider these questions:

- ◉ How does this topic or activity align with my mission and vision?

- ◉ How does this topic or activity support my culture and values?

- ◉ What does the data tell me? How can I stay on course with the facts?

- ◉ What systems do I need in place to keep things flowing?

- ◉ How does what I'm doing feed my soul?

- ◉ Before I move forward, let's reflect on this and make sure I am all clear on my purpose and direction.

If you need to ponder or talk about something serious, take a walk near a body of water or meet over a cup of tea.

In your office and personal spaces, add colors (blue or black) and objects (a fountain, black and white photos, seashells, watercolor paintings, a bowl of water) that reflect Water. Consider using blue or sea-green bedding.

Wear blue or black clothes and accents (scarf or tie), especially if you are under stress or speaking in public. Wear water-derived (pearls) or water-inspired jewelry like turquoise, lapis and blue topaz.

Keep yourself hydrated, especially with warm drinks.

Live near or regularly visit a body of water. Engage in activities that involve water, such as boating, fishing, surfing and swimming.

Develop a practice or activity that you can do alone or with a group that involves hearing/listening—music, podcasts, audio books, storytelling or the spoken word.

Cultivate stillness. Take time each day to be silent and listen to the unspoken messages that may arise.

A hot bath or shower is highly recommended!

Tend the Garden
Featured Element: Wood
Recommendations for Profiles 914 959, 995

In all that you do, hold a sense of curiosity and wonder toward a new way of imagining the world.

The body parts that correlate with Wood are the hands and feet. Start and end your day with a quick hand or foot massage, focusing on what's in store for the future.

Be an advocate for Wood through language that inspires learning, innovation and optimism. Consider these questions:

⊙ What are three out-of-the-box ways I can do to get this job done?

- ⊙ How does this topic or activity allow me to stay on the cutting edge?

- ⊙ How does this topic or activity differentiate me from the competition?

- ⊙ What have I not tried? What am I missing?

- ⊙ Am I having fun yet?

Be very visual with your processes; chart, write and draw things out so you can focus.

Rub your hands together for energy.

In your office and personal spaces, add colors (green) and objects (plants, wood furniture, frames and accessories) that symbolize Wood. Lamps that illuminate upward also invoke Wood. Consider using green or wood-toned bedding.

Wear green clothes and accents (scarf or tie), especially if you are under stress or speaking in public. Wear wood-derived or wood-inspired jewelry such as aquamarine, garnet and sapphire.

If you need to ponder or talk about something serious, take a walk outside, especially among trees.

Develop a meditation or reflection practice that involves movement, especially coordination with the hands and feet. Take a dance, *tai chi* or gymnastics class. Gardening is the best activity to cultivate Wood.

Let the Sun Shine In

Featured Element: Fire
Recommendations for Profiles 234, 243, 297, 335, 353, 445, 454, 472

In all that you do, seek confidence, clarity and alignment.

The body part that correlates with Fire is the eyes. It is important to be aware of how you view the world and how the world views you. Start and end your day with a visualization of the message or impression you wish to impart on others.

Be an advocate for Fire through language that inspires people to expand and connect. Consider these questions:

- How can I shed some light on this topic and look at the big picture?

- Am I seeing things eye to eye with others?

- Am I clear on my intention, messages and priorities?

- What can I do or say to get people to support and join my effort?

- How does this topic or activity improve my reputation and image?

⊙ How does this topic or activity lead to new or expanded opportunities?

Be very visual with your processes; chart, write and draw things out so you can focus.

Rub your hands together for energy.

In your office and personal spaces, add colors (red, purple) and objects (candles, plants with red or purple leaves) that symbolize Fire. Consider using red or purple bedding.

Wear red or purple clothes and accents (scarf or tie), especially if you are under stress or speaking in public. Wear fire-inspired jewelry such as opal, amber or ruby.

If you need to ponder or talk about something serious, take a walk in the sun or light a candle.

Cultivate discernment by drawing out your ideas before talking about them.

Take a least three photos each day to sharpen your sense of vision, both what you see and what you don't see. You do not have to share your photos.

Develop a meditation or reflection practice that you can do alone or with a group that involves visual movement. Take a dance, *tai chi*, photography or painting class.

Get Grounded

Featured Element: Earth
Recommendations for Profiles 297, 656, 665, 757, 775 977

In all that you do, seek connection, consensus and stability.

The body part that correlates with Earth is the abdomen. Start and end your day by rubbing your hands together and placing them on your belly. When in doubt or in need of reassurance, rub your belly and breathe into your abdomen. Trust your gut.

Be an advocate for Earth through language that nurtures and supports. Consider these questions:

⊙ Before I get started, how should I establish our ground rules?

⊙ How does this topic or activity support or not support group confidence, cohesion and morale?

⊙ What are the needs and implications from a human perspective? What are the operational needs?

⊙ What do we need to do work together in a spirit of support?

⊙ Let's dig in!

In your office and personal spaces, add colors (brown, yellow, orange) and objects (rocks, earthenware) that symbolize Earth. Consider using earth-toned bedding.

Wear earth-toned clothing or accents (a scarf or a tie) everyday, especially if you are under stress or speaking in public. Wear earth-inspired jewelry such as quartz, jade or tiger eye.

Try to have direct contact with Earth (bare hands and feet to the ground) every day.

Develop a practical nature to all aspects of your life. Intentionally give and seek support every day. Do something that builds your community every day; for instance, have daily contact with a friend or loved one, make a daily to-do list or cook more often.

If you need to ponder or talk about something serious, take a walk and find a way to connect directly to the Earth. Have modeling clay or blocks on hand to build out your ideas instead of talking about them.

Develop a meditation or reflection practice that you do with a group that engages in community service. Your best spiritual food is helping others.

Put the Pedal to the Metal
Featured Element: Metal
Recommendations for Profiles 115, 151

In all that you do, seek solutions that involve action.

The body part that correlates with Metal is the head. Invoking Metal means thinking strategically. The head and body are always in alignment with the mission to be accomplished.

Start and end your day with a quick scalp massage to engage your mind with your body.

Be an advocate for Metal through language that inspires right action and results. Consider these questions:

- What is the fastest way I can get this out the door?

- How can I make these ideas actionable?

- What three things can I accomplish today?

- Who or what is holding me up?

- How can I maximize my gain with the least effort?

- Let's do it!

Identify small tasks that you can accomplish in a short period of time. Think daily or weekly tasks versus monthly or annual tasks. By breaking your big goals into small steps, you will be less prone to procrastination. When you accomplish those tasks, make sure you celebrate.

In your office and personal spaces, add colors (gold, grey, silver) and objects that symbolize Metal. Consider using white, gold or grey bedding.

Wear white, grey or gold clothing or accents (a scarf or a tie), especially if you are under stress or speaking in public. Wear metal-derived (gold, silver, copper) or metal-inspired jewelry such as hematite, moonstone or cat's eye.

Take regular walking breaks and try to stand or move around while working.

When in doubt, seek counsel from mentors or trusted colleagues. You don't have to go it alone.

Develop a meditation or reflection practice that you can do alone or with a group that involves kinesthetic activity. Brisk, aerobic exercise and breathwork is ideal. Mix exercise with a project, such as gardening or construction.

Water the Seeds

Featured Elements: Water ↦ Wood

Recommendations for Profiles 279, 317, 629, 692, 968, 986

This represents early spring as the seedlings emerge from the frozen ground. It marks the sign of new beginnings.

In all that you do, seek clarity and alignment to understand and be understood.

Be an advocate for the transition of Water to Wood through language that inspires clarity through the creative process. Consider these questions:

- ⊙ What are three out-of-the-box ways I can do to accomplish our mission?

- ⊙ How can I build upon my past experiences?

- ⊙ Where do I have a common understanding with others?

- ⊙ What do I need to release or reinvent into order move forward in a good way?

- ⊙ Am I having fun yet?

Listen intently, then be very visual with your processes; chart, write and draw things out so you can focus.

Rub your hands together for energy.

In your office and personal spaces, add colors (red, purple, blue) and objects (candles, fountains) that symbolize Water and Fire. Consider using blue and green bedding.

Arrange your meeting space to allow for maximum creativity. Take away the desks and tables, play some music, and allow for room to explore new ways of thinking.

Wear red, purple or blue clothes and accents (a scarf or a tie), especially if you are under stress or speaking in public. Wear water-derived (pearls) or water- and wood-inspired jewelry like turquoise, lapis, blue topaz, aquamarine, garnet and sapphire.

If you need to ponder or talk about something serious, have some hot coffee or tea. Light a candle or take a walk near water.

Develop a meditation or reflection practice that you can do alone or with a group that involves the ears and the eyes. Do something you can listen to and apply visually, like a dance, tai chi, painting or a photography class.

Feed the Fire

Featured Elements: Wood ⊢→ Fire

Recommendations for Profile 178, 187, 216, 261, 418, 712, 721, 849, 867, 876

This transition is about preparation and anticipation, as the concept of a Fire suggests a meal or a gathering, both of which involve the combining of different things to form a cohesive whole.

In all that you do, be mindful of the balance between curiosity and clarity, focus and ambiguity.

Be an advocate for Wood and Fire through language that leads to a win-win outcome. Consider these questions:

⊙ How can I narrow these ideas down to set me up for success?

⊙ Which of these ideas will be the most unique and effective?

⊙ Which of these ideas bring out my best thinking?

⊙ How do these ideas align with my current skills and capacity?

- ◉ What are the specific pros and cons of each idea?

- ◉ Where are the unforeseen shadows?

Listen intently, then be very visual with your processes; chart, write and draw things out so you can focus.

Rub your hands together for energy.

In your office and personal spaces, add colors (red, purple, green) and objects (candles, plants) that symbolize Wood and Fire.

Wear red, purple and green clothes or accents (a scarf or a tie) to bring focus and attention. Wear wood-derived or wood- and fire-inspired jewelry like aquamarine, garnet, sapphire, opal, amber and ruby.

Be more deliberate and formal in setting your meeting space. Have chairs and tables set up on an orderly fashion with space to walk around and post things on the walls.

If you need to ponder or talk about something serious, light a candle or take a walk in a wooded area.

Develop a meditation or reflection practice that involves visual movement. Take a dance, *tai chi*, painting or a photography class.

Lay Your Foundation
Featured Elements: Fire ↦ Earth
Recommendations for Profile 371

The transition from Fire to Earth is like a lava flow that has cooled and begun to settle into fertile, mineral-rich soil. Concepts and visions become tangible teams, facilities and organizations. As the container is created, the commitment deepens.

In all that you do, seek confidence and unity.

Be an advocate for Fire and Earth through language that allows the group and the shared vision to lead the process. Consider these questions:

- ◉ What do I specifically need to know in order to move forward with confidence?

- ◉ Let's make sure everyone is clear on their roles and responsibilities.

- ◉ I feel great now that the vision is clear. Let's get organized and move forward.

Listen intently, then be very visual with your processes; chart, write and draw things out so you can focus.

Rub your hands together for energy.

In your office and personal spaces, add colors (red, purple, green) and objects (candles, plants) that symbolize Wood and Fire.

Wear deeper earth-toned clothes and accents like brown, burgundy, orange or plum to provide a sense of ease and unity. Wear fire- and earth-inspired jewelry such as opal, amber, ruby, quartz, jade and tiger eye.

Have a more open meeting arrangement that encourages dialogue and equity. Chairs arranged in a circle is ideal.

If you need to ponder or talk about something serious, light a candle or take a walk in the sun.

Develop a meditation or reflection practice that you can do alone or with a group that involves teamwork or community building.

Get it in Gear
Featured Elements: Earth ↦ Metal
Recommendations for Profile 115, 151

In all that you do, seek confidence and unity toward a plan of action.

Be an advocate for Earth and Metal through language that keeps the group coordinated and motivated. Consider these statements and questions:

- Am I feeling overwhelmed? What support do I need?

- Let's take a quick look at the workplan and see where I stand. What adjustments, if any, do I need to make?

- What can I do to make sure I stay organized and coordinated?

- Thank you for your hard work! It is much appreciated!

Even though you may be focused on "the work", take time to continually think before taking action.

In your office and personal spaces, add colors (earth tones, gold, silver,) and objects (geodes, landscape paintings) that symbolize Earth and Metal.

Wear brighter earth- and metal-toned clothes and accents like yellow, orange, grey and white to encourage agility and lightness. Wear earth- and metal-inspired jewelry such as quartz, jade, tiger eye, gold, silver, copper, hematite, moonstone and cat's eye.

Acknowledge that people are busy and will likely not want to devote time for long meetings. Organize short "standing meetings" focused on troubleshooting and mutual support. Serve coffee and snacks to help build an environment of camaraderie.

Develop a meditation or reflection practice that you can do alone or with a group that involves teamwork or community building. The more active and kinesthetic, the better.

Power Through It
Featured Elements: Metal ⟼ Water
Recommendations for Profile 398, 894, 923, 932

In all that you do, seek solutions that involve action toward deeper understanding and impact.

This recommendation lies at the bottom of the circle. Like the final mile of a marathon, maintain momentum and energy, while keeping focused on the finish line.

Be an advocate for Metal and Water through language that decreases stress while increasing compassion and teamwork. Consider these statements and questions:

- ⦿ Let's keep communicating! What does everyone need and how can we support each other?

- ⦿ Let's take a quick look at the workplan and see where I stand. What adjustments, if any, do I need to make?

- ⦿ What can I do to make sure I stay organized and coordinated?

- ⦿ Keep up the good work! You're almost there!

Focus on small tasks and maintain a checklist. When you accomplish those tasks, make sure you celebrate.

Wear white, grey or gold with black or blue clothing or accents (a scarf or a tie), especially if you are under stress or speaking in public. Wear metal-derived (gold, silver, copper) or metal- and water-inspired jewelry such as hematite, moonstone, cat's eye, turquoise, lapis and blue topaz.

In your office and personal spaces, add colors (gold, silver, blue, black and white) and objects (black and white photos, metal frames, fountains) that symbolize Metal and Water.

Acknowledge that people are busy and will likely not want to devote time for long meetings. Organize short "standing meetings" focused on troubleshooting and mutual support. Serve coffee and snacks to help build an environment of camaraderie.

If you need to ponder or talk about something serious, do so over a warm, soothing beverage.

Develop a meditation or reflection practice that sustains your energy. Breathwork, yoga, even a quick shower or washing your face will help.

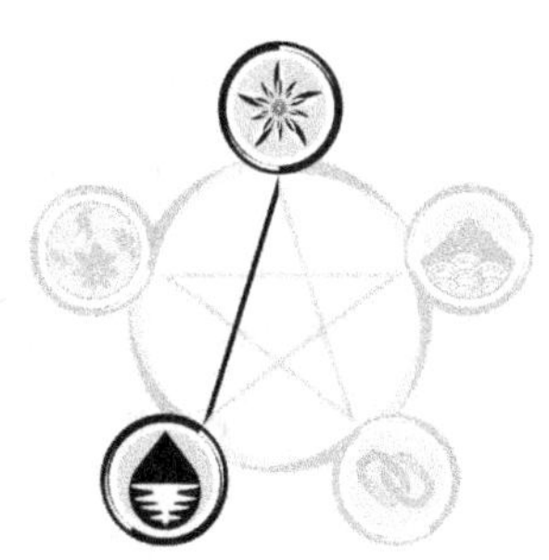

Follow Goldilocks

Featured Elements: Water ↦ Fire
Recommendations for Profiles 326, 344, 362, 389, 427, 537, 546, 564, 573, 638, 683, 748

The dynamic between Water and Fire can lead to a lot of steam (excess Fire) or smoldering ashes (excess Water). But with the right balance of Fire and Water, the result is a simmering pot of nourishing soup or that perfect soothing bath temperature. This is the Goldilocks effect—not too hot nor too cold, but just right.

In all that you do, be mindful of the alignment between your purpose (mission and values) and your message (priorities and outreach).

Be an advocate for Water and Fire through language that leads to a balance between listening and visualizing. Consider these questions:

- ◉ What is the best way for me to communicate my mission?

- ◉ What would success look like in a story?

- ◉ Am I in right relationship with others and the path forward? Or do I need to take a step back and reflect?

◉ Let's recap the main points we want to convey and make sure we're clear.

Listen intently, then be very visual with your processes; chart, write and draw things out so you can focus.

Rub your hands together for energy.

In your office and personal spaces, add colors (red, purple, blue, black) and objects (floating candles) that symbolize Water and Fire. Wear red, purple, blue and black clothes or accents (a scarf or a tie) to bring perspective. Wear water-derived or water- and fire-inspired jewelry like turquoise, lapis, blue topaz, opal, amber and ruby.

Make sure your meeting space is warm and inviting. Arrange comfortable chairs in a circle and have plenty of wall space to post charts. Serve hot, calming drinks like herbal tea.

If you need to ponder or talk about something serious, light a candle and set it by a fountain or bowl of water. Better yet, arrange some floating candles in a bowl of water.

Forge Your Tools

Featured Elements: Fire ↦ Metal
Recommendations for Profiles 124, 133, 142, 225, 252, 288, 481, 528, 555, 582, 813, 822, 831, 858, 885

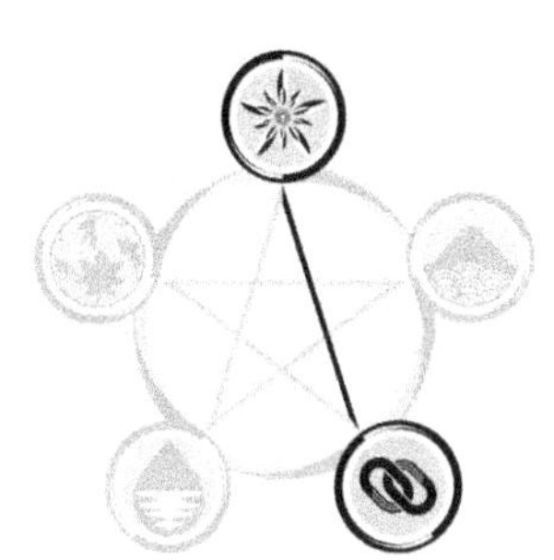

This dynamic is the most precarious of all the transitions, as it is so difficult to regulate. Alchemy is the nature of the relationship between Fire and Metal. Fire can heat Metal so it can be forged into tools and other useful structures. In all that you do, seek clarity and focus to assist you in accomplishing your goals.

The key is to find and maintain the right amount of focus and direction to maximize productivity.

Be an advocate for Fire and Metal and through language that affirms and encourages the power of the team and the values of cooperation and compassion. Consider these statements and questions:

- ◉ Let's keep communicating! What do people need and how can I support everyone?

- ◉ Let's take a quick look at the workplan. What adjustments, if any, do I need to make?

- ◉ What can I do to make sure everyone stays organized and coordinated?

- ◉ Keep up the good work! I believe in you!

Focus on small tasks and maintain a checklist. When you accomplish those tasks, make sure you celebrate.

Wear white, grey, or gold with red or purple clothing or accents (a scarf or a tie), especially if you are under stress or speaking in public. Wear metal-derived (gold, silver, copper) or metal- and fire-inspired jewelry like hematite, moonstone, cat's eye, opal, amber and ruby.

In your office and personal spaces, add colors (gold, silver, red, purple, white) and objects (metal candlesticks, red or purple candles) that symbolize Fire and Metal.

Acknowledge that people are busy and will likely not want to devote time for long meetings. Organize short "standing meetings" focusing on troubleshooting and mutual support. Serve coffee and snacks to help build a sense of teamwork and camaraderie.

Develop a meditation or reflection practice that keeps you focused and energized.

Rub your hands for energy. Take frequent stretch or walking breaks.

Check in with each other often to see if people are coming from their Primary or Secondary perspectives. Ask them to assess how stressed they are. Keep in mind that the higher the stress level, the greater the chances that the Secondary characteristics will arise.

Trim the Branches
Featured Elements: Metal ↦ Wood
Recommendations for Profiles 519, 591

This dynamic underscores the tension between Metal and Wood. It can be subtle, like a gardener pruning a tree; or drastic, like chopping down the tree. The intensity of the interaction depends on the attitudes and actions of the power of Metal. The most positive outcomes result in a controlled pruning of ideas, thereby providing a realistic framework for the creative process. Stepping back and reflecting on the bigger picture will provide a deeper perspective and prevent ideas from getting too out of hand.

In all that you do, seek creative solutions toward a path of action.

Be an advocate for Metal and Wood through language that keeps the bigger picture and strategy at the forefront. Consider these questions:

> ⊙ How does this suggestion help me get my work done today?

> ⊙ I'm taking on too much. What can I cut so I can get the job done?

> ⊙ Let my take a quick moment and reflect on my mission and values. Is everything I am doing today in alignment with them?

⊙ Let me take a quick look at the workplan. What adjustments, if any, do I need to make?

⊙ What can I do to make sure I stay organized and coordinated?

Identify small tasks that you can accomplish in a short period of time. Think daily or weekly tasks instead of monthly or annual tasks. By breaking big goals into small steps, you will be less prone to procrastination. When you accomplish those tasks, make sure you celebrate.

Wear white, grey, or gold with green clothing or accents (a scarf or a tie), especially if you are under stress or speaking in public. Wear metal-derived (gold, silver, copper) or metal- and wood-inspired jewelry like aquamarine, garnet and sapphire.

In your office and personal spaces, add colors (gold, silver, red, purple, white) and objects (metal candlesticks, red or purple candles) that symbolize Fire and Metal.

If you need to ponder or talk about something serious, organize walking meetings, especially among trees.

Develop a meditation or reflection practice that involves being in nature. Gardening is an ideal activity.

Till the Soil

Featured Elements: Wood ↦ Earth
Recommendations for Profiles 169, 196, 611

This transition is about preparation and anticipation, as the concept of seedlings breaking ground in the early spring suggests a new beginning. Be mindful, however, of depleting the soil with too many plants, or ideas.

In all that you do, consider how to infuse fun and creativity in staying organized and connected. The transitions between these two elements are Breakthrough and Depletion. Be mindful of the balance

Be an advocate for Wood and Fire through language that leads to a win-win outcome.

- ◉ How can we narrow these ideas down so we can set ourselves up for success?

- ◉ Which of these ideas will be the most unique and effective?

- ◉ Which of these ideas bring out our best thinking?

- ◉ How do these ideas align with our current skills and capacity?

⊙ What are the specific pros and cons of each idea? Where are the unforeseen shadows?

Listen intently, then be very visual with your processes – chart, write and draw things out so you can focus. Rub your hands together for energy. In your office and personal spaces, add colors (red, purple, green) and objects (candles, plants) that symbolize wood and fire. Wear red, purple and green clothes or accents (a scarf or a tie) to bring focus and attention. Wear wood-derived or wood- and fire-inspired jewelry (e.g. aquamarine, garnet, sapphire, opal, amber, ruby).

Be more deliberate and formal in setting your meeting space. Have chairs and tables set up on an orderly fashion with space to walk around and post things on the walls.

If you need to ponder or talk about something serious, light a candle or take a walk in a wooded area. Develop a meditation, reflection practice that involves visual movement. Take a dance, *tai chi*, painting, or a photography class.

Channel the Current
Featured Elements: Earth ⟼ Water
Recommendations for Profiles 499, 739, 766, 793

In all that you do, seek connection to understand and be understood.

Be an advocate for Water and Earth through language that leads to a balance between listening and visualizing. Consider these questions and statements:

- ◉ How can I dig into this topic and keep things flowing?

- ◉ Are the relationships in my life supportive of my purpose and mission, and vice versa?

- ◉ Let's reflect on and support this activity in a positive way.

In your office and personal spaces, add colors (blue, black and earth tones) and objects (a ceramic fountain, soapstone or limestone sculptures) that symbolize Water and Earth. Wear blue, black and earth-toned clothes or accents (a scarf or a tie) to bring perspective.

Establish a meeting space that allows for reflection and ceremony. Presenting a process as a historical timeline, noting important people partnerships, and milestones, will set a good tone for the work to be done.

If you need to ponder or talk about something serious, go for a walk and try to have direct contact with Earth—bare hands and feet to the ground.

Do something that builds your community every day; for example, have daily contact with a friend or loved one, make a daily to-do list, or cook more often.

Develop a practice or activity that involves hearing or listening, like music, podcasts, audio books, storytelling or the spoken word. Spend less time with visual activities such as videos and reading. It would be great if these practices and activities are engaged in community service. Your best spiritual food is helping others.

FREQUENTLY ASKED QUESTIONS

Q: As a beginner to understanding The Five Elements, how and where might I begin to apply the recommendations?

First look to the recommendations that apply to your specific chart. Start with what feels natural for you. If you are a verbal person, look at the questions that you might ask and write one or two of these on a sticky note. Place these questions in a visible place where you see them often over the course of your day.

Consider how you can integrate the language of a particular element into how you characterize a question or a direction. For example, if Fire is an element that you need to bring forth, you might ponder, *How can I shed some light on this topic? What are the shadows?* If it is Water that you need to bring forth, you might consider asking how to dive in and see what the data says. For Earth, you might ask, *Where do we find common ground?*

If you are more visual in your orientation, bring in colors and surround your work and home spaces with those colors. Determine your natural orientation and go from there.

Q: How is The Five Elements different from Western astrology?

Most astrological traditions, including Western astrology, chart the placement of planets and stars according to an individual's birth date, time, and location. Astrology readings compare one's birth chart to the placement of planets and stars at a given place and point in time. Thus, the primary reference point of astrology is in relation to space.

The foundation of **The Five Elements** is the *Lo Square*, whose formulas are based upon mathematical equations in cycles of nine. Thus, the primary reference point of this system is time. In this manner, the only information required to utilize this system is one's birthdate, not their location.

Q: What is the mathematical formula for calculating the Primary attribute?

The mathematical formula for calculating your Primary attribute is as follows:

I. **Take all the numbers of your birth year and add them together.**

Using Terry's birth year, 1989, as an example:
1 + 9 + 8 + 9 = 27

II.   **If the sum is a double digit, continue adding the numbers until you get a single digit.**

Example: 2 + 7 = 9

III.   **Once you get a single digit, subtract that number from 11. The result is your Primary attribute number.**

Example: 11 - 9 = 2
Terry's Primary attribute is 2|Caregiver.

Q: What is the mathematical formula for calculating the Secondary and Developmental attribute?

I.   **Find your Primary attribute number in columns A-C on the chart below.**

Using Sam as an example: His Primary attribute is 6|Protector. The placement of the 6 is the bottom row of column B.

A	B	C	D
1	4	7	8 - Earth
2	5	8	2 - Earth
3	6	9	5 - Earth

II.   **Identify the Earth number in column D of that row. That number represents the most previous month from your birthdate.**

Example: Column D of the bottom row is 5-Earth. Since Sam was born in January, the 5-Earth represents November 4 of the previous year.

III.   **As you move forward on the calendar, each month decreases by one. Subtract one from the number in the previous step for each month until you reach your birth month.**

Example: Since our starting point on November 4 is 5-Earth, the month number decreases to 4 on December 4. It decreases to 3 on January 4, and to 2 on February 4.

Sam's birthday is on January 25, so his Secondary and Developmental number is 3|Visionary.

Note: February 4 and November 4 of every year begin with an Earth number (2, 5 or 8).

Hint: If your birthday falls on a cusp, check the archetype profiles on both sides of the cusp and determine which Secondary and Developmental attribute is the best fit.

Q: What is the mathematical formula for calculating the Relational attribute?

If your Secondary and Developmental attribute is _**5 or lower**_:

I.   **Subtract that number from 5.**

Example: Sam's (638) Secondary and Developmental attribute is 3|Visionary, so Sam would subtract 3 from 5.

5 - 3 = 2

II.   **Add the difference from step 1 to your Primary Attribute number.**

Example: Sam's Primary attribute number, 6/Protector.

6 + 2 = 8

Sam's Relational attribute is 8/Rock.

If your Secondary and Developmental attribute is _**higher than 5**_:

I.   **Subtract 5 from your Secondary and Developmental attribute number.**

Example: Nyle's (885) Secondary and Developmental attribute is 8|Rock, so Nyle would subtract 5 from 8.

8 - 5 = 3

II.   Take that difference and subtract it from your Primary attribute number.

Example: Nyle's Primary attribute number, 8|Rock

8 - 3 = 5

Nyle's Relational attribute is 5|Facilitator.

Note: If the remainder is "0" then the attribute will be 9/Networker. This applies to profiles 169, 279. 389, and 499.

Example: Terry's (279) Secondary and Developmental attribute is 7/Achiever, so Terry would subtract 5 from 7.

7 - 5 = 2

We then take that difference and subtract it from Terry's Primary Attribute, 2|Caregiver

2 - 2 = 0

Since the difference is "0", Terry's attribute will be 9.

Terry's Relational attribute is 9/Networker.

If the difference is a negative number then add that difference to 9. This applies to profiles 178, 187, 196, 297, and 288.

Example:Grace's (187) Secondary and Developmental attribute is 8|Rock, so Grace would subtract 5 from 8.

8 - 5 = 3

We then take that difference and subtract it from Grace's Primary Attribute, 1|Philosopher

1 – 3 = -2

Add this difference to 9.

9 + -2 = 7

Grace's Relational attribute is 7/Achiever.

Q: What is the origin of the nine archetypes? How do they relate to The Five Elements?

The nine archetypes originated from *Chiu Kung Ming Li*, one of the oldest forms of astrology. The ancient Chinese believed that the source of *qi* came from nine stars. Polaris (the North Star), known in Chinese as *Ta Shin*, or the Emperor's Seat, held one end of the spectrum. This star represents complete *Yang* energy, or Fire. Vega (the Zero star) is known in Chinese astrology as *Zhi Nu*, or the Maiden Star, and occupies the other end of the spectrum. It represents complete *Yin* energy, or Water. The seven stars of Ursa Major (the Big Dipper), or *Beidou*, the Palace of the Immortals, sit between Polaris/*Ta Shin* and Vega/*Zhi Nu*.

Together, these nine stars represent the universal lifeforce that exists within and between all of us.

In contrast to the ultimate *Yang* and ultimate *Yin* energies of Polaris/*Ta Shin* and Vega/*Zhi Nu*, respectfully, the seven stars contain both *Yin* and *Yang* natures, and the assigned elements of Wood, Metal and Earth. The order of the elements reflects in the *Yin* and *Yang* energies of each; for example, the third star in the *Baidu* constellation is *Yang*/Wood, and the fourth star is *Yin*/Wood. The sixth and seventh stars are *Yang*/Metal and *Yin*/Metal. The second, fifth, and eighth stars, representing Earth, act as buffers among the elements.

Ta Shin/The Emperor's Seat (Polaris)
Yang – Fire
9/Networker

Tian Shu/Celestial Pivot
Yang – Earth
8/Rock

Tian Xuan/Celestial Rotating Jade
Yin - Metal
7/Achiever

Tianji/Celestial Shining Pearl
Yang - Metal
6/Protector

Tianquan/Celestial Balance
Yin and *Yang* - Earth
5/Facilitator

Yuheng/Jade Sighting
Yang - Wood
4/Optimist

Kaiyang/Opening of the Heart
Yang - Wood
3/Visionary

Yaoguang/Twinkling Brilliance
Yin - Earth
2/Caregiver

Zhi nu/Maiden Star/Vega
Yin - Water
1/Philosopher

The *Chiu Kung Ming Li* system has evolved over time, resulting in its modern manifestation, Nine Star Ki, upon which this book is based.

Q: What if I don't completely agree with the readings and the findings? How can I reconcile what I believe to be true about myself with what the readings and findings are telling me?

The Five Elements is a tool among many tools to provide guidance and clarity and help you navigate your particular way. It may be that some of the guidance you receive works for you and some feels less relevant. Take what works for you and leave the rest. Also, consult a practitioner who is trained in this system. Many times, there are nuances depending on the orientation of your particular chart and how the elements relate to each other. An experienced practitioner may look at your chart and provide you with a different way of seeing things that will help you understand how this information might prove useful.

Q: Will The Five Elements framework evolve or develop further over time?

The Five Elements are based on a philosophy that is thousands of years old. Over time, the system has evolved according to the particular needs of society at that time. I, for instance, have taken the language of the archetypes and modernized them. So now we have names for these archetypes such as Philosopher, Visionary, Optimist, and so on. Such names recast these archetypes in ways that are more applicable now. One hundred years hence, I look forward to the further evolution and development of **The Five Elements**. What I would hope is that the integrity of the system is never compromised—that there are five elements; that there are the Supporting and the Restraining cycles in which they interact with each other; and that what we are looking for is balance. Those primary principles have been embedded for thousands of years, and I hope that those would be consistent.

Q: How would you explain the scientific basis of The Five Elements?

Modern science is a system that approaches the universe by way of repeated inquiry. Hunches, hypotheses, theories, and empirical evidence are woven into this system and its conclusions. While much effort has gone into attempts to meld East Asian philosophy and approaches with modern science, this has not been applied to **The Five Elements**.

I do not make any scientific claims about **The Five Elements**. It is an ancient system that has found its own form of benefit and proof over many centuries. At some point, I can imagine a beneficial partnership with organizations and universities to see what the basis of this system is. Such partnerships have yet to exist, but I am hopeful that they will come to fruition.

Q: What are the advantages and disadvantages of The Five Elements for understanding human behavior versus Western-based frameworks?

Leadership assessment approaches such as Myers-Briggs (MBTI), DISC, StrengthsFinder® and Enneagram align and differ with **The Five Elements**. What fascinates and compels me is how these approaches appear to be complementary. A given approach may speak to an individual and if the goal is to achieve insight and benefit, it follows that one should identify a system that speaks their language. **The Five Elements** can work in conjunction with these Western-based frameworks, allowing us to apply and combine their offerings in new and exciting ways.

RESOURCES

Between Heaven and Earth: A Guide to Chinese Medicine, Harriet Beinfield, L.Ac. and Efrem Korngold, L.Ac., O.M.D. Ballentine Books, 1991.

Feng Shui Astrology, Jon Sandifer. Ballentine Books, 1997

Nine Star Ki, Michio Kushi. One Peaceful World Press, 1992.

The Book of Changes and the Unchanging Truth, Hua-Ching Ni. Sevenstar Communications, 1983.

The Complete Guide to Nine Star Ki, Bob Sachs. Element Books, 1992.

The Ki, Takashi Yoshikawa. St. Martin's Press, 1986.

ACKNOWLEDGEMENTS

This book is a manifestation of my journey in discovering the profound wisdom garnered from my East Asian heritage. I have sought to bring these practices forward in ways that are relevant to our 21st century workplaces, communities, and homes. The journey has spanned 30 years, and I hold deep gratitude to the following people whose guidance, wisdom, support, and love have seen me through.

To Suey Sum Yee Fong, and Kwong Lai Fong Gee, my esteemed grandmothers, who cultivated and nurtured **The Five Elements** in my young life, reminding me that it was already coded in my DNA.

To HH Professor Lin Yun Rinpoche, Professor K.C. Liu, Bob Sachs, and especially Katherine Metz—revered teachers who provided the roadmap for my journey and held my hand along the way.

To Grace Lee Boggs, Aunty Puanani Burgess, Mama Lila Cabbil, Kumu Robert Uluwehi Cazimero, Kathy Ko Chin, Dolores Huerta, Martha Lee, Ms. Jacqueline Martin, john a. powell, Maestro Jerry Tello, and Pat Turner—mentors upon whose shoulders I stand. I would not be who I am if not for each of you.

To Tessie Guillermo, my stalwart who gave me my first opportunity to bring **The Five Elements** into her organization in 1996, and has cheered me on ever since.

To my dear friends and companions who cultivate communities of belonging and make this world a better place for all: Daniel Nane Alejandrez, Maestra Susanna Armijo, Ignatius Bau, Mama Carol Bebelle, Lecia Brooks, Juanita Capri Brown, Dr. Ruby Cain, Maestra Debra Camarillo, Isaac "Papa Bear" Cardenas, Cristy Chung, Tiffany Curtis, Portia Espy, Allen Kwabena Frimpong, Susan M. Glisson, Vondaris Gordon, Monica Haslip, Baba Greg Hodge, Deepa Iyer, Kolene and Lyle James, Valarie Kaur, Jeanné Lewis, La quen naay Elizabeth Medicine Crow, Chris Messinger, Sandra Meucci, Mee Moua, Dan Mulhern, Simran Noor, Michelle Otero, Theresa Pascual, Amate Perez, Sylvia Perez, Maggie Potapchuk, Ayyu Qassataq, Walter Quan, Hector Sanchez-Flores, Linda Sarsour, Trish Adobea Tchume, Jacqueline John Tsingaris, Charles H. Tucker, aa Valdivia, Tony Watkins, Joe Weston, Akaya Windwood, Stan Yogi, and my brothers at Hālau Nā Kamalei O Līlīlehua. In the best and toughest of times, I can count on you to make my life better through music, dance, laughter, and ice cream.

To my readers and supporters Rosie Abriam, Michela Fong, and Ryan Fong. Thank you for your insight and wisdom.

To my colleagues Karen Rezai, Brandon Hadi, Bouapha Toommaly, Joshua Feliz Martinez, and Christopher Caldara. I couldn't have done this without your support.

To my friends at Roots and Branches Farm and Gilchrist Retreat Center who provided sanctuary for me to write, and to be.

To Russell Regan, for his support in my early years of this journey.

To my editor Gina Mazza; design team Vanessa Bowen, Chase Chang, Jody Luzier, James Kwolyk; and IT maven Nathan Martel. Your gifts have made **The Five Elements** accessible to the world.

To my fellow Triple Earth, Todd Hoskins, who knew what I needed before I did, and masterfully wove this journey together with elegance, simplicity, beauty, and compassion.

To my parents, Bob and Mary Fong, and the Fong clan for their unconditional love and care from day one.

To my sons Rafael, Santiago, and Conner, who fill my life with joy, wonder, and pride. Love you to the moon and beyond.

To R. Gregory John, the kindest and very best of men. Thank you for being my protector, my rock, my visionary and my love.

ABOUT THE AUTHOR

From the beginning, Kevin Kahakula'akea John Fong has sought to shift narratives and patterns that limit our potential and tear apart our social fabric. Whether on personal, interpersonal, or organizational levels, Kevin has promoted fundamental change that would allow us to live with greater compassion, efficacy, and well-being.

The Five Elements: An East Asian Approach to Achieve Organizational Health, Professional Growth, and Personal Well Being resides at the root of all that Kevin does. Kevin has brought **The Five Elements** to hundreds of organizations and thousands of people—from Silicon Valley to rural Mississippi, from primary schools in New Mexico to the White House.

As Founder of the Kahakulei Institute, Kevin has gathered a team of bold leaders who work to weave people and possibilities to cultivate communities of belonging. Through decades of tenacious practice, Kevin has become an internationally recognized cultural translator, facilitator, and speaker in transformative justice. Through his work, Kevin helps to develop leaders who can, by building beloved communities, push back on the existential threats that people around the world now face. Kevin believes that, under the right conditions, truth can partner with accountability to bring healing and reconciliation, even in communities that have resisted positive change.

A graduate of the University of California with a degree in East Asian Studies, Kevin resides in the San Francisco Bay Area, the traditional land of the *Ohlone* People.

my5elements.life